International Standard Book Number (ISBN):
978-0-9918554-0-7

Printed in the United States of America

First Printing: February 2013

Trademarks

All terms mentioned in this book that are known to be trademarks or service marks have been appropriately capitalized. User of a term in this book should not be regarded as affecting the validity of any trademark or service mark.

Warning and Disclaimer

Every effort has been made to make this book as complete and as accurate as possible, but no warranty of fitness is implied. The information provided is on an as-is basis. The author and publisher shall have neither liability nor responsibility to any person or entity with respect to any loss or damages arising from the information contained in this book.

For My Family

Proceeds from this book will be donated to charity. By purchasing this book, you are doing something to give back. Thank you.

If you have a favourite charity that you would like to let us know about, please visit our website and let us know: www.tjgalda.com

In effort to protect the environment, this book does not come with a DVD. Rather, you can download everything you need from the website. To download the tutorial files and tools, visit: www.tjgalda.com

Table of Contents

Preface...9

How to Use This Book..12

Getting Started...14

Architecture 21

Introduction 21

Parenting and Hierarchies 24

Groups 28

Freezing Out Your Rigs 31

Constraints 36

Joints 60

Joint Chains 62

Local Rotation Axis 74

Forward Kinematics (FK).. 80

Inverse Kinematics (IK) 92

Pole Vectors 114

Controls 120

Custom Attributes... 140

Direct Connections.. 150

Expressions 157

Set Driven Keys 174

Other Things to Consider in Architecture 182

Rigging Architecture Summary 184

Deformation... 185

Introduction 185

Preparing Your Model for Deformations 187

Double Transformations and Considerations..................... 191

Clusters.. 195

Weights and Envelopes.. 200

Lattice.. 205

Blend Shapes.. 222

Rigid Binding and Edit Membership Tool 231

Smooth Binding... 247

Painting Weights: The Tool Explained............................ 250

Painting Weights: Tips and Tricks 266

Component Editor and Pruning Weights....................... 281

Bind Pose 290

Adding Influences.. 295

Non-linear Deformers: Overview 304

Non-linear Deformers: Bend.. 307

Non-linear Deformers: Flare.. 313

Non-linear Deformers: Sine 320

Non-linear Deformers: Squash 327

Non-linear Deformers: Twist.. 339

Non-linear Deformers: Wave... 345

Wires... 358

Deformation Order 373

Input List... 376

Other Things to Consider for Deformation......................... 379

Rigging Deformation Summary... 382

Conclusion 383

Key Terms 385

About the Author.. 393

Index 395

Preface

Character rigging is the art of putting in all the "strings of the marionette". It is the work that goes into creating all of the controls that take a model in the computer from simply a model, to a fully production ready puppet that can be animated. Because of all the controls need to be "wired" together, this is often referred to as "rigging", much like how the rigging of a sailboat allows the sails to work and propel the boat forward gracefully.

Rigging can be broken down into two major sections, building the controls, and how the model deforms. The first is termed architecture and the latter deformation. We have modeled the book along those lines, and it is broken down into these two sections as well: Architecture and Deformation. At major studios, it is even a common practice to have people who specialize in one or the other, as it can take years to perfect.

As you work through the book, you should keep in mind that the ultimate design of a good rig is for it to be one that "just works" and fades into the background. The goal should be to make your puppet one that is simple to use, and fast to animate with. It should be one that is reliable and bug-free, and one that does not take any complex instructions or training. Having a rig such as this will allow the animation to happen quickly and will be a joy to use. This is ultimately the goal to remember, since speed will allow your animators to have more time to work on making the animation look even better. At the same time, fast rigs providing speed will save your production money.

Although this book is designed for the beginner, it does make some assumptions that you are comfortable in moving around within Maya. We have tried our best to ensure that the tutorials are clear and understandable, and easy to follow.

This book is geared to have a few major differences from the typical "how-to" rigging book on the market today. I am striving to write all the explanations to the WHY things happen. It is far too important a question that gets often over looked. There are tutorials in the book that will show you how to hit the buttons and which buttons to hit in what order, but before each tutorial is a theory section that explains WHY things happen the way they do.

Knowing WHY will allow you to not only be able to create a rig from a tutorial, but to understand what is going on and why. This will also allow you to understand how to fix something when it breaks and allow you to move into the trouble shooting realm. Understanding WHY is critical to being able to fix random issues when they show up and this is a critical skill in the production environment whether you are a technical director or an animator.

Understanding WHY will also allow you to grow forward from the tutorials and start to innovate and create your own rigs and solutions. One thing you will discover is that since the art of rigging is pulling pieces together, there often a multitude of "correct" ways to create a rig and solve a problem. Rigging can be a creative realm where you can explore and come up with your own unique answers to the problem "how do I make this simple and easy to use, yet fast and powerful?".

Enjoy!

How to Use This Book

To get the most out of this book, we have made use of several different formatting techniques to help you quickly identify which section is which.

Theory sections are written in normal body text. These sections help by explaining the context and important techniques and theories you need to know about each topic. Everything from Joints to Smooth Weights are outlined in full detail.

Tutorials are sprinkled throughout the book. In fact, many feel like the best way to learn something is by actively doing it. To that end, each major theory section has several tutorials specific to that section and will help you learn as you go. These tutorials are made in such a way to be quick to complete, thus allowing you to work at your own pace and put the book down for breaks. They are also thoroughly tested as I remember being frustrated going through tutorials when I was learning, only to find one step was missing or broken. Like putting a puzzle together, it is only possible if all the pieces are there! **Tutorials** are listed in a step by step fashion, with numbered steps. **Example files** are listed at the end of the tutorials, but it is best to try to complete the tutorial on your own first.

Menu Commands are indented, written in a bold font and are found in the menus within Maya. For example:

File -> Save Preferences

MEL commands and expressions are written in a plain, terminal font. This will identify exactly what you could write into Maya's script editor to run your commands. For example:

```
tj_createToggleHotkeys;
```

Of course, as with all the books in the series, key terms are found at the end of the book. These terms are a definition guide that will help you quickly find and remember what each piece of lexicon means to a rigger.

Beyond the table of contents, you might also find using the index as a useful way to speed up how you find the exact page of each item in the book. An extensive index can be found at the end of the book.

Finally, if you have any questions, please feel free to contact us. Contact details can be found on the website and we will do our best to help you through your questions.

Getting Started

In effort to protect the environment, this book does not come with a DVD. Rather, you can download everything you need from the website. To download the tutorial files and tools, visit: www.tjgalda.com

Moving around within Maya in the most efficient fashion will not only make your workflow faster, but also make your life easier. Working faster than your counterparts will make you more desirable by any employer, and allow you to simply DO BETTER WORK IN THE SAME AMOUNT OF TIME. To help you out, I have written a tool that will allow you to choose a number of hotkeys to create. These toggles are simple but important speed enhancers that I use every day.

Some of the scripts to source that work well with this book:

tj_createToggleHotkeys

This will open a window to allow you to choose what toggling hotkeys you would like to start working with.

tj_circleAtJoint

This will create a circle as a control object for any object(s) you have selected. We discuss how and why this works in our Controllers section of the book.

tj_bind poseReset

This will reset the bind pose for the selected joints, allowing you to add influences and new joints even if the automatic "go to bind pose" option within Maya does not work. This works on selected joints. If no joints are selected, the tool works on all joints in the scene.

There are even more goodies, like a toggle for all smooth nodes in your scene, a few attribute adding buttons, and more. These can all found on the shelf:

shelf_tj_advancedCharRigging.mel

This shelf can be downloaded from our website and loaded using the shelf editor.

Tutorial: Load Shelf

1. Click and hold on the down arrow icon beside the shelf area.

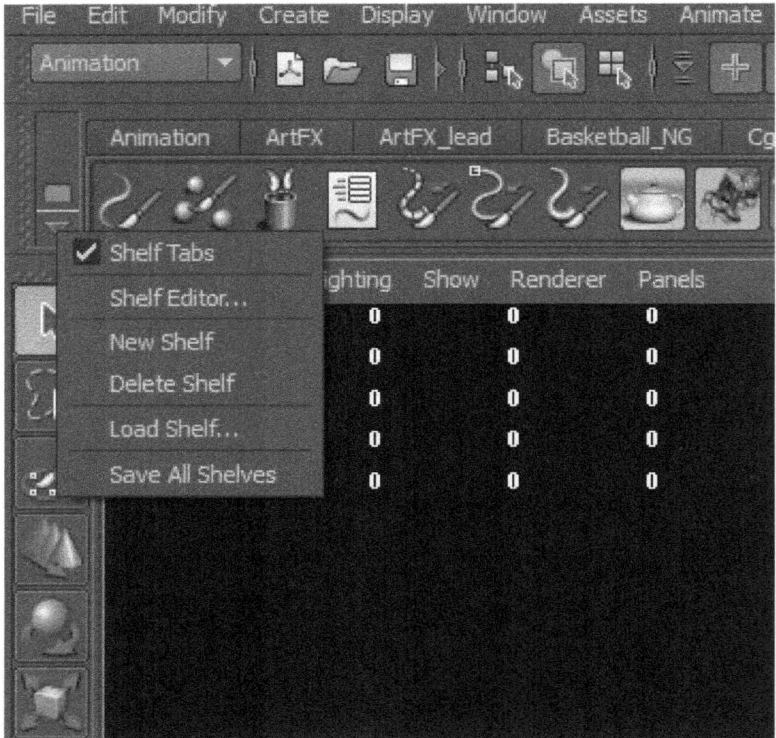

Figure 1. Shelf Menu

2. Select "Load Shelf…"
3. Browse to your shelf and select the Open button.

If you prefer, you can download the scripts individually, source the scripts, and type their names individually such as:

```
tj_createToggleHotkeys;
```

Tutorial: Source Script

1. Open your script editor using the two stacked rectangles button in the bottom right corner of Maya.

Figure 2. Open Script Editor

2. Select
   a. **File -> Source Script...**
3. Browse to your script and select the Open button.
4. Your script is now sourced into memory, and you can now run the command above by typing the command into the script editor:

```
tj_createToggleHotkeys;
```

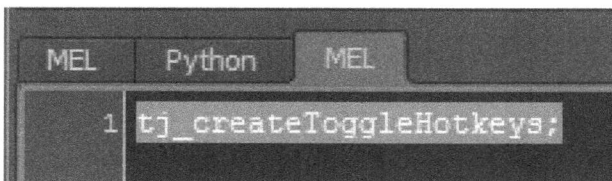

Figure 3. Mel command

5. Hit the numeric enter key or use the combination of CTRL
    + Enter to run your script.

By running this in your script editor, you should see a
window that looks like this:

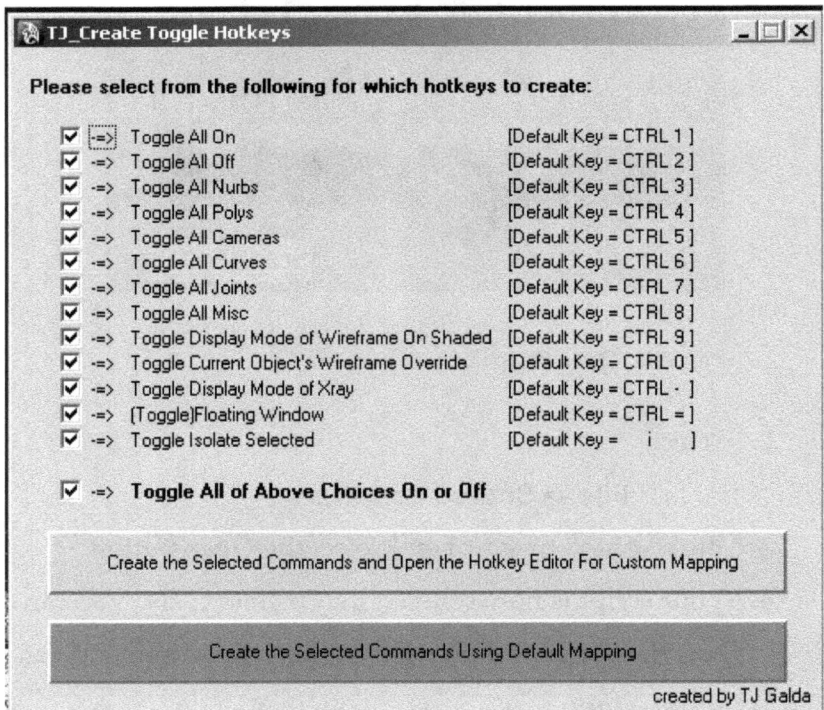

Figure 4. Toggle Hotkeys tool

Choose your keys, map them, and work faster. Once you have created your hotkeys, simply save your preferences and they will be there every time you open Maya.

1. To save your preferences, you can use the command:

File -> Save Preferences

Architecture

Introduction

Character setup or "rigging" can be broken in to two sections. The first half is all about creating the systems and controls for how the character will move. This half focuses on everything from how your scene is laid out to where individual pivot points are. Think of this half as creating all the "wires" and controls that your digital marionette will require in order to move it. The second half is all about creating the look of how the objects and models will change as they are moved or how they deform.

This section deals with architecture or the movement system that is sometimes referred to as the "motion system". We will discuss how to create various setups and keep it boiled down to what you really need to know. We will move quickly through all the basic building blocks and sum up with a tutorial at the end of the section that will walk you through how to create your rig from beginning to end. By the time you have completed this section, you should be able to create your own skeleton system and add in all the basic appropriate controls.

Scattered throughout the theory and explanations are tutorials that will walk you through specific applications for making use of what was just explained. You should take the time to complete each of these to fully get a handle on all of the content provided here.

Without creating proper underlying architecture, your characters will simply not be able to move correctly and will look wrong. Take your hand for example. If your knuckles are in the wrong spot, your fingers will be too long and poke into your hand when you make a fist and will not bend properly. On the other hand, your fingers will not be long enough and will not even be able to make a fist!

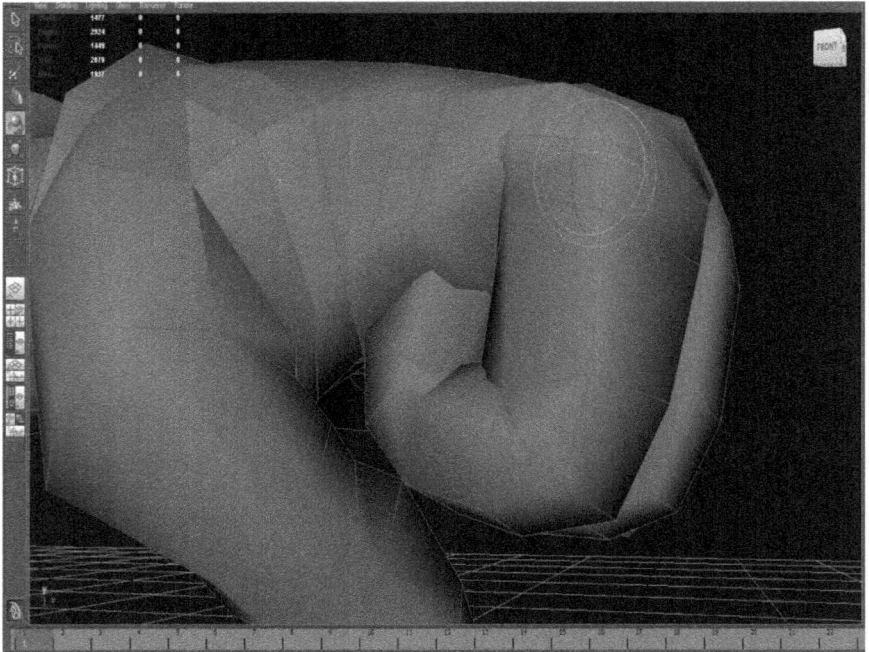

Figure 5. The fingers are too long and stick into the palm.

As you can see, paying attention to how your characters are built is vital.

Beyond pure mechanics of how things move, it is important to keep your scene clean and understandable. Taking the extra time at the beginning to have a consistent naming convention will allow for you to write scripts more easily, write expressions and copy them from one item to the next (we will underline the importance of this later by copying an expression from one finger to all of the others) and even more importantly will allow everyone who has to use the rig to work faster. After all, the faster you work, the more you can accomplish and the better things will work out in the end.

Parenting and Hierarchies

We will start on our journey of discussing motion systems by discussing parenting and hierarchies. Luckily, this is straightforward. Each object can have a relationship with one parent and/or any number of children. Like families of ducks, the children will faithfully follow along wherever the parent goes. This means if you move the parent, any children of that parent will move the exact same way.

Tutorial: Parent Objects

1. Select the child (or children, with a multiple selection) of the hierarchy.
2. Hold SHIFT down and select the parent of the hierarchy.
3. Use the command:
   a. **Edit -> Parent**
   b. Or you can use the hotkey of: p

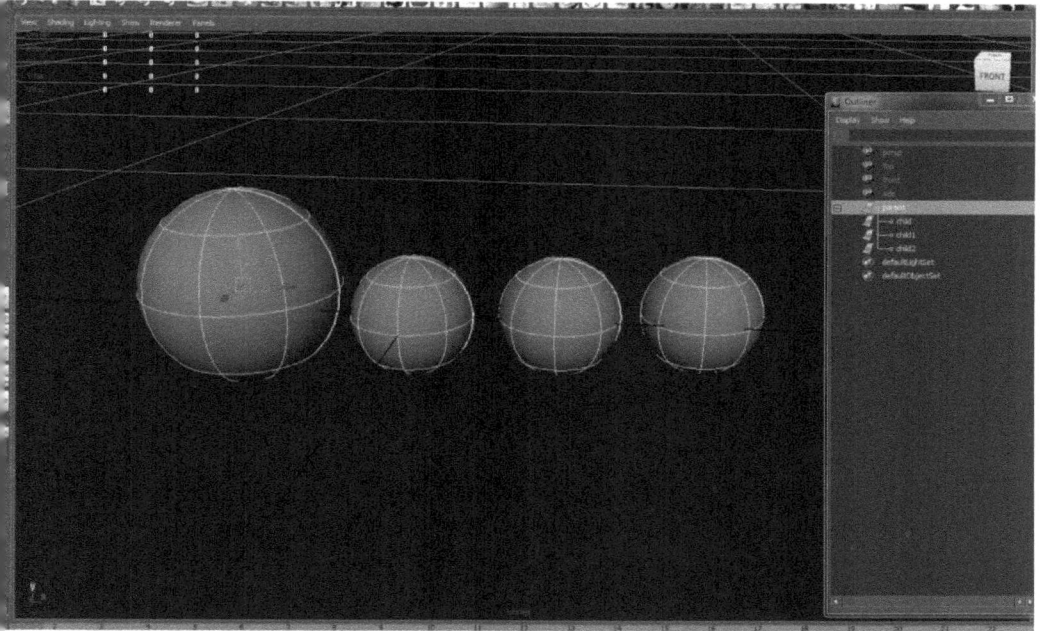

Figure 7. The parent is set up.

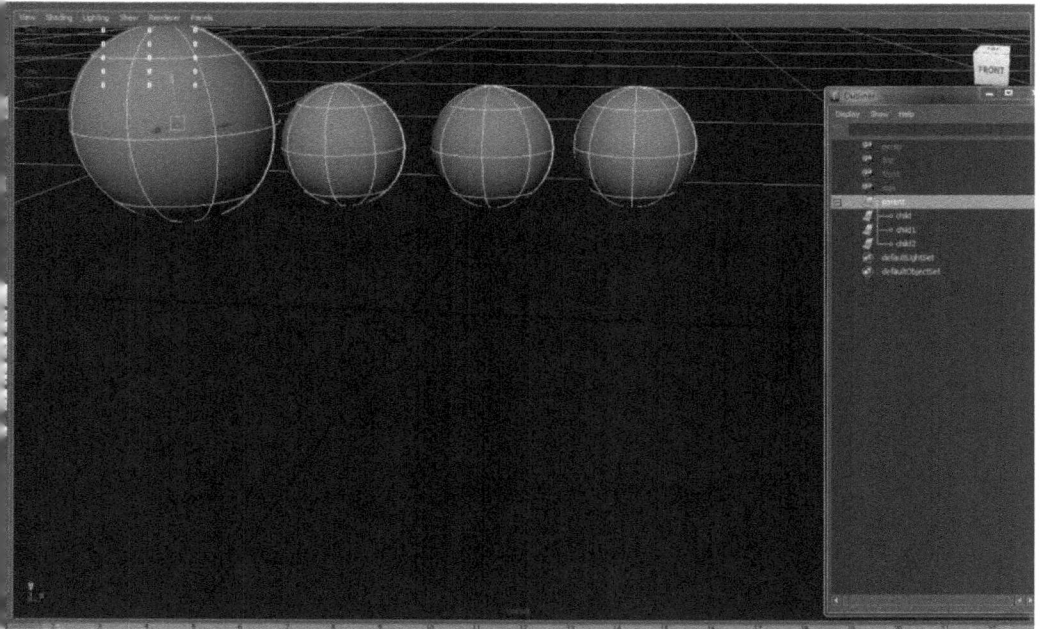

Figure 6. When the parent moves up, the children follow along.

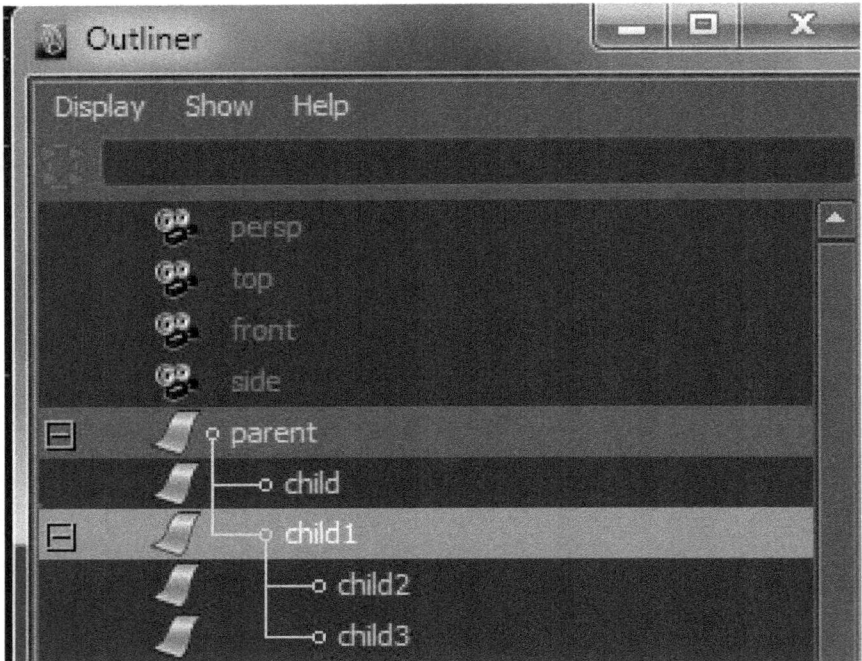

Figure 8. The large ball has 3 children.

Stack up several layers of parents and children and suddenly you have what is termed a hierarchy, with each level affecting those below it in a logical fashion.

This can be especially useful in many situations. Take for instance a robot. You can quickly attach your robot together via parenting. Since robots tend to be rigid and have pieces that do not bend, no deformations are required. This means, after having parented your pieces to each other, you are essentially done rigging. Of course, you can add layers of complexity with better controls or areas that bend, or even a skeleton, but in essence, the simple act of parenting is all that is generally required, if your pivot points are all in the right place. A pivot point is of course where the object will rotate or pivot from. In the case of our robot's ball joints, these pivot points are in the center of the ball. You can move the pivot around as required, and you will be able to bend in the correct position all with parenting.

A good practice is to have the hips drive all of the motion. Parenting all your objects together in a robot until the box around his hips will achieve this. If you do so and select the hip box you should be able to move your entire robot around. This lower box is the top of the hierarchy or the root parent of everything. For this reason, this is sometimes referred to as the "root" object or the "center of gravity (cog)". This is an important concept, since later on you will want to be able to move your entire robot to a new position (to start a new animation scene for instance).

Every rig you create from now on should have a root object or even better a root group. Why is a root group better? Well, this brings us to the concept of grouping.

Groups

Much like parenting, groups are a way to collect objects together and affect them all at once. You can just as easily create an empty group (or transform node) with nothing in the group itself.

Tutorial: Create Empty Group

1. Click in the scene anywhere to deselect all objects.
2. Use the command:
   a. **Edit -> Group**
   b. or you can use the hotkey of CTRL + g

To add items into the group, you can parent objects individually to the group using the parenting command that we just discussed.

Alternatively, you will likely find it far faster to select the nodes you would like to place into a group and use the group command with the items still selected. This will perform the same function as parenting all of those nodes to the empty group, but do so much faster.

Tutorial: Grouping

1. Select all the objects you would like in your group.
2. Use the command:
   a. **Edit -> Group**
   b. or you can use the hotkey of CTRL + g

Although a fundamental, grouping is a great way to keep your hierarchies clean and easily understandable. As your scene becomes more and more complex, it is important to keep your hierarchies together in an orderly fashion.

Grouping becomes particularly important later on when we discuss gimbal lock. In our robot example, you will notice for instance that we have three group nodes at the top of the hierarchy that are built in for animation later on. These were each constructed as empty group nodes and then parented into the right place in the hierarchy. This will allow you to pin your robot down (or constrain) your robot on one group node to a vehicle perhaps. This will make your robot go anywhere the vehicle goes. However, since we have several group nodes, we can also still be able to animate the robot around even though it is constrained. By having the main parent constrained down, the children groups are able to follow along while still providing a way to offer the animator the ability to offset the position of the robot if necessary.

Another nice benefit to having several groups at the top of your hierarchy is that each group can have its' own pivot point placed in a separate place. One pivot could be at the feet perhaps, which would make it great for constraining to a surfboard. Another group could have its' pivot at the hips, which would make it easier for something like a big claw to pick up the robot.

Yet even another large benefit is that having multiple groups also saves you in the case of one of your groups entering gimbal lock. Both constraining and gimbal locks are described later on, but it is important to remember to keep a few extra groups at the top of your hierarchy. Even if these are never used, which is not likely, having the extra group is no hardship.

In addition, condensed, why having three groups at the top of your hierarchy is important:

1. Constraining and still being able to animate as required.
2. Multiple pivot point locations are possible.
3. The ability to avoid gimbal lock is increased.

Freezing Out Your Rigs

Any good rig should be able to move back to the default pose in a quick and intuitive fashion. This makes it far easier when your character is handed off to someone else or when you are starting a scene to be able to reset quickly the character into position. In order to do so, taking your default positions as a starting point and making them equate to zero is a great way to allow someone to orient themselves quickly. In other words, if you have moved, rotated, and even scaled and object to get it to a place that is the starting position, that new starting position should be position zero (and the starting scales should be at one). A group of translates, rotates, and scales (and shear) is considered a transform matrix. If you remember from your high school math, a matrix with 0's and 1's is your identity matrix, so forcing your translate and rotates to zero and your scales to one is sometimes called forcing your transforms to their identity matrix (even though this isn't a true identity matrix). You can force Maya to create the identity matrix for this, and move all the information out of the channel box to more hidden attributes by making use of the tool "Freeze Transformations". Doing so will then take the starting position and make the channel box read 0 for the attributes frozen at that particular place.

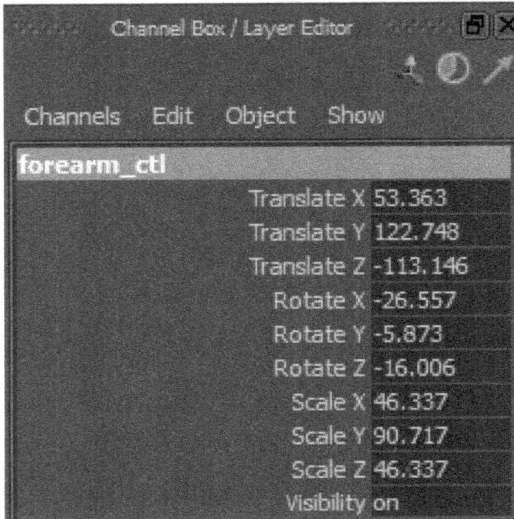

Figure 9. Non Zeroed attributes

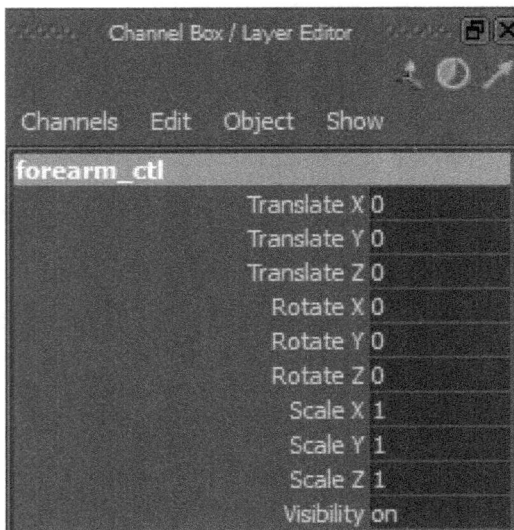

Figure 10. After freeze transformations is run, the attributes are "zeroed out".

The freeze transformation command is simply:

Modify -> Freeze Transformations []

Opening the options, you will see that you can freeze any or all of the translate, rotate, or scale values, as well as joint orient. We will discuss joint orientation in full detail a little further along. Typically, you will want to have the translate, rotate and scale values all checked on and the joint orientation turned off. It is important to note, that the scale values will be frozen to a value of one, while the rotations and translations will be frozen to zero.

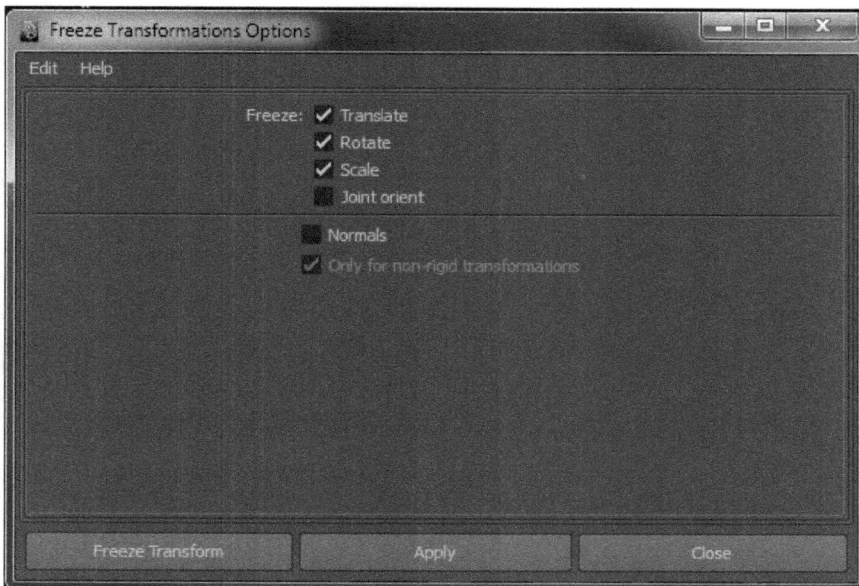

Figure 11. Freeze Transformation Options

Tutorial: How to Freeze Transformations

1. Select the transform(s) that you would like to zero out the values.

2. Run the command from the menu:

   a. **Modify -> Freeze Transformations []**

3. Ensure you have the choice(s) you wish to zero out selected and hit the Freeze Transform button.

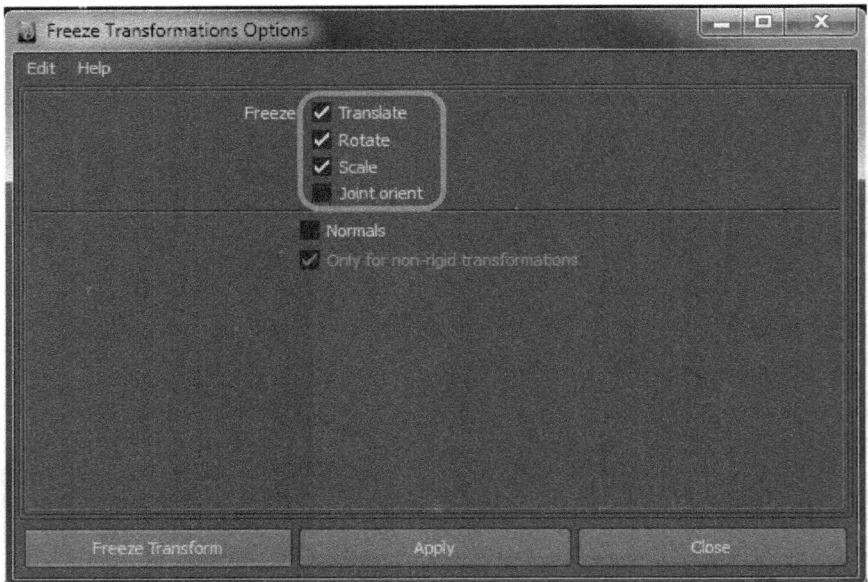

Figure 12. Ensure the proper checkboxes are on.

Condensed, the reason why you freeze all of your transformations is so that you can go back to the initial pose quickly from any pose or animation later on which makes animation far easier.

Constraints

Now, let us take the idea of parenting one step further. What if you wanted an object to have not only one parent, but two? Or Three? Enter our friend the constraint. A constraint is simply a way of telling one object to behave according to another. You have a number of different choices of constraints: point, aim, orient, scale, and parent. Let us start with point constraints.

Point constraints are ways of making one object's TRANSLATIONS affect another object's translations. If you point constrain one object to another, it will follow along faithfully. The difference between this and parenting is that it will ONLY copy the translations. It will NOT copy the scales or rotations.

Tutorial: Point Constraint

1. Select the transform you wish to constrain to. This transform will drive the other transform.

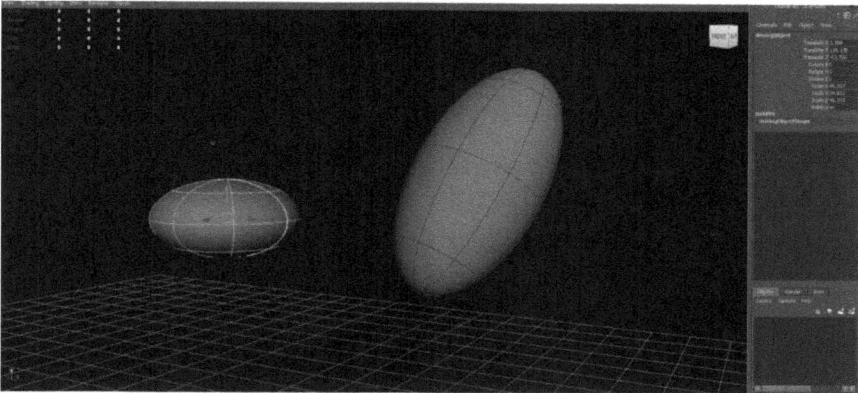

Figure 13. Select one object.

2. Hold SHIFT down and select the object that you wish to constrain. This is the transform that will be driven by the transform you selected first in step one.

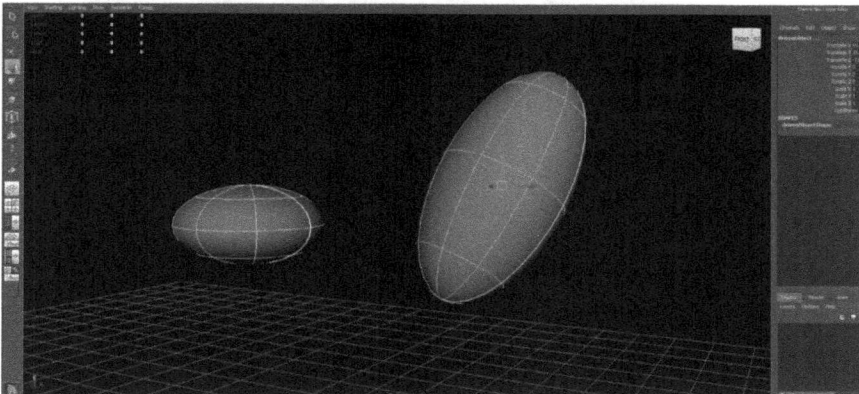

Figure 14. Shift select the second object.

3. Run the command from the menu:

    i. **Constrain -> Point**

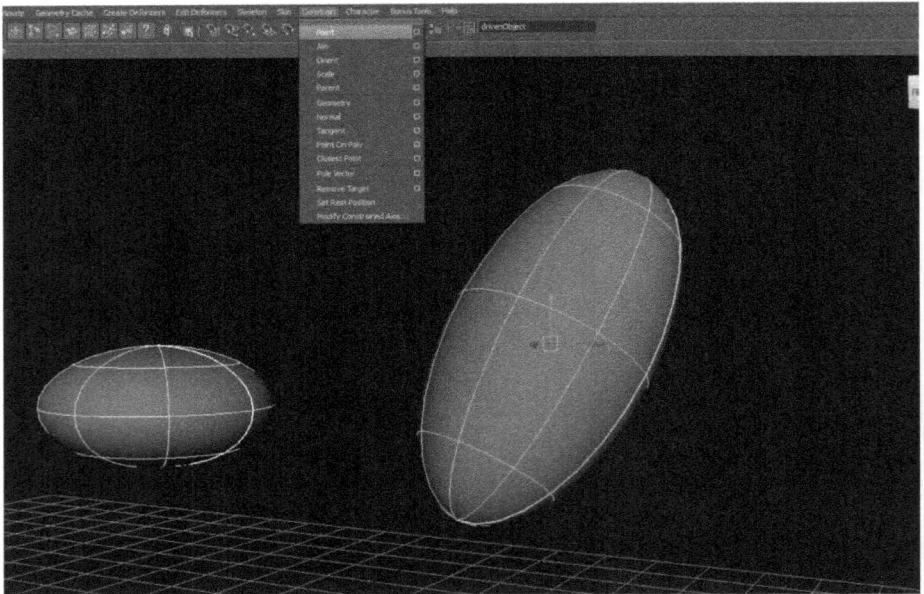

Figure 15. Point Constraint.

You can also point constrain an object to more than one object. In other words, it can be constrained to two objects as in the following example:

Tutorial: Point Constraint Two Objects

1. Select the first transform you wish to constrain to. This is one of the transforms that will drive the controlled transform.

2. Hold SHIFT down and select the object that you wish to constrain. This is the transform that will be driven by the transform you selected first in step one.

3. Run the command from the menu:

   a. **Constrain -> Point**

4. Repeat step one with a slight variation by select the second transform you wish to constrain to.   This is the other transform that will drive the controlled transform.

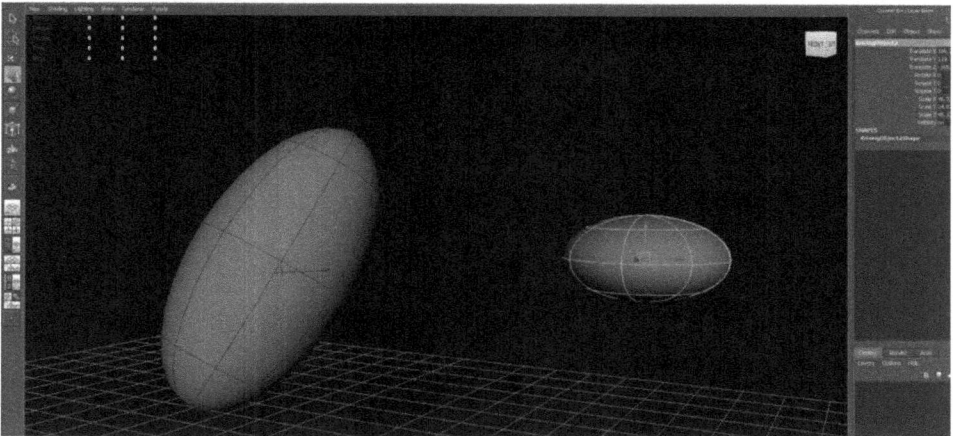

Figure 16. Selected a third object.

5. Hold SHIFT down and select the object that you wish to constrain as you did in step two. This is the transform that will be driven by the transform you selected first in step one.

6. Run the command from the menu again:

    a. **Constrain -> Point**

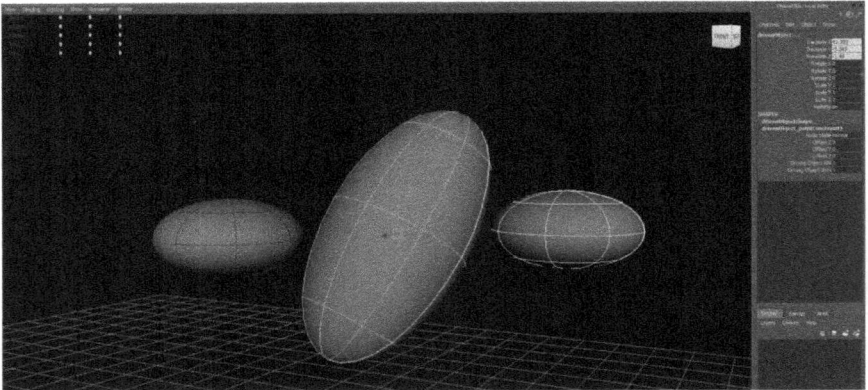

Figure 17. Constrained to two objects.

The point constraint has a "weight" associated with it. In other words, you can control how much one object affects the other. By default, this is 1. This also means 100%, as a weight value ranges from 0 to 1, or in percentage terms from 0% to 100%. If you have an object constrained to two objects, it will be 50% of each by default. This is because by default, each will be at a value of 1. However, since there are now two constraints, a value of 1 out of a total of 2 (weight) is ½ or 50%. If both weights are equal, it will remain half way between the two. By changing the weight value, you can control how much each object can control the constrained object.

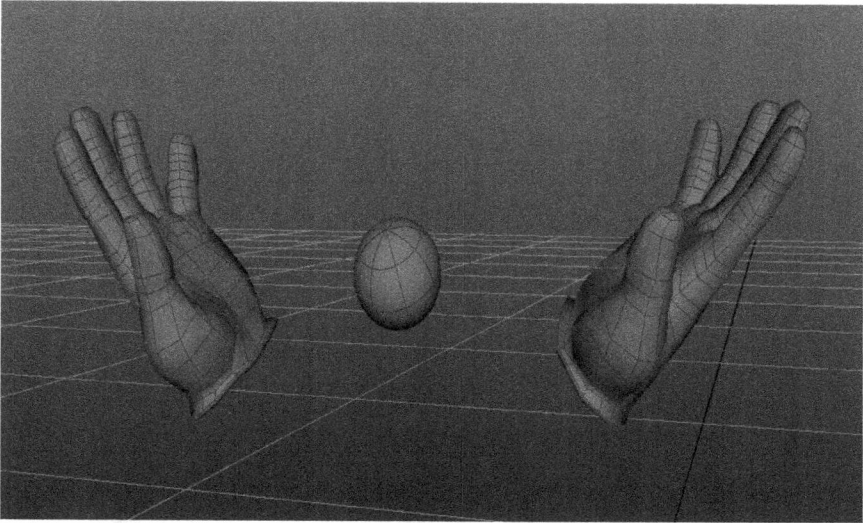

Figure 18. Ball constrained to two hands.

This can be useful for many things. A simple animation example is likely to be clearest way to show this. Let us examine the constraint swap. In this example, we will constrain a ball to two hands in order to easily "throw" the ball from one hand to another.

Tutorial: Constraint Swapping for Animation

1. Create your models of your left hand, right hand and a ball.

2. Create a locator for the left hand and place it in the palm. Name it "lf_palm_constraint_loc".

   a. **Create -> Locator**

Figure 19. Left palm locator is created.

3. Repeat the process for the right hand, resulting in "rt_palm_constraint_loc".

   a. **Create -> Locator**

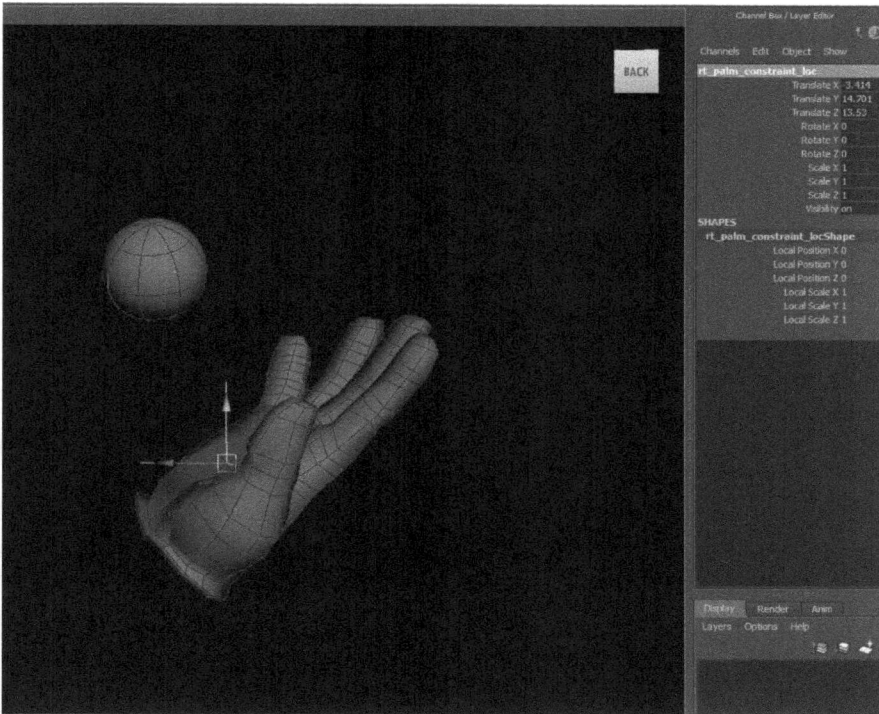

Figure 20. Right palm locator is created.

4. Select the lf_palm_constraint_loc, then the ball and create a point constraint.

   a. **Constrain -> Point Constrain**

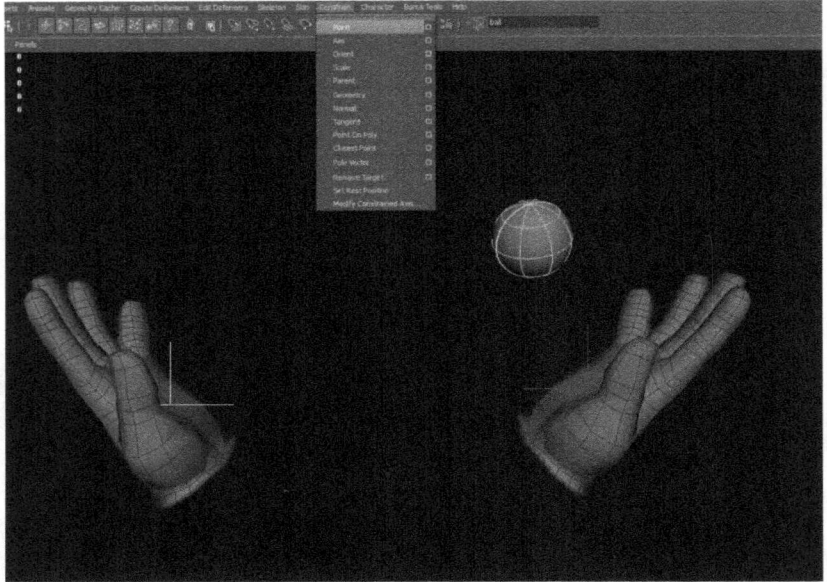

Figure 21. Left point constraint.

5. Repeat the process for the right hand. Select the rt_palm_constraint_loc, then the ball and create a point constraint.

   a. **Constrain -> Point Constrain**

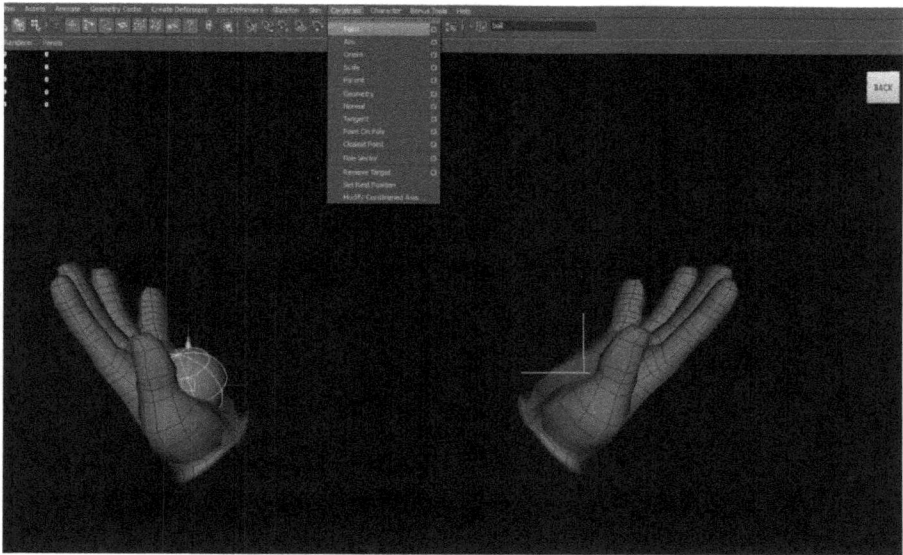

Figure 22. Right palm point constraint.

6. You will now have a ball that is constrained to both hands and will be halfway between the two. By moving either locator, you will move the ball "somewhat" (only half of the motion). This is because both locators are controlling the ball equally. Select the ball and click on the channel box to examine the point constraint settings.

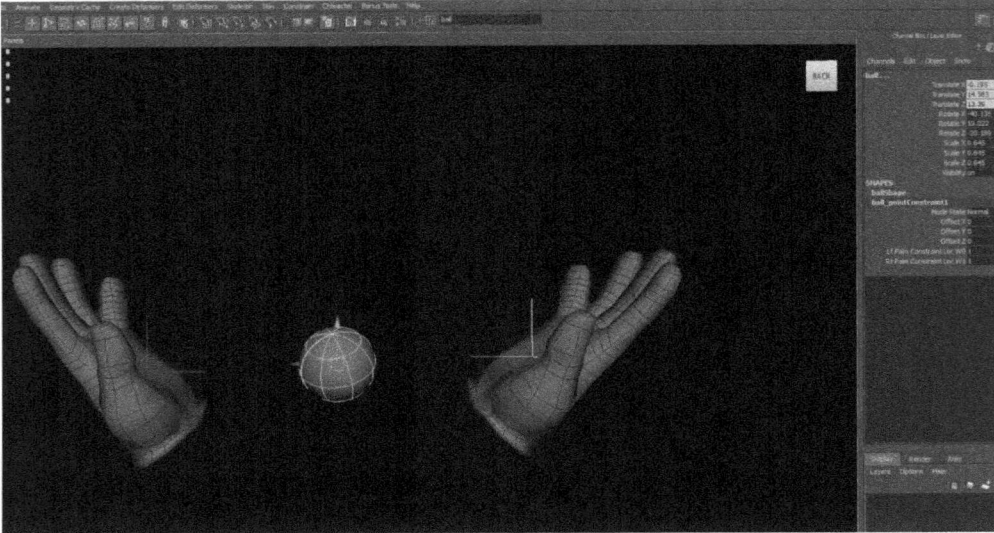

Figure 23. Ball constrained to both locators.

7. Adjust the two weight values to control the balls motion. Change the attribute of lf_palm_constraint_loc_W0 to 0 and the attribute of rt_palm_constraint_loc_W1 to 1. The ball should be all the way into the right hand. You can adjust its position by moving the rt_palm_constraint_loc around.

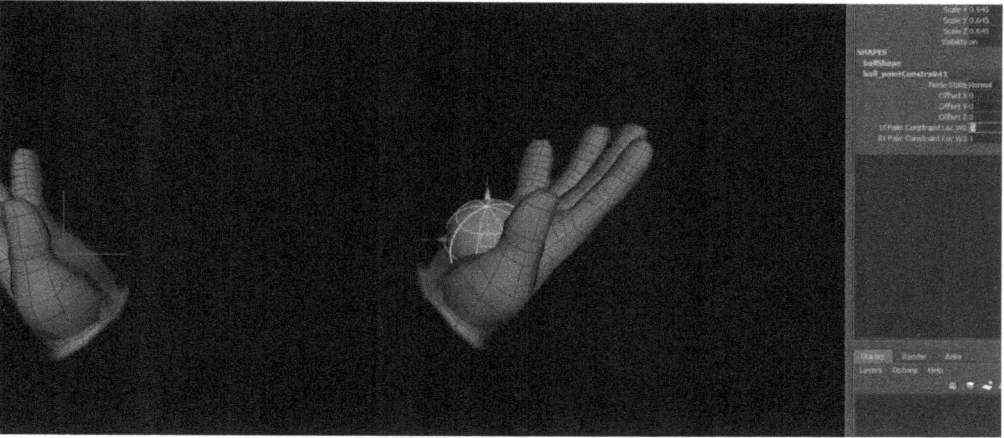

Figure 24. Changing weights moves the ball.

8. Go to frame 1 and set a key for the weight values. Select the rt_palm_constraint_loc_W1 attribute in the channel box and use the command:

    a. **Right click -> Key Selected**

    b. Repeat this for the lf_palm_constraint_loc_W0 attribute.

9. Go to frame 20 and reverse the attribute values.

    a. lf_palm_constraint_loc_W0 = 1

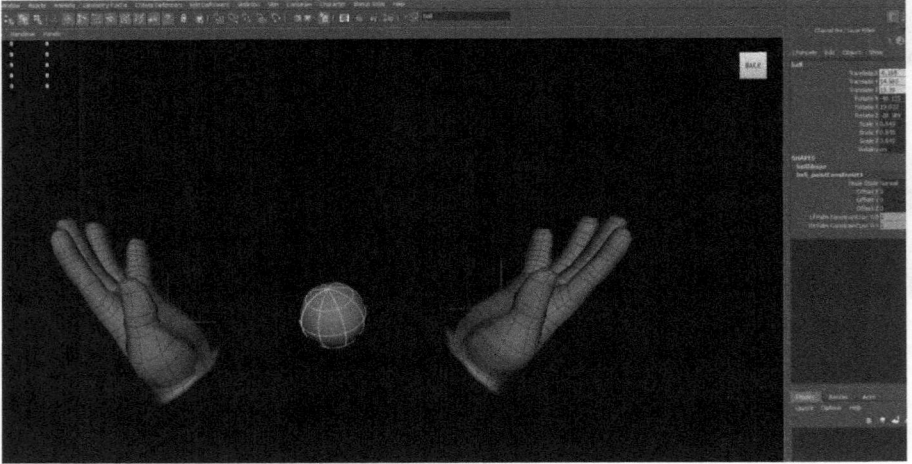

Figure 25. Weights move the ball.

    b. rt_palm_constraint_loc_W1 = 0

    c. The ball should move all the way to the left hand

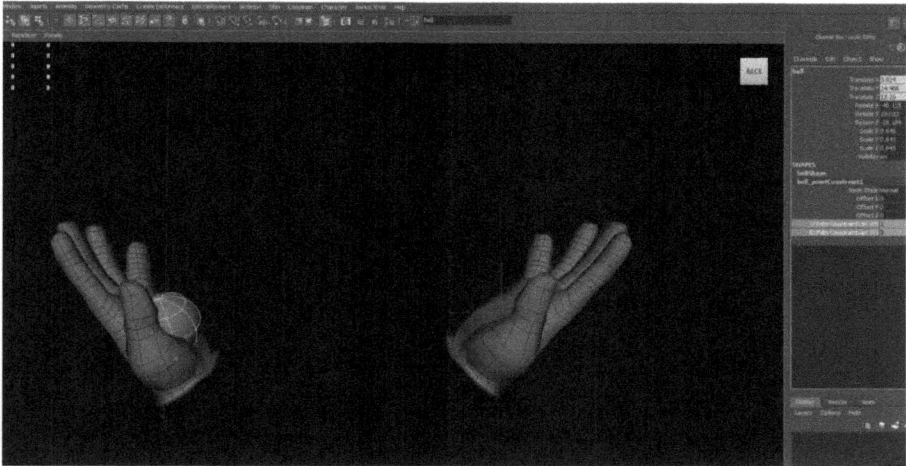

Figure 26. Ball moves all the way over.

10. Key the values in for frame 20. Select the rt_palm_constraint_loc_W1 attribute in the channel box and use the command:

   a. **Right click -> Key Selected**

   b. Repeat this for the lf_palm_constraint_loc_W0 attribute.

11. Now scrub the animation time slider and see the ball move from the right hand to the left hand.

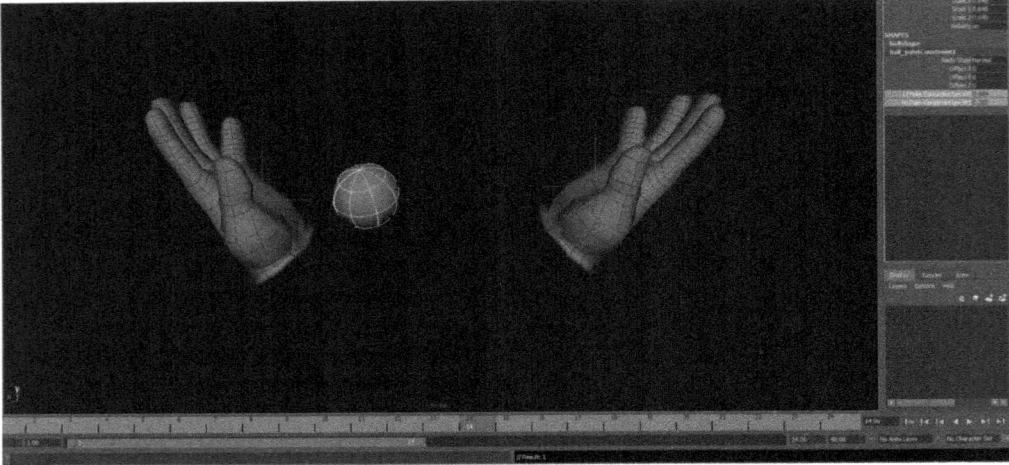

Figure 27. Scrubbing the animation of the ball.

Example File: 1_ball_constraint_tutorial.ma

To complicate the example further, often you will need to have the ball moving differently and not exactly in straight line from one hand to the other. To do so, one method is to have a third constraint to a locator. "Throwing" the ball from the left hand to the locator than to the right hand will result in the same look. However, if you then animate the locator appropriately, you can move the ball in the air. Play with this idea in this next tutorial.

Tutorial: Constraint Swapping for Animation Using 3 Constraints

1. Create your models of your left hand, right hand and a ball.

2. Create a locator for the left hand and place it in the palm. Name it "lf_palm_constraint_loc".

   a. **Create -> Locator**

3. Repeat the process for the right hand, resulting in "rt_palm_constraint_loc".

   a. **Create -> Locator**

4. Select the lf_palm_constraint_loc, then the ball and create a point constraint.

   a. **Constrain -> Point Constrain**

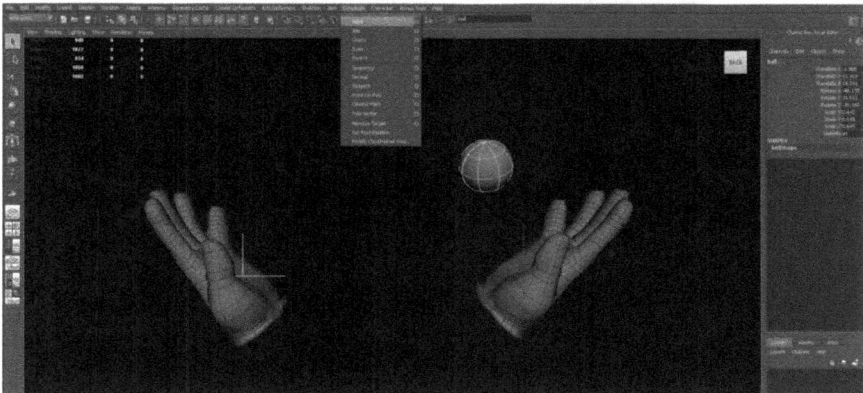

Figure 28. Ball constrained to left palm.

5. Repeat the process for the right hand. Select the rt_palm_constraint_loc, then the ball and create a point constraint.

   a. **Constrain -> Point Constrain**

6. You will now have a ball that is constrained to both hands and will be halfway between the two. By moving either locator, you will move the ball "somewhat" (only half of the motion). This is because both locators are controlling the ball equally. Select the ball and click on the channel box to examine the point constraint settings.

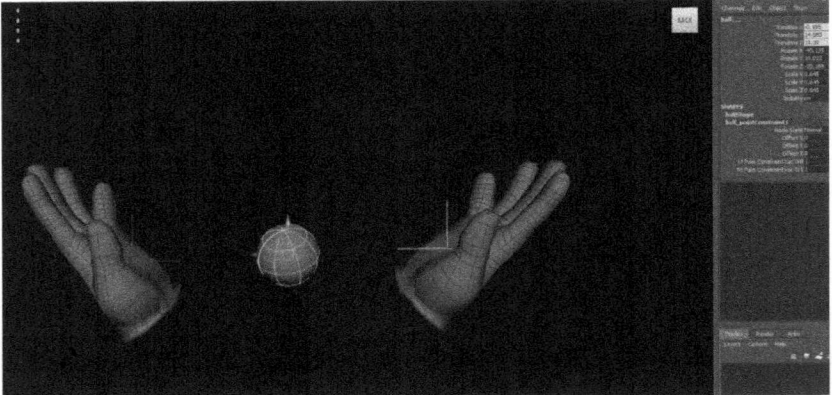

Figure 29. Ball has two masters.

7. Adjust the two weight values to control the balls motion. Change the attribute of lf_palm_constraint_loc_W0 to 0 and the attribute of rt_palm_constraint_loc_W1 to 1. The ball should be all the way into the right hand. You can

adjust its position by moving the rt_palm_constraint_loc around.

8. Go to frame 1 and set a key for the weight values. Select the rt_palm_constraint_loc_W1 attribute in the channel box and use the command:

    a. **Right click -> Key Selected**

    b. Repeat this for the lf_palm_constraint_loc_W0 attribute.

9. Go to frame 20 and reverse the attribute values.

    a. rt_palm_constraint_loc_W1 = 0

    b. lf_palm_constraint_loc_W0 = 1

    c. The ball should move all the way to the left hand

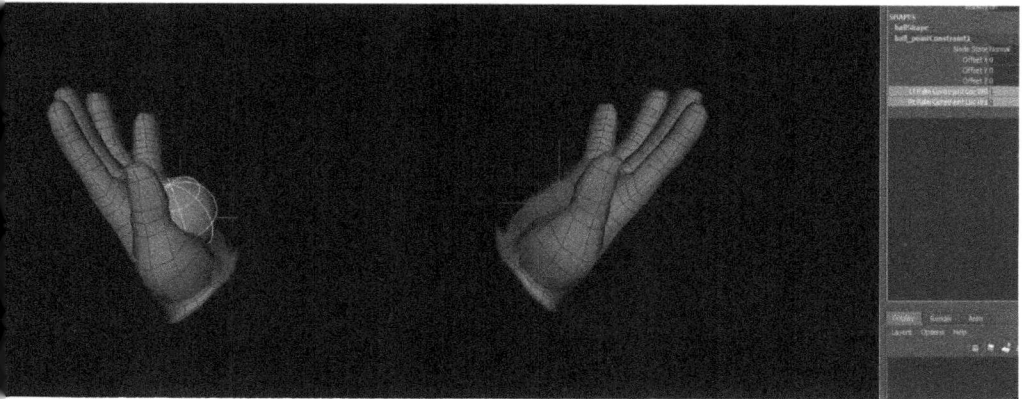

Figure 30. Ball keyed into left hand.

10. Key the values in for frame 20. Select the rt_palm_constraint_loc_W1 attribute in the channel box and use the command:

   a. **Right click -> Key Selected**

   b. Repeat this for the lf_palm_constraint_loc_W0 attribute.

11. Now scrub the animation time slider and see the ball move from the right hand to the left hand.

12. Create a third locator and name it "ball_flight_loc".

   a. **Create -> Locator**

13. Position the locator in between the two other locators and slightly above.

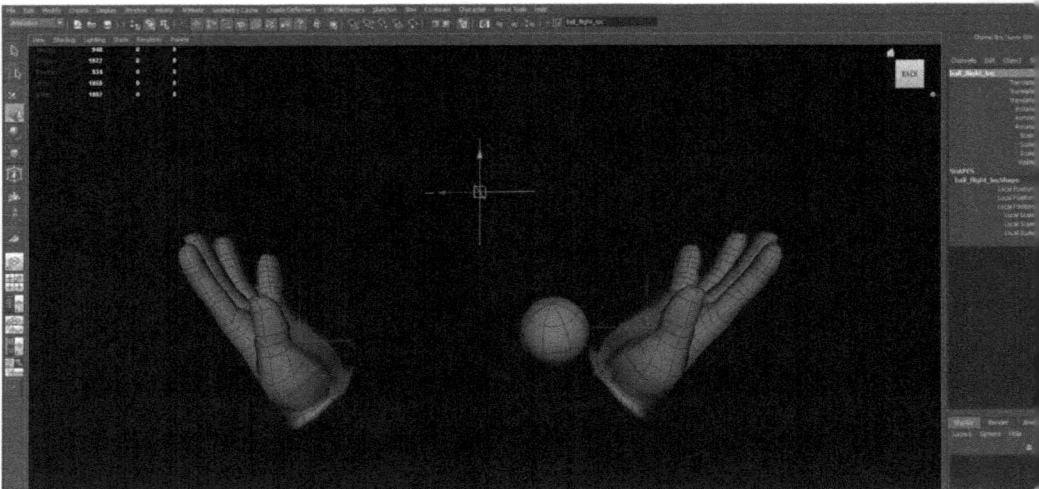

Figure 31. Ball flight locator.

14. Next, create a point constraint between the ball and the new ball_flight_loc. Select the ball_flight_loc, then the ball and create a point constraint.

    a. **Constrain -> Point Constrain**

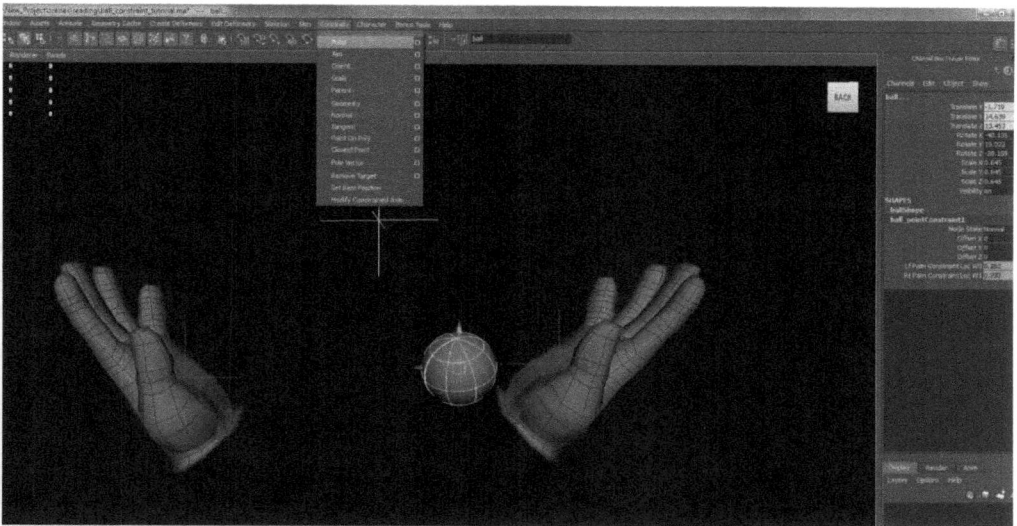

Figure 32. Constrain to new locator.

15. Let us key the values again. This time, go to frame 1. Select the point constraint in the outliner and then select the new attribute of ball_flight_loc_W2 in the channel box. Key it at 0 on frame one, using the command:

    a. **Right click -> Key Selected**

16. Move to frame 20, and set another key at 0 again.

17. Now let us go half way, to frame 10. Select the two palm attributes, and set them to 0. Set the ball flight locator to 1 while you're at it:

    a.   rt_palm_constraint_loc_W1 = 0

    b.   lf_palm_constraint_loc_W0 = 0

    c.   ball_flight_loc_W2 = 1

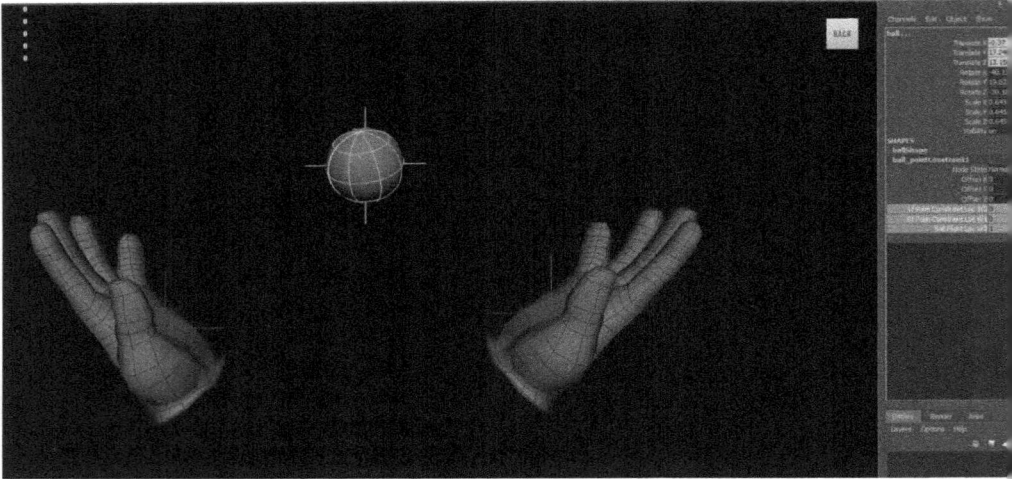

Figure 33. The ball flies to the middle locator.

18. Key each of the values for frame 10. Select the attributes and:

    a. Right click -> Key Selected

19. Now you can scrub the timeline and see the ball fly from the palm to the ball flight locator and then on to the other palm. Experiment by animating the ball flight locator a

little and you will see the ball inherit this motion as the constraint turns on and then still return to the other palm.

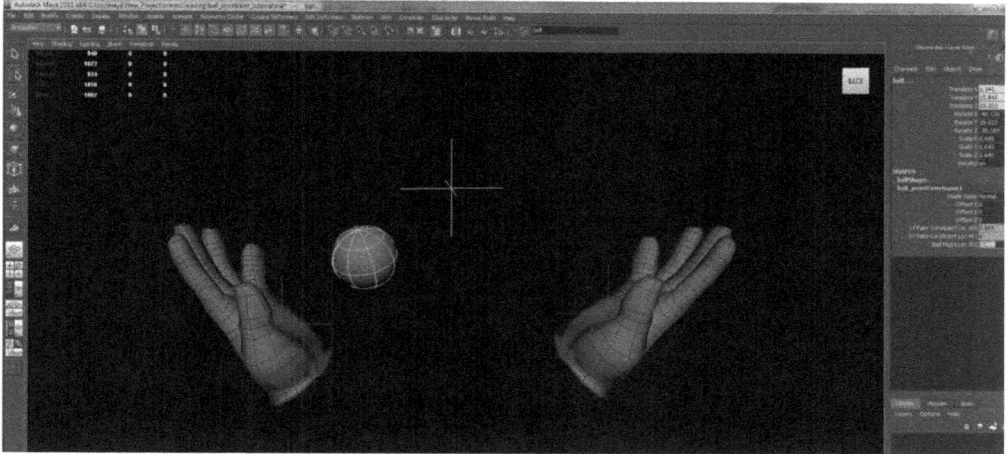

Figure 34. The ball flies to left palm.

Example File: 2_ball_3_constraint_anim_tutorial.ma

Of course, you could also have the ball constrained to locators at either hand that are parented and animate to adjust the ball's flight. As with many things in digital animation, there is a variety of options to get you to the same result.

One more thing to note: once you constrain an object, you can no longer just turn the constraint off or back to 0 without having problems occur. This is because once the object has been constrained it no longer "remembers" where it was originally. It has taken on the location of the object it was constrained to, and only remembers that. That means if you turn it the constraint off, by lowering the weight to zero, the object has to "guess" at where it was originally, since that original position has been "forgotten". The result is an object that seemingly pops around without rhyme or reason each time your animation is played back. This is typically solved by always having at least one constraint active for any object that has ever been constrained. This is not a big deal or concern to have a constraint always on, but it is something you should remember to avoid the object popping around all over your scene.

To continue on the constraint theme, an orient constraint will control the rotations, and a scale constraint will control the scales. These act exactly the same way the point constraint does, just with different types of the transform (rotate or scale) and so we will not waste your time or trees with pages of in-depth repetition.

A parent constraint will do all of these three combined. The reason that a parent constraint exists is to allow two "parents" to share a "child". This can be replicated by putting on both a point and orient constraint on an object.

The caveat to using parent constraints is that they leave the actual hierarchy alone. This means that someone opening your scene for the first time will have a harder time understanding relationships at a glance when you use a parent constraint versus outright parenting. For this reason, where possible, the preferred method is to use ordinary parenting.

Therefore, condensed, why constraining is great:

1. It is an easy way of copying translations, rotations, and/or scales from one object to another.
2. An object can have "multiple parents" if it is constrained to more than one object.

Joints

A joint within Maya is nothing more than a point in space that has its own local rotation axis. Sometimes referred to as a bone, the joint is a visual way to represent a point. The joint has a special icon that draws an arrow shape towards the joint below it, or its child joint. This arrow portion is the depiction of the joint length, and is often referred to as a "bone" since it represents the bones in an anatomical sense while the joints represent the pivot points of those bones. You will often see the term bone or joint used interchangeably in reference to Maya.

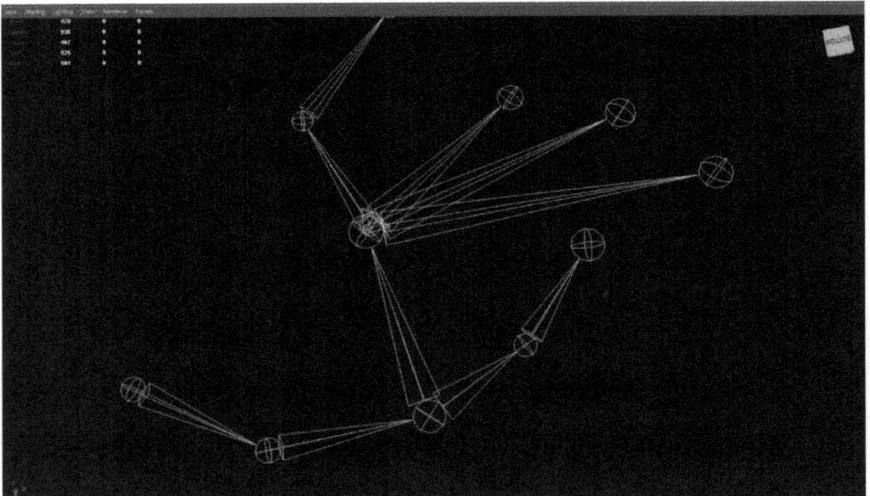

Figure 35. Joints in Maya.

It is important to note that while in some software packages this arrow or bone actually does have their own characteristics and effects, the arrow portion within Maya has no real effect or relation to any deformation, and merely serves as a visual guide. It may be for this reason that many people use joints and bones as interchangeable names. Within Maya, they can easily be considered one and the same.

The main advantage of a joint within Maya is the local rotation axis. The caveats to this is covered in detail a little further on, but suffice it to say for now that the local rotation axis allows for the joint to rotate on a different axis than the world axis and can be adjusted to the user's liking. This is one of the main differences between a joint and just a normal transform.

Another main difference between a transform and a joint is that joints are the default choice for binding. While it is possible to use actually anything for binding, utilizing influence objects, joints are the "proper way" of going about doing so. We will discuss deformation a little later on, but suffice it to say the properties of joints (LRA's, only drawn/not rendered, etc.) make joints the best choice to bind your character. So, why joints are good:

1. They have a bone drawn to show you the skeleton yet do not actually render.
2. They are the default choice for binding.
3. They have their own local rotation axis (LRA), allowing them to rotate differently.

Joint Chains

Continuing onwards, we can now talk about putting joints together in joint chains. Using the joint tool, you will automatically be able to create joints parented to each other. In fact, the tool defaults to doing so and will continue doing so until you hit enter to stop using it.

Tutorial: Drawing Joints

1. Drawing joints works best in an orthographic view (Front, Top or Side), so first switch to the Front Camera:

   a. Hotbox (Spacebar) -> Left click and hold in the very center -> Front

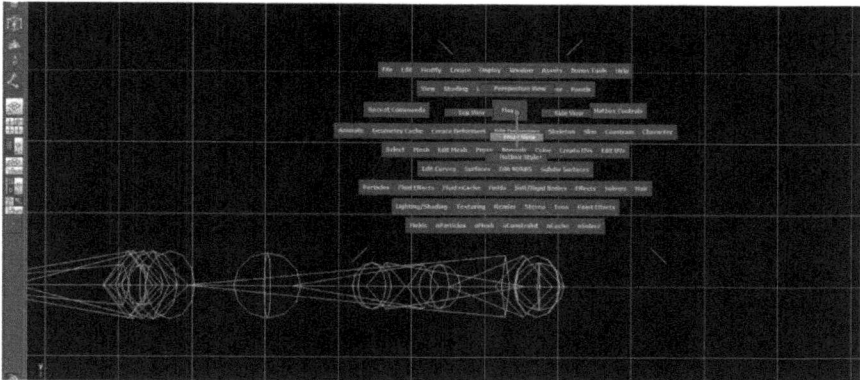

Figure 36. Hotbox to select front view.

2. Next we can make use of the joint drawing tool:

   a. Skeleton -> Joint Tool

   b. Each left click will draw a new joint in the hierarchy

   c. Hit Enter when you are finished.

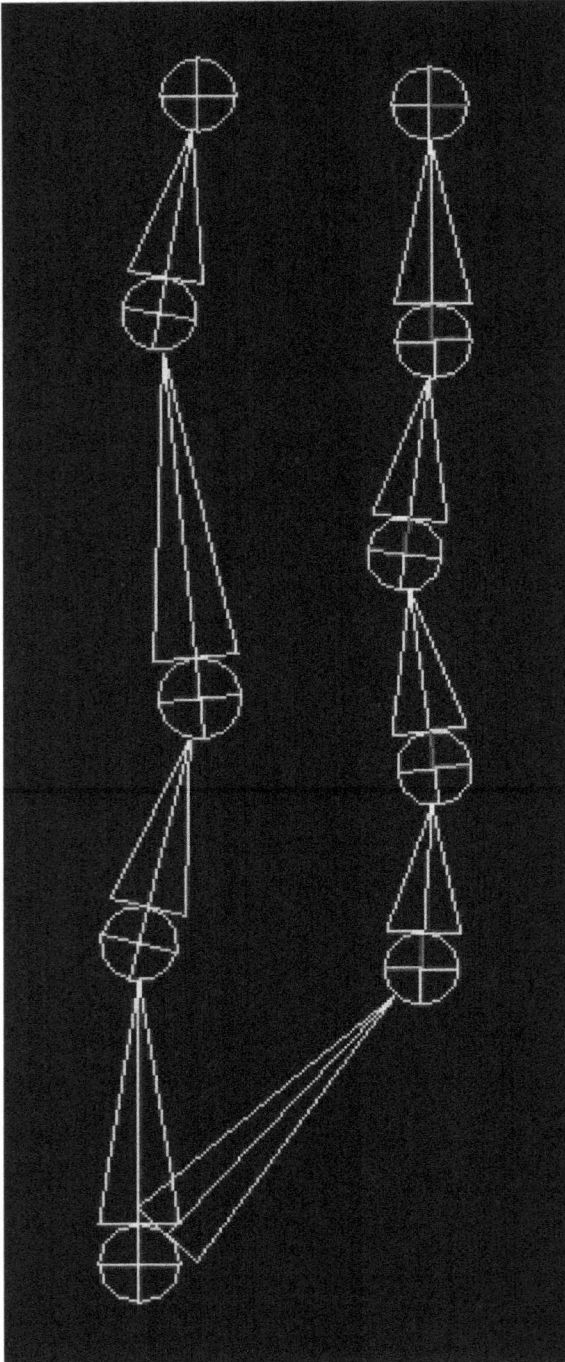

Joints can be parented together to form more complex chains. Try drawing two joint chains and parenting them together in the following example.

Figure 37. Parenting joints.

Tutorial: Joint Parenting

1. Start in the Front camera as in the tutorial above.

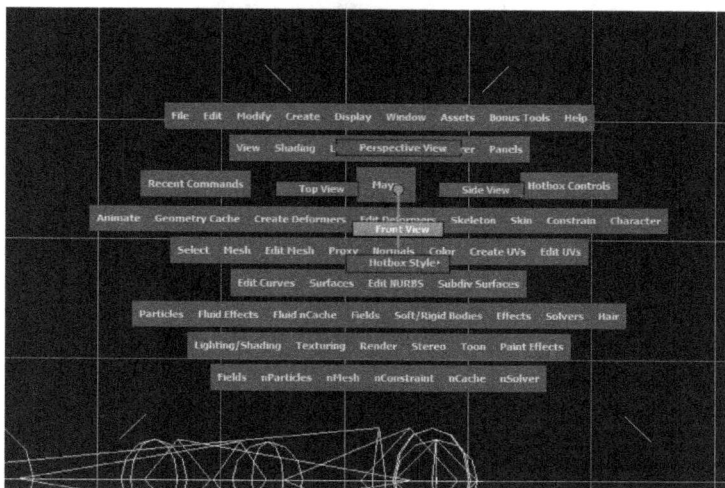

Figure 38. Front camera select.

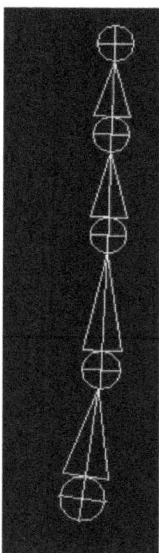

2. Let us build a hand. Draw one joint chain with 4 joints as shown in the example image to create a finger.

3.   Skeleton -> Joint Tool

4. Each left click will draw a new joint in the hierarchy

5. Hit Enter when you are finished.

6. Repeat this 3 more times for your other 4 fingers.

Figure 39. One joint chain.

7. Draw in one more joint to act as base and parent the finger chains to this joint by using the p key.

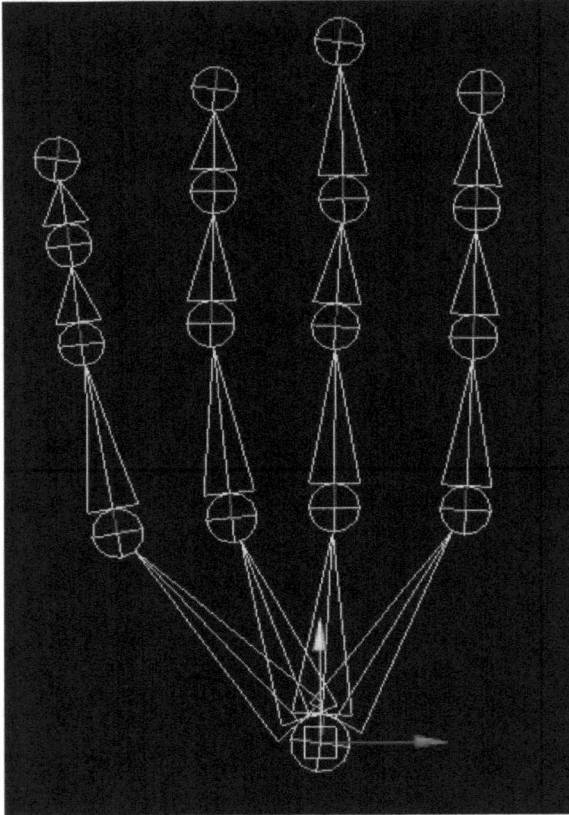

Figure 40. Four fingers drawn.

8. Now draw a 3 joint chain to represent the arm. Start with the shoulder, and then draw an elbow and a wrist as in the image.

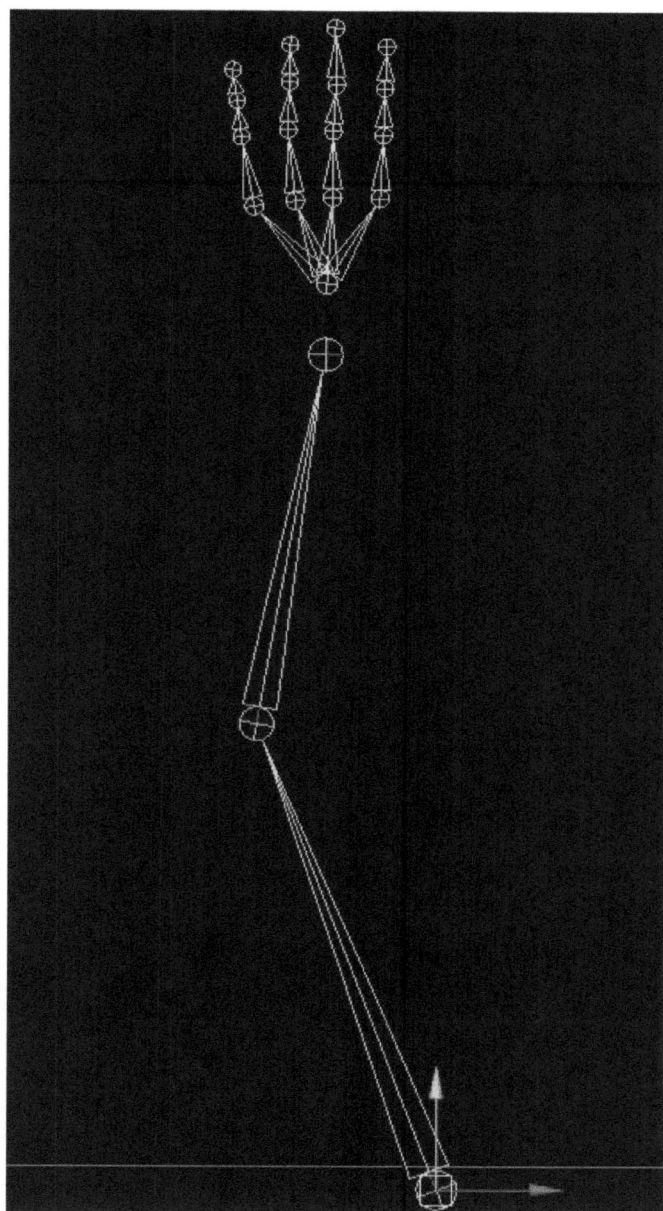

Figure 41. Arm joints drawn.

9. Select the topmost joint in your index finger, or the "root" joint of that finger.

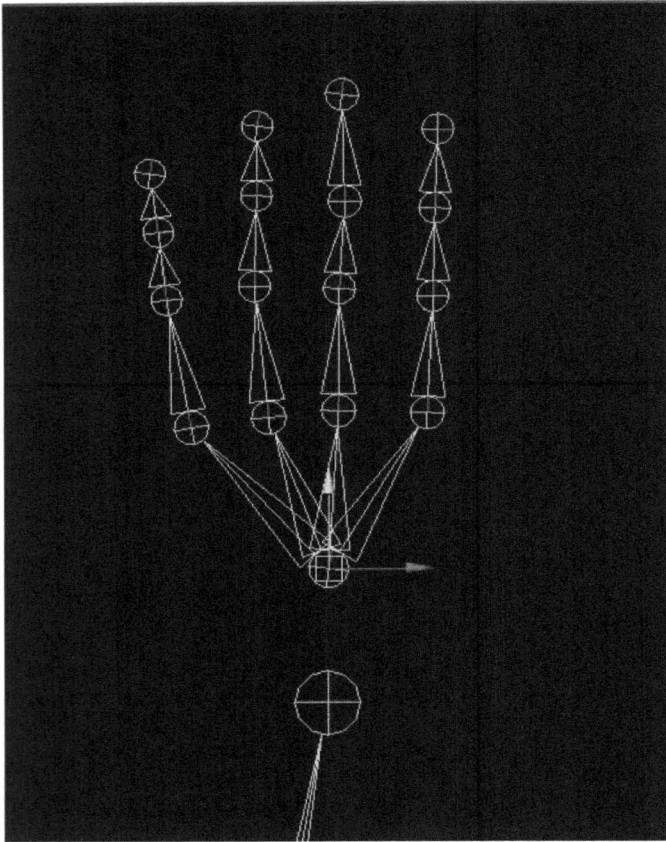

Figure 42. Finger base selected.

10. Hold shift and select the wrist joint.

11. Parent the joint by hitting:

    a. p

12. You can also parent multiple joints at once. Try drawing another hand and this time selecting each of the root joints for your fingers, or the topmost joints of each finger, and parenting them all at once. Remember to hold shift.

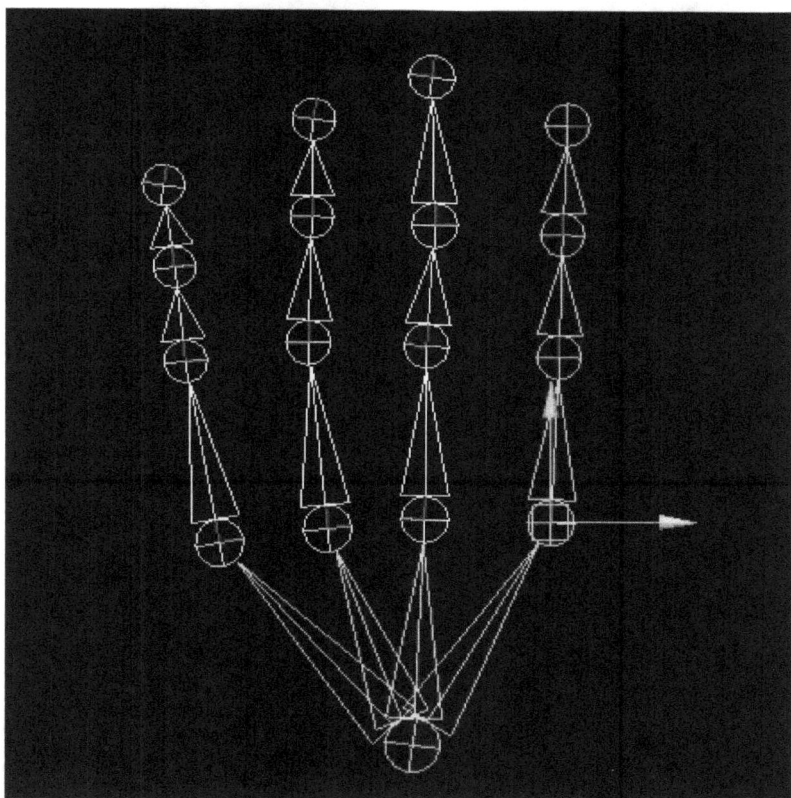

Figure 43. Select all fingers at once.

13. Whichever you select last will become the parent, as discussed above. Hold shift and select the wrist joint.

14. Parent the joints by hitting:

   a. p

15. Now you have a beginning of an arm with 4 fingers. Try adding a thumb on your own.

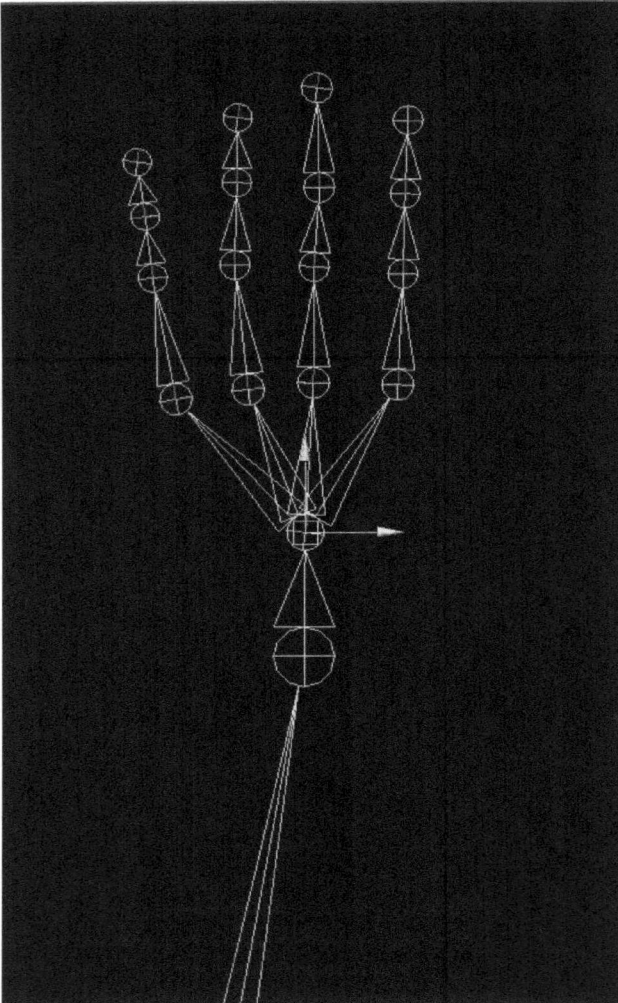

Alternatively, you can accomplish this same task by moving up and down the hierarchy as you are creating your chains as explained in the following tutorial.

Figure 44. Missing thumb required.

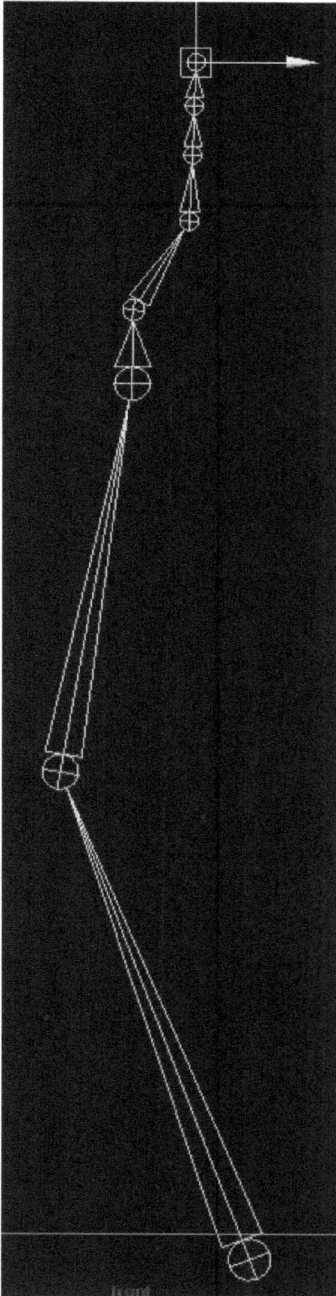

Tutorial: Drawing all at once.

1. This time start by drawing your shoulder, elbow, and wrist joints in the Front view.

2. Next, draw your index finger's 4 joints.

Figure 45. Drawn all the way to a finger.

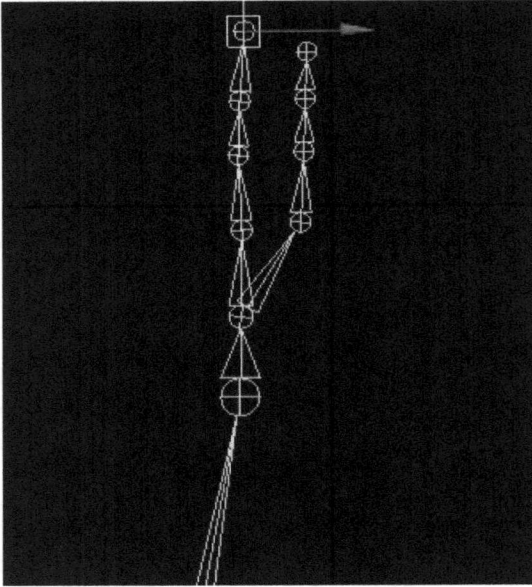

Figure 46. Use up arrow and then draw the next finger.

3. Now, use the up arrow key to move back up the hierarchy until the wrist joint is highlighted.

a. Up arrow key

4. Draw your middle finger's 4 joints.

5. Move up the hierarchy back to the wrist once again using the up arrow key.

6. Repeat the process drawing the other two fingers and a thumb.

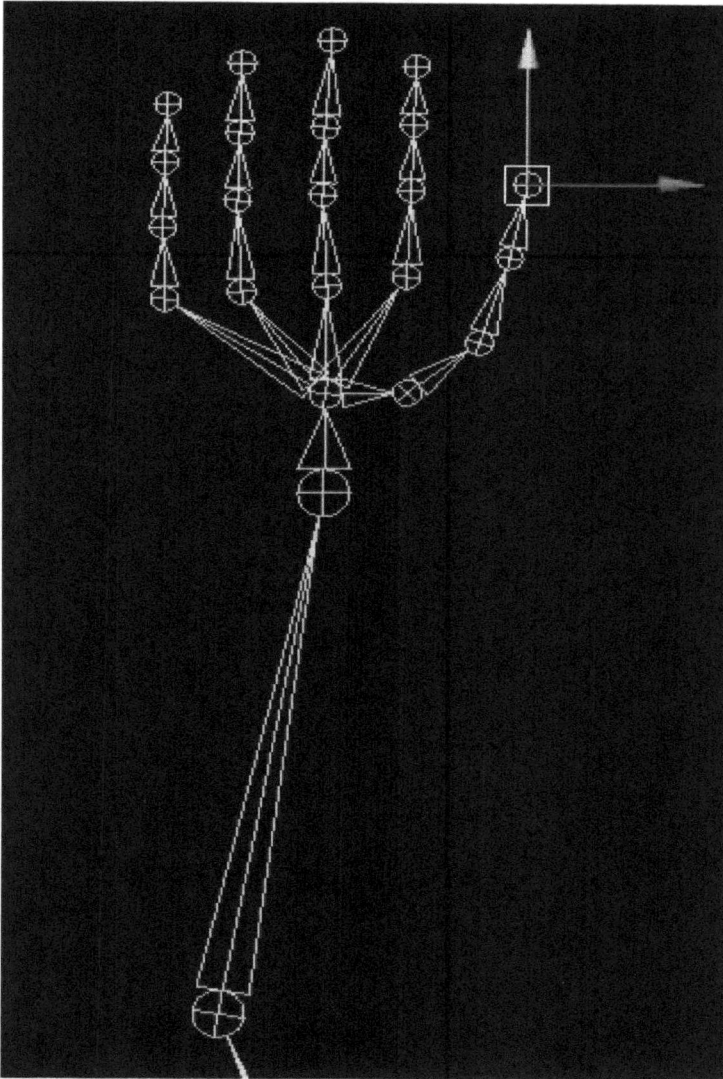

Figure 47. Completed arm is drawn all at once.

Local Rotation Axis

Once you have created your joints, it is also wise to setup the various local rotation axes of the joints. You can show your local rotation axis of a joint by selecting the joint and using

Display -> Transform Display -> Local Rotation Axis

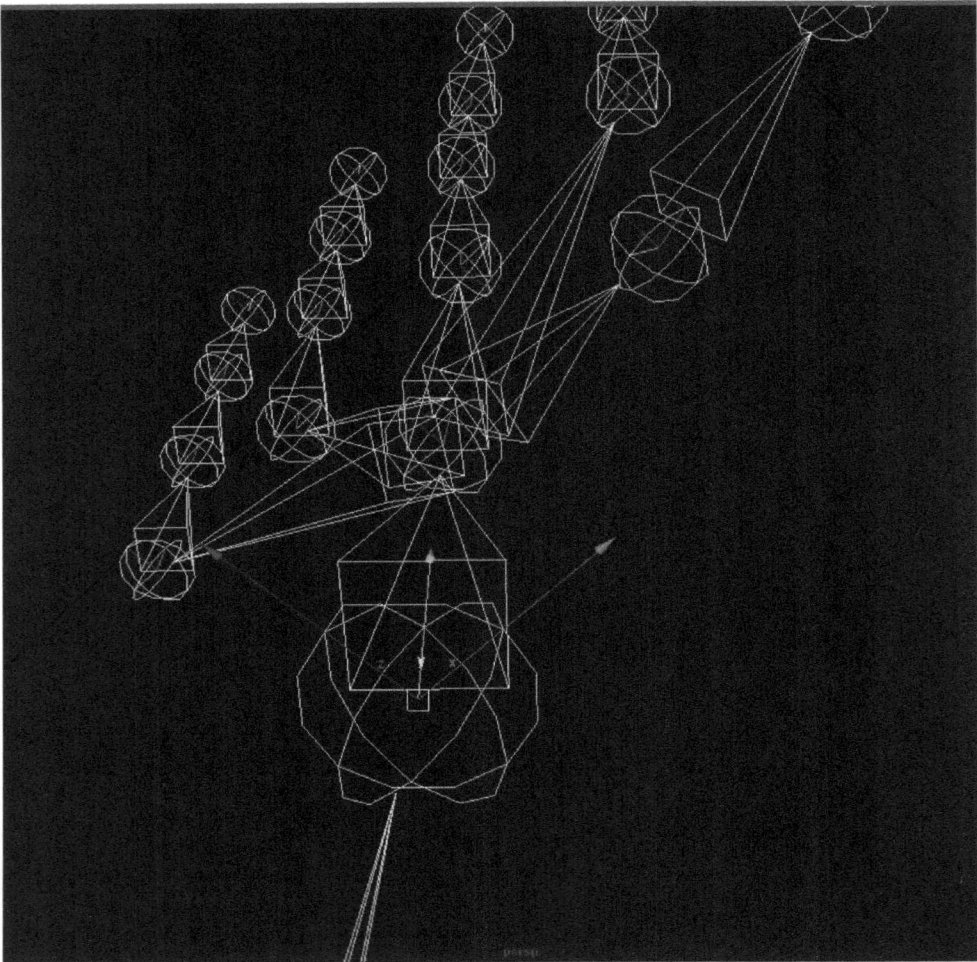

Figure 48. Local Rotation Axis.

Each local rotation axis (LRA) will need to be adjusted for its particular position. We want to orient the LRA's to point in such a fashion that Z becomes the primary axis of rotation. This is due to the math that centers on gimbal lock, which is a well-known flaw of Euler angles. To keep this simple, suffice it to say that certain orientations are difficult or impossible to attain. This will result in your rotation gimbal "breaking" to avoid mathematical errors like dividing by zero.

What do you really need to know about LRA's? With gimbal lock, we can predict that the first axis to break will be either X or Y. The

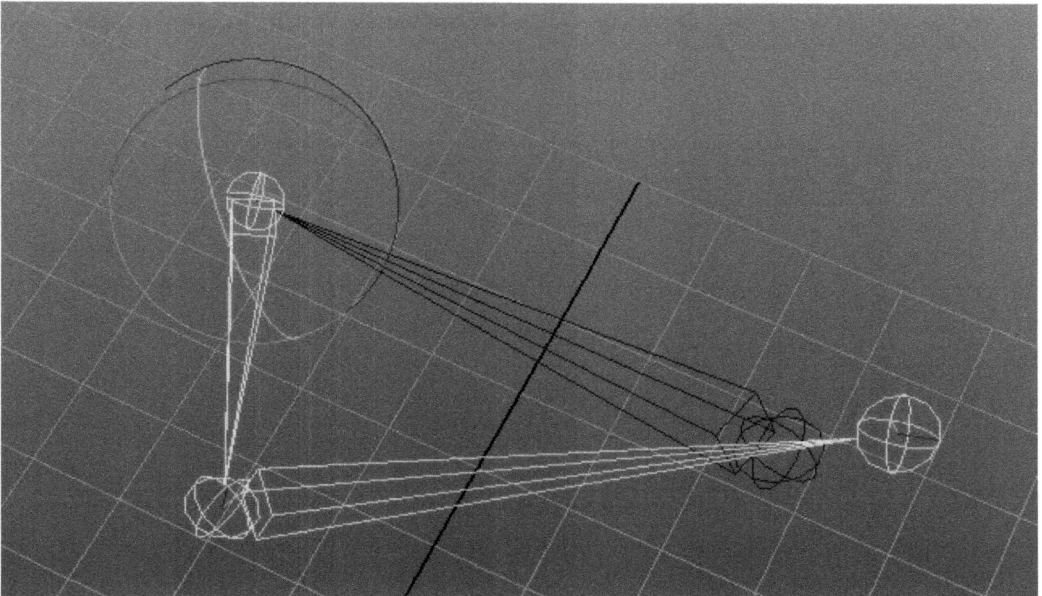

Figure 49. Broken gimbal.

second will be the other, so either Y or X. The last troublemaker will always be Z. Thus, if we setup our LRA's to make use of this understanding, we should avoid gimbal lock in most situations. To do so, we orient the joints so that Z is the primary axis of rotation. There are two ways to do so. You can make use of Maya's built in joint orientation tool or do so manually yourself. The following tutorial will show you both methods.

Tutorial: Orient Local Rotation Axis

1. Start by creating a hand as outlined in the previous tutorial.
2. Select all of your joints and display the LRA's
   a. **Display -> Transform Display -> Local Rotation Axis**

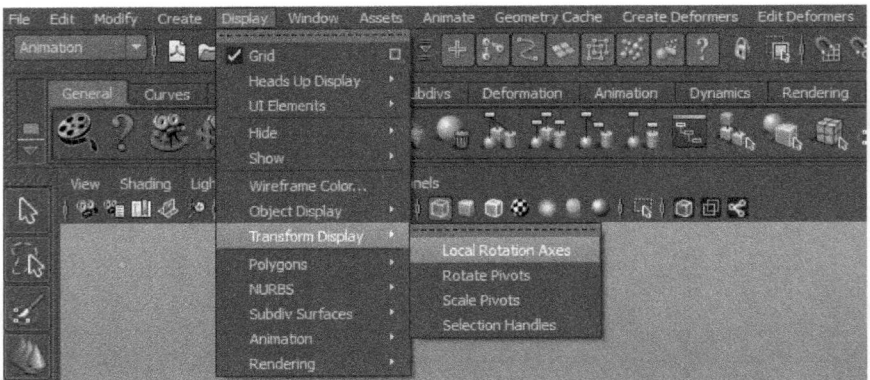

Figure 50. LRA menu

3. Select the joints in your fingers and use the joint orientation tool:

a. **Skeleton -> Orient Joint []**

b. There are several different options here, based upon the rotate order. Experiment with the settings to understand which method does what. Essentially, each setting will setup your joint LRA's in a different fashion. In the case of the fingers, we want to have the Z-axis pointing perpendicular to the joint direction, and the Y-axis pointing up. This will allow the fingers to all rotate on the z-axis as the primary axis.

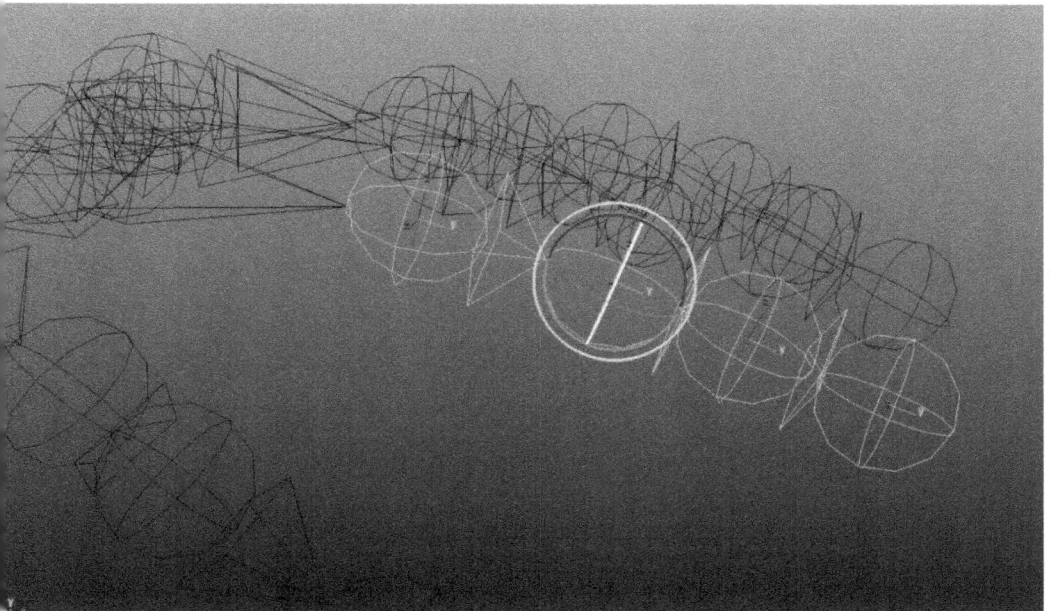

Figure 51. Z is the primary axis.

4. Sometimes using the tool will not result in getting the result that you wish. In these cases, it is very good to know how to do the orientation manually yourself. Select the joint, and enter the component (blue) mode:

   a. F8 toggles modes on the status bar

5. Turn off all options

   a. Click and hold, select "turn all off"

6. Turn on just the Local Rotation Axis:

   a. Right Click and hold on the ? mark icon

   b. Select/toggle on Local Rotation Axis

7. Now you will be able to select the LRA's themselves. Select one, and use the rotate tool to rotate the LRA in the orientation you desire.

   a. r to rotate

After you have drawn your joints, it is a good practice to zero out the transforms or freeze them. This will allow you to get back quickly to the rest pose when you are animating and in general make your life a lot easier.

Modify -> Freeze Transformations []

Please note, once you have put in the hard work of drawing and orienting your LRA's for all your joints, you will want to freeze your transforms. Make sure you check the options and turn off "Joint Orientation" in this case, since you do not want to lose all your hard work! If you do not turn off the "joint orientation" option, the orientation too will be reset back to the default rotation of the joint.

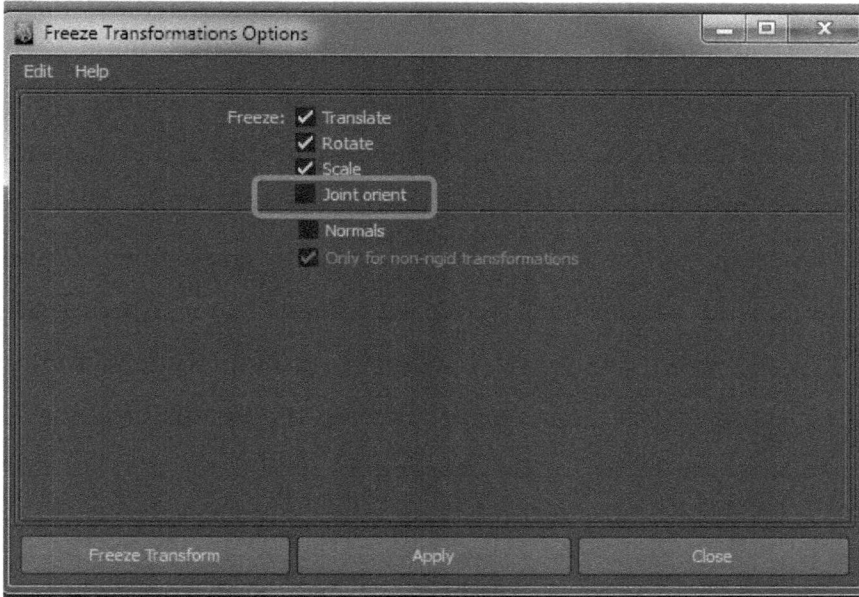

Figure 52. Deselect joint orient.

Once you have created, oriented and frozen out your skeleton, we can then progress on to how to move the skeleton in animation. There are two main systems that we will cover in this book; Forward Kinematics (FK) and Inverse Kinematics (IK). In the next book in the series, our intermediate book, we will progress to even more ways to move joints such as using a curve, dynamics, double-jointed systems, or a variety of other methods. Let us begin with the basics.

Forward Kinematics (FK)

By default, when you draw your joint chain, you have created a forward kinematic system. In forward kinematics, the motion progress forward down the chain. Take for example your shoulder. When you rotate your shoulder upward in a FK system, your elbow automatically moves upward as well, following along for the ride. In fact, all the other joints below come along for the ride as well, namely your wrist, and finger joints. Moving the elbow will move the wrist, etc. The forward kinematic system is the most basic but is capable of allowing for smooth arcs and is often used for situations that require this like dangling your feet

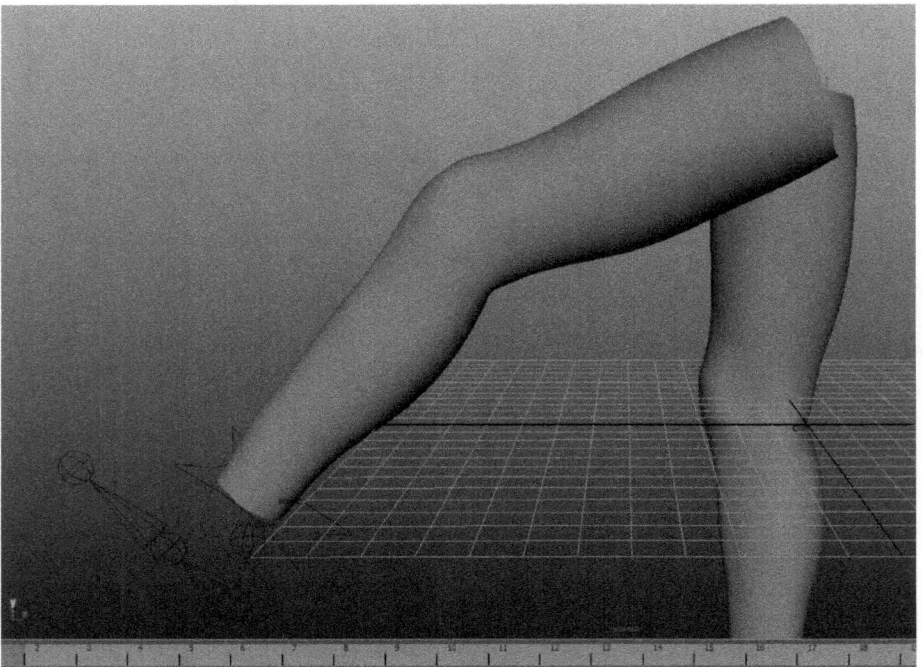

Figure 53. FK legs.

when you are sitting on a bench.

One thing to note is that generally people only rotate their joints when using FK. That is for good reason. When you translate or scale your joints in an FK system, the bone length changes. This of course is a rarity in an anatomical sense. To avoid the volume changes or bone length errors, it is far easier to impress the "golden rule" of saying, "only ever rotate in FK". Once you know this, you CAN translate or scale your joints, but just make sure you are being careful or doing so for the right reasons. For most of your animation scenarios, you will indeed rely on only rotating your joints since the bone length will need to remain the same. It is not often that you would see your forearm stretch and shrink after all. Regardless of how you move, rotate, or scale your joints, you should ultimately try to keep your skeletons reflecting their anatomy and that means that lengths generally stay the same.

In this next tutorial, we will build a proper hand. Note that because joints are simply a point in space, we will use the trick of creating two joints at the knuckles to help simulate knuckle thickness. This technique will help later on when we discuss weighting and deformations later in the book.

Tutorial: Building a Hand

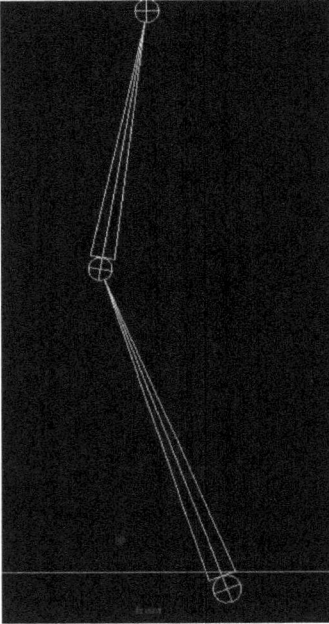

Figure 54.   Draw   arm joints.

1. Start by using the skeleton tool and drawing in the top view your shoulder, elbow, and wrist as before.

    a. **Skeleton -> Joint Tool**

2. Name your joints properly by clicking on them in the outliner and writing in the proper name

    a. **Window -> Outliner**

    b. Double click on joint1

    c. Rename   it   to "rt_shoulder_jnt"

    d. Repeat this process for rt_elbow_jnt and rt_wrist_jnt

3. Use the orient techniques discussed above to ensure the LRA's are in the proper direction, and that Z is the primary axis at your elbow.

4. Next, we will draw the pinky finger. Start by selecting the rt_wrist_jnt and then

    a. **Skeleton -> Joint Tool**

    b. Draw the joint at the base of your pinky, and continue to draw your joints to look like this image.

The key tip to remember here is the double joints for each knuckle will provide space for a thickness in deformation.

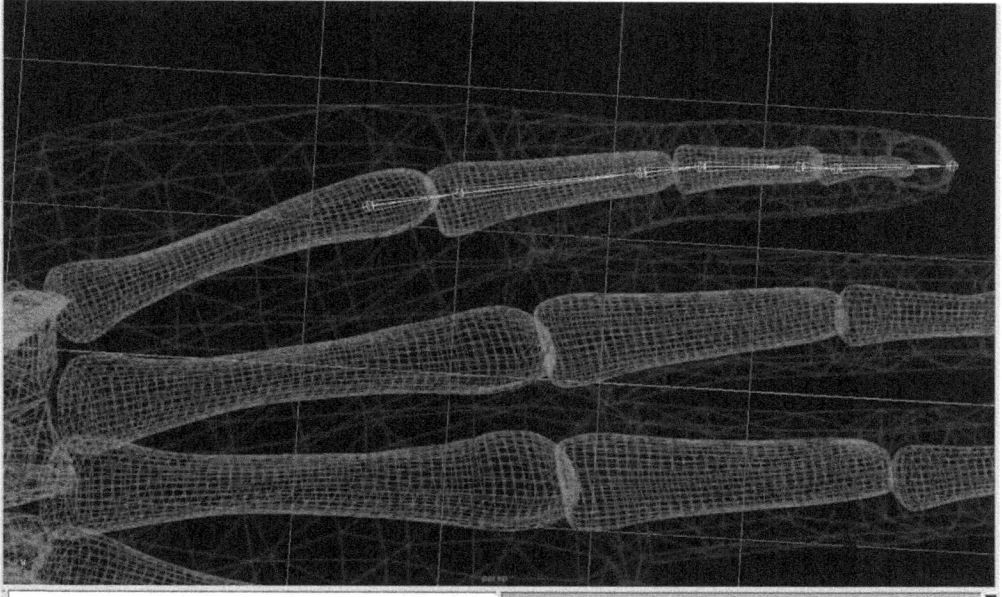

Figure 55. Joints have two joints to provide knuckle thickness.

c. Draw a second joint at the base of the pinky a little further out. Draw two joints at the next knuckle (medial joint) of your finger in the same fashion

d. Draw two joints at the next knuckle (distal joint) again.

e. Draw one more joint to symbolize the tip of the finger. Note that this tip joint will not get any weight during the deformation setup, but it will allow for easier animation since you will be able to see where the finger ends even if you hide the model and only show the skeleton. If you did not have this tip joint present, the skeleton can be misleading to an animator that uses only the joints for a fast silhouette.

    f.   Hit enter to complete the finger

5. Now that you have drawn the finger, align the LRA's so that their primary axis is Z for the main rotation. As explained above, you may find this easiest to do manually.

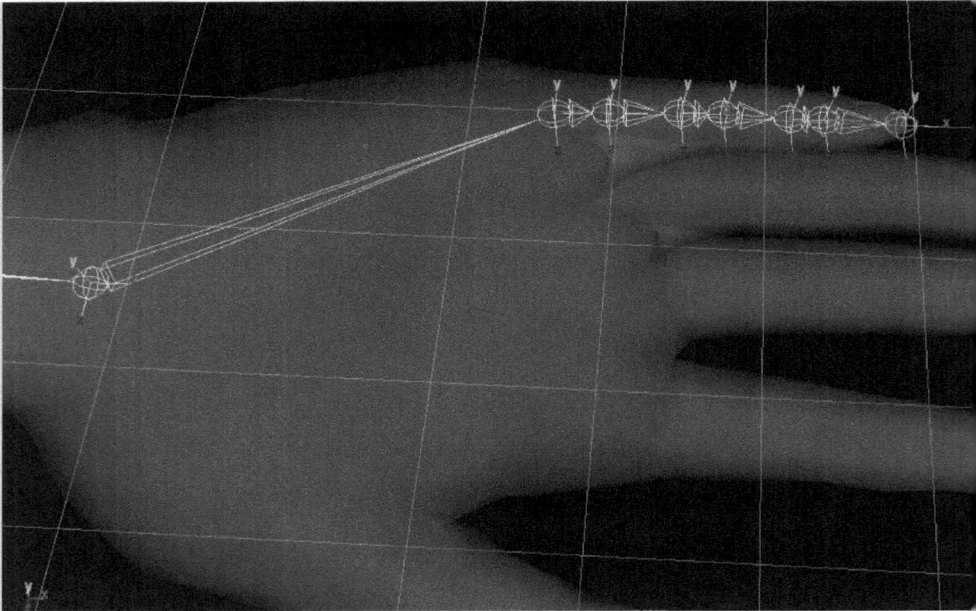

Figure 56. Get the first finger right before moving on.

6. Once you have aligned your first finger, take the time to name the joints properly.

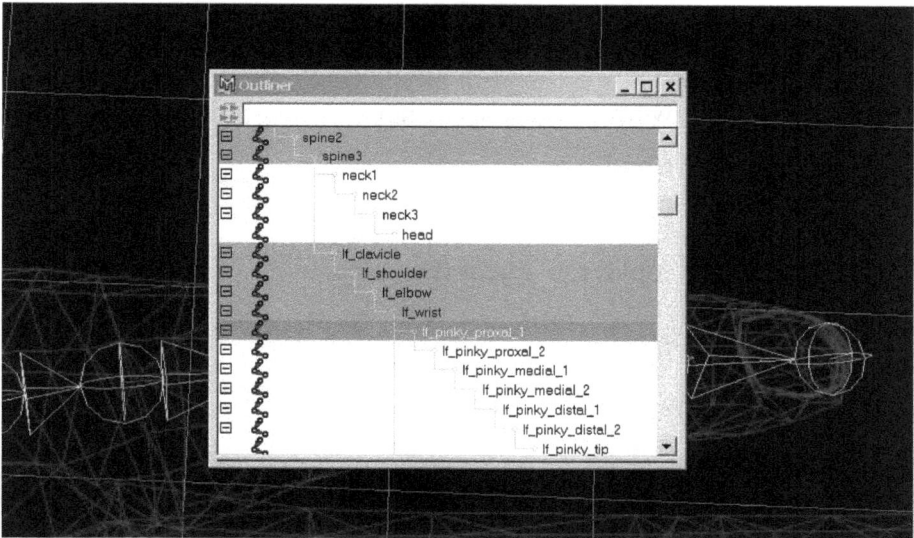

Figure 57. Name the hierarchy properly.

7. Do not forget to Freeze Transformations to zero out your joints

   a. **Modify -> Freeze Transformations []**

   b. Make sure that "joint orient" is NOT checked on; since you do not want to lose the work you did fixing the LRA's.

8. Now that you have aligned and named your finger, you can save yourself a lot of work on the other three fingers

by duplicating this finger. Since you have already fixed the LRA's, you only need to do this once (on the pinky) and the work is done "for free" on the other fingers. Look for other shortcuts like this throughout the book. ☺

a. Select the lf_pinky_proximal1_jnt.

b. Ctrl – d to duplicate the joint

c. w and translate the new finger to the position of the ring finger.

d. Select all of the new joints and use search and replace to adjust the names

    i. **Edit -> Search Replace Names -> Replace** "pinky" with "ring"

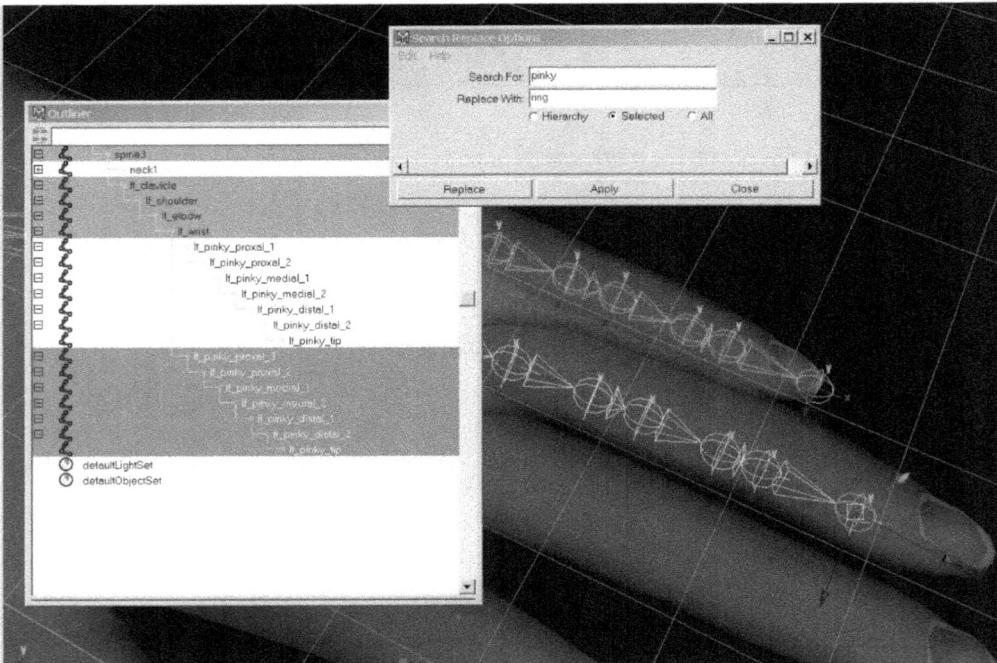

Figure 58. Search and replace to make the next finger.

9. Move the individual joints into the right position

    a. w and translate, e and rotate individual joints as necessary to adjust for the ring finger positions.

10. Do not forget to Freeze Transformations to zero out your joints on your ring finger.

    a. **Modify -> Freeze Transformations []**

    b. Make sure that "joint orient" is NOT checked on; since you do not want to lose the work you did fixing the LRA's.

11. Repeat steps 8 and 9 for the middle and index fingers.

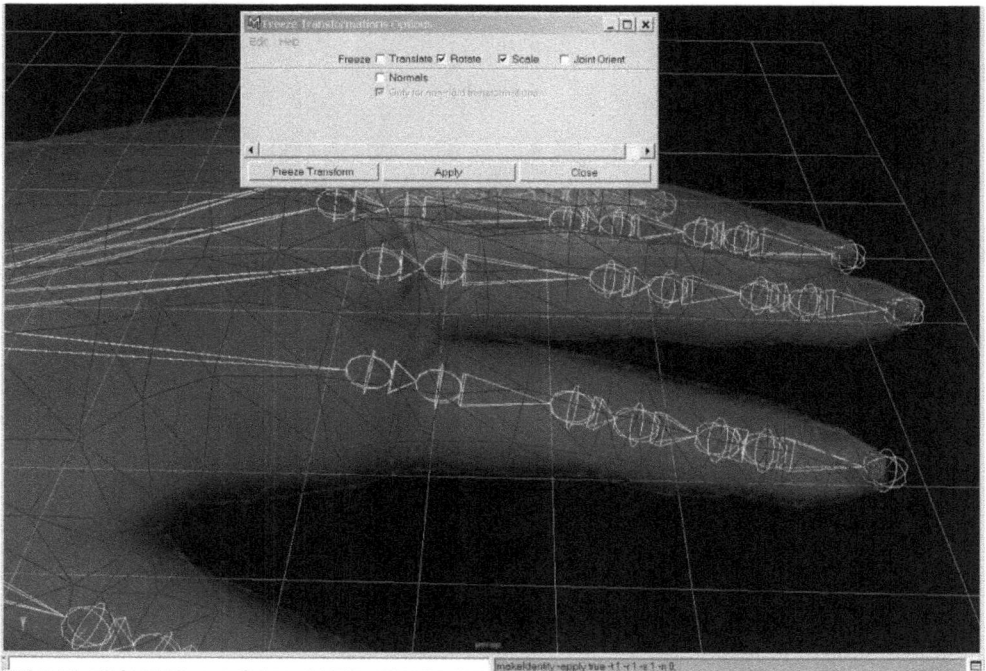

Figure 59. Freeze transforms for the fingers.

12. You can also repeat this process for your thumb, but with one important note. Look at your own thumb and you will note that it is the same as your finger, but rotated 90 degrees when relaxed. Repeat step 8 and duplicate a finger for your thumb, then

   a. e and rotate the lf_thumb_proximal1_jnt 90 degrees to adjust the LRA and joint positions.

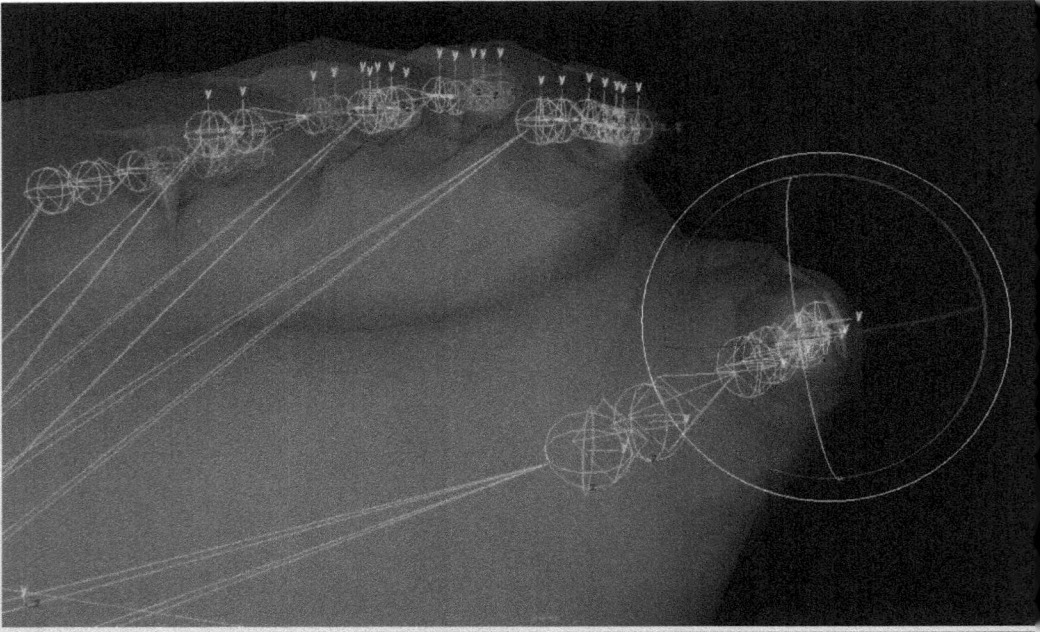

Figure 60. Rotate thumb into position.

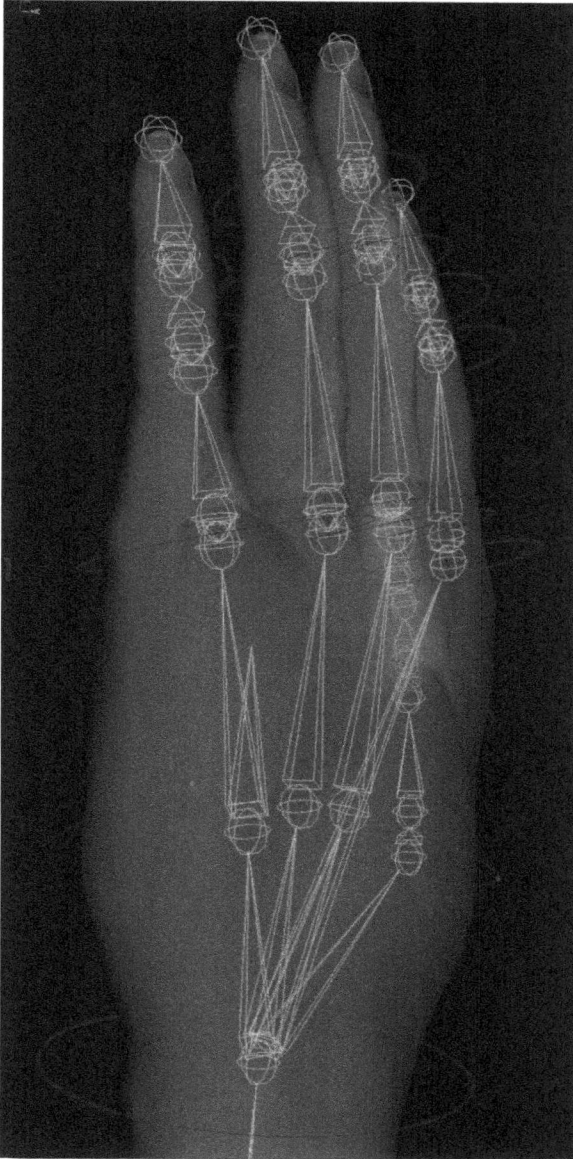

Figure 61. Completed hand.

13. Continue on your process of placing the joints and freezing the transformations at the end. You will see in this image control curves added to help with animation. These were created by a simple script that you can download from the website to make it very easy to add controllers to your own rig.

Later in the book, we will discuss expressions. One great expression to write is one that rotates the second knuckle joint the same as the first knuckle joint. This will cut the amount of animation you need to do in half for the finger rotations. For example:

```
  lf_pinky_proximal2_jnt.rotateX =
lf_pinky_proximal1_jnt.rotateX;
  lf_pinky_proximal2_jnt.rotateX =
lf_pinky_proximal1_jnt.rotateX;
  lf_pinky_proximal2_jnt.rotateX =
lf_pinky_proximal1_jnt.rotateX;
```

Knowing this ahead of time, having named all your joints properly will save you a lot of time. This is because of the simple fact that you can write the above piece of the expression, and then quickly copy that for the other fingers by replacing "pinky" with ring, middle, etc. and not having to type it all out. Two things are important to note then. First, adhering to a naming convention is will allow you to search and replace, saving time. After all, once you have set up one hand, would it not be great to duplicate it, do a quick search and replace for the names to create the opposite hand in rapid fashion? Second, naming the pinky right off the bat will save you work down the road. Remember, the faster you can do these processes, the more you can get done and thus the more time have to create better work.

Getting back to the point of this section, FK, we should discuss the major drawback of an FK system. An FK system can make it difficult to keep something in place. For instance, if you wanted to keep your hand on a table, rotating your shoulder in an FK system would require you to rotate your elbow in an opposite fashion to bring your hand back to the table. This is termed as counter-animating, and can be frustrating in that it often requires double the work. For this reason, an alternative method was required to make locking something in space easier to animate.

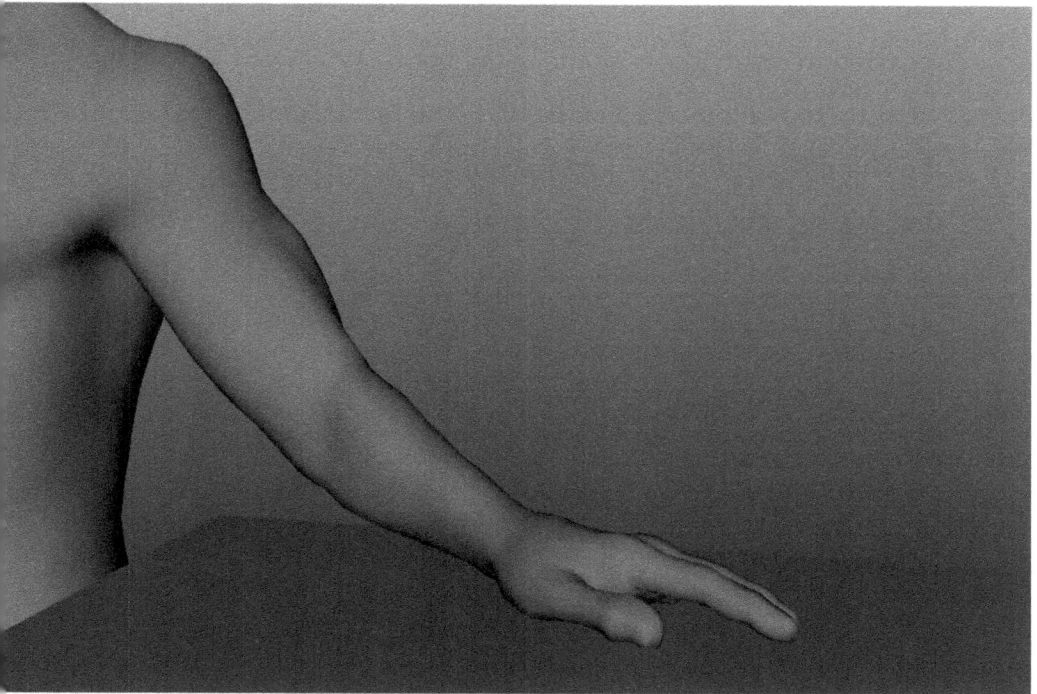

Figure 62. Hand resting on table.

Inverse Kinematics (IK)

To solve the problem of locking something down in space, the solution of inverse kinematics came along. In an inverse kinematics system, the motion of the joints propagates backwards or inversely. In other words, in our example of the arm, if we had an IK system running from the shoulder to the wrist, by moving the handle at the wrist, we would move the elbow and the shoulder. IK systems work in that they allow the user to pick the end position, and the system figures out the joint rotations required in order for the joints to get there. When you move your wrist by moving the IK handle, the system constantly figures out the shoulder and elbow rotations in order to get the positions of the elbow and shoulder. In this sense, you are working backwards mathematically or inversely since you solve the last position first and deduce the rotations it takes to get to that position. This is why it is called Inverse Kinematics. Typically, an IK system runs through 3 joints, as our arm example.

Tutorial: How to Create an IK Solver

1. Start by drawing three joints. Starting at the shoulder, draw a shoulder, elbow, and wrist by using the joint tool.
   a. **Skeleton -> Joint Tool**
   b. Left click to draw the joints, hit enter when you are done.
2. Name the joints shoulder, elbow and wrist

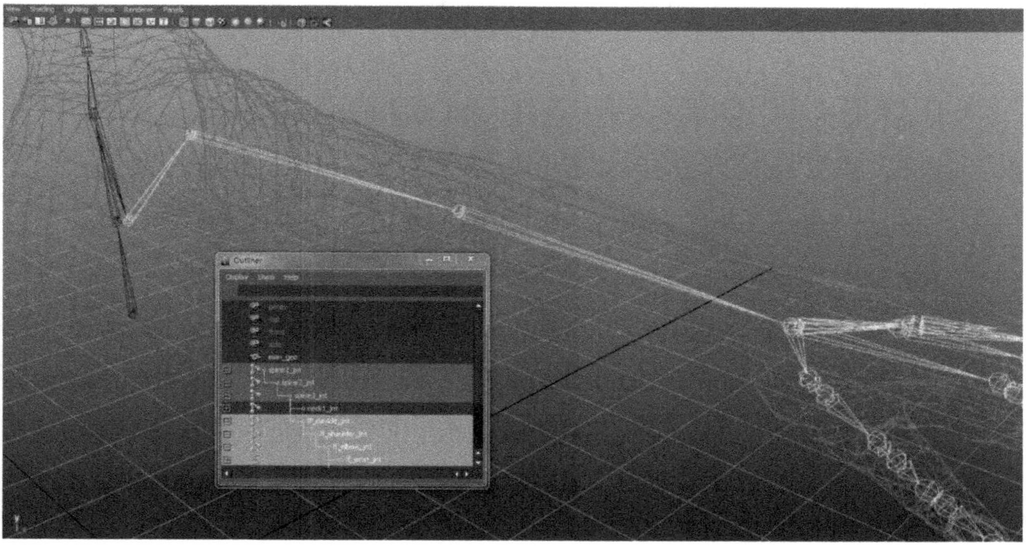

Figure 63. Arm drawn and named.

3. Create an IK handle by using the tool:
   a. **Skeleton -> IK Handle Tool []**
   b. Choose the ikSCSolver
4. Click on your shoulder then wrist to create the handle.

There are two types of solvers: the single chain (SC) solver and the rotational plane (RP) solver. Using a single chain solver, we are able to move our wrist. The arm will bend in the preferred angle and keep its bone lengths constant. The direction in which the elbow bends is referred to as the preferred angle since it needs to choose the "best" angle in which to bend. Mathematically, there are many directions you could bend for the same end position, but we have a direction in mind or one that we "prefer". This allows us to tell the computer which way is the "right" way to bend our elbow, and which way is "backwards". To set up your preferred angle, or the angle you want your arm to bend, the simplest way is to create your bones with a slight angle already in place. This simple feature embedded within Maya makes your life a little easier. The system will look for this angle when creating the IK handle and assume it is the preferred one. If you draw your joints perfectly straight, you then have to enter a preferred angle in the attributes of the IK system. The simplest approach is to draw your arm with a slight bend so it will bend the proper way.

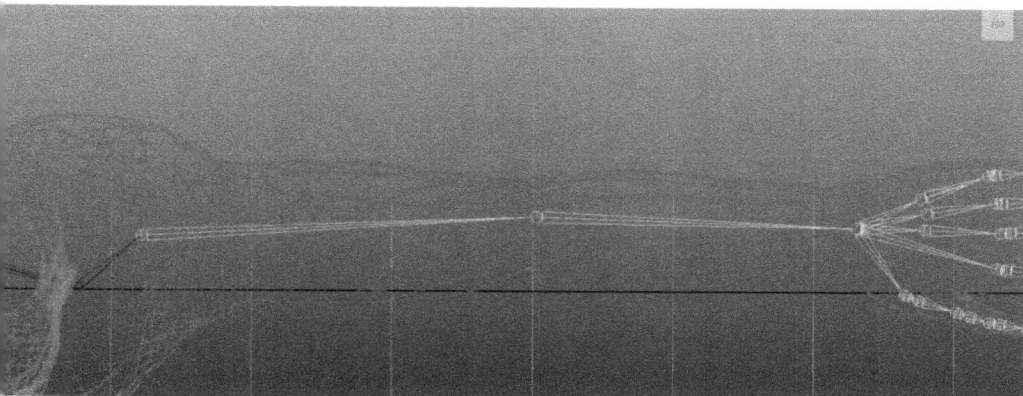

Figure 64. Arm has slight angle at elbow.

One quick point to make clear: the preferred angle typically does not change nor is animated. After all, you usually want your elbow to bend in a specific fashion.

However, this is not the whole story, is it? After all, if I move my wrist to a position, my elbow may be in any number of correct positions, depending on how I wanted to twist my arm and how my shoulder has rotated. This brings us to the next type of solver we could use, the rotational plane (RP) solver.

Tutorial: Create an IK RP Solver

1. Draw your shoulder, elbow, and wrist joints and name them appropriately using the tools outlined previously.
2. This time, create an RP solver:
   1. **Skeleton -> IK Handle Tool []**
   2. Choose the ikRPSolver

3. Click on your shoulder then wrist to create the handle.

It is important to know though, that an IK system can solve for any number of joints, not only just three. The greater the number, the more complex this can be and the more prone to error. Error you say? Well, maybe error is too strong a word, and we should say estimation error. Try drawing four joints and creating an IK handle to control them. Notice how your elbow always has the same bend to it, and you have a hard time pointing it to where you want it? Now try this same example with 5 joints or 8.

Let us backtrack now to our 3 joint arm example, the shoulder, elbow, and wrist. When you move your wrist to a position and you know your shoulder position, the elbow can be in any number of positions around a rotation plane. The rotation plane is simply the triangle that makes up the flat plane between the shoulder, elbow, and wrist.

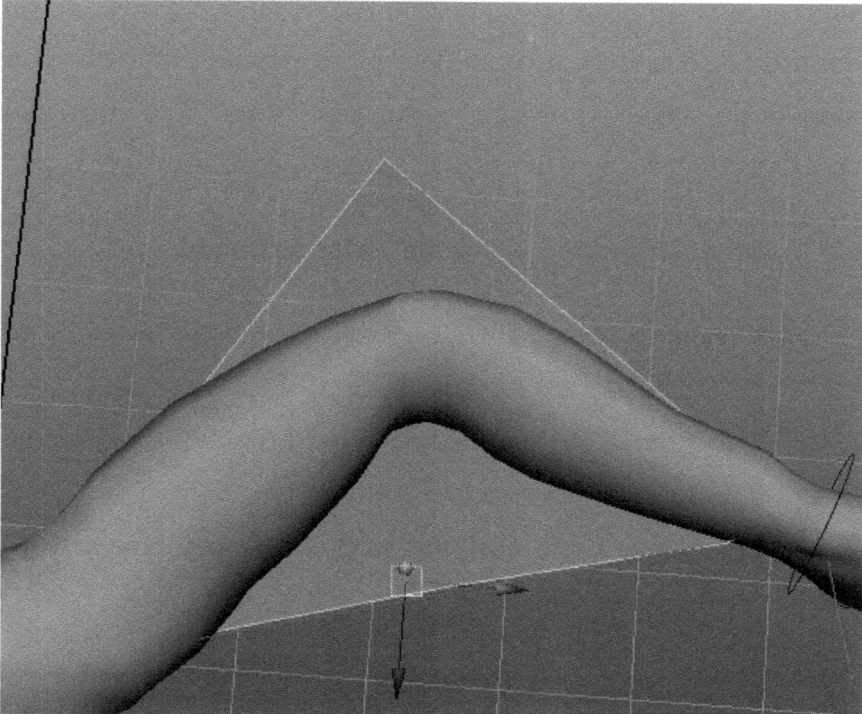

Figure 65. Rotation plane.

Now that the computer knows the wrist position and where the rotation plane is, it always places the elbow on the rotation plane (our triangle) in the position that is mathematically correct. The boiled down mathematical version is that assuming the length of the upper arm and lower arm stay the same, the elbow must be on a correct rotational plane.

To account for this, we need to also control this rotation plane. After all, once we can control the rotation plane, we can control the twist of our example arm. Animating the twist is as simple   as   using   the   twist   attributes:

Tutorial: Animating using the Twist Attribute

1. Create an arm, name it properly, and create an IK RP Handle using the previous tutorial.

2. Select the IK RP Handle and move it towards the shoulder. This will flex your arm, or bend it.

3. Select the twist attribute in the channel box and try changing the values.

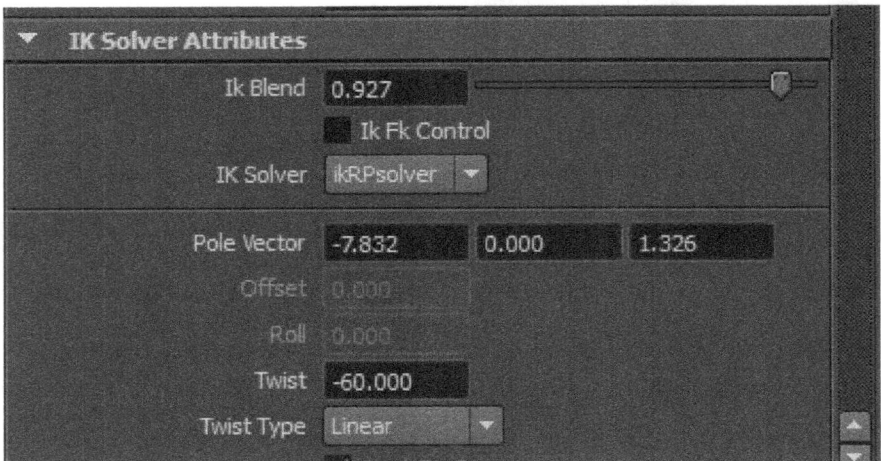

Figure 66. Twist attributes can be animated.

You can use the twist attribute to control the direction of the rotational plane and thus control the rotation or twist of the arm.

However, this can be cumbersome. This twist value needs to change based on where we want our elbow or knee to point and not some arbitrary number. The twist attribute can be animated, but would it not be easier if this were handled automatically for you? This brings us to our next topic, the pole vector. But first, let us pull all of the IK knowledge you have just learned together and build a proper foot rig to ensure you really understand how to make use of the various handles.

Tutorial: Rigging a Foot and Leg

1. Switch to side view.
    a. Spacebar (hold down for hotbox) -> Left click and hold in the center -> drag to the right to select side view
2. Draw your joints for your leg and foot
    a. Skeleton -> Joint Tool

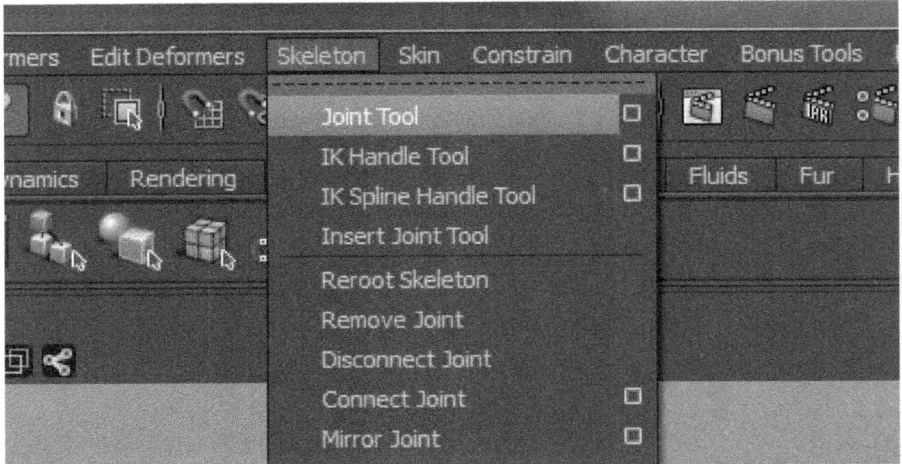

Figure 67. Joint tool menu.

3. Click and draw your hip, knee, ankle joints.

4. Continue to draw your heel, ball, and toe joints.

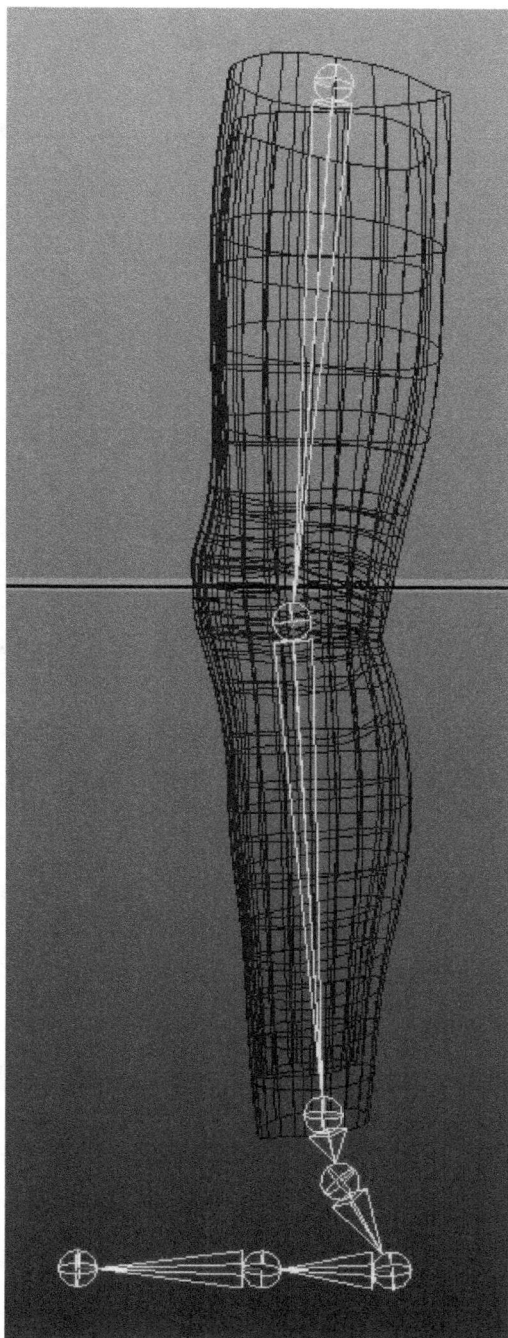

Figure 68. The leg is drawn as illustrated.

5. Hit enter to exit the tool.

6. Use the translate tool to move the joints as necessary to ensure a proper fit in your leg.

7. Ensure there is a slight bend at the knee.

8. This is a good time to stop and name your joints properly.

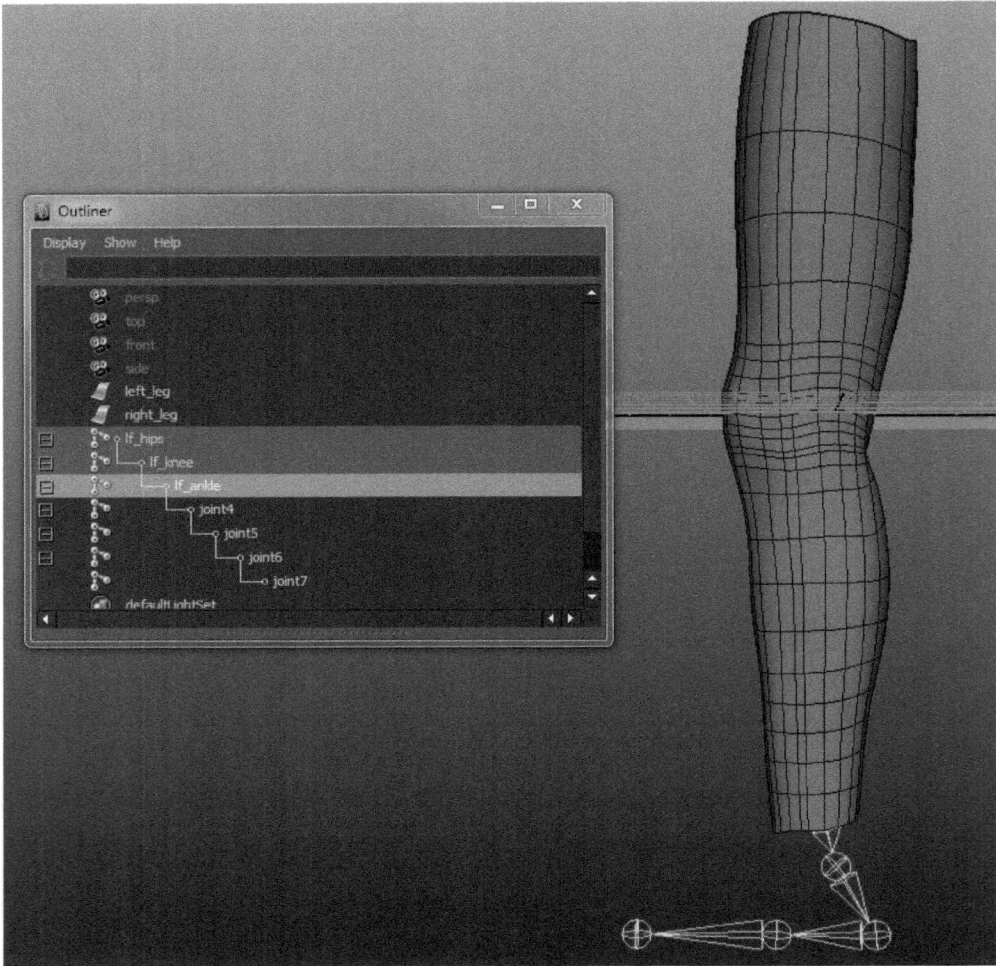

Figure 69. Leg joints positioned and named properly.

9. In order to control your leg, we will use the RP solver for an IK handle.

    a. **Skeleton -> IK Handle Tool []**

    b. Choose current solver to be ikRPsolver

    c. Click on your hip joint than your ankle joint to create the ik handle

    d. Rename the handle to "ankle_ikHandle"

10. Of course, a rotational plane solver IK will require a pole vector to be more animator friendly.

    a. **Create -> Locator**

    b. Snap the locator to the knee by selecting translate, holding down the "v" key and middle mouse dragging on the knee joint.

    c. Move the locator in front of the knee and rename it "knee_pole_vector_loc".

    d. Select the locator

    e. Shift select the ik handle "ankle_ikHandle"

    f. **Constrain -> Pole Vector**

11. We will also use two other ik systems to make the foot lock appropriately to the ground. One from the ankle_jnt to the ball_jnt, and one from the ball_jnt to the toe_jnt

    a. **Skeleton -> IK Handle Tool []**

    b. Choose the current solver to be ikSCsolver

    c. Turn on the "Sticky" option

    d.   Click on your ankle_jnt than your ball_jnt to create the ik handle

    e.   Rename the handle to "ball_ikHandle"

12. In order for this last ik handle to work properly, we will need to ensure our "heel joint" never rotates. That is because it is simply a solid bone in the human foot, and in the digital world is used for nothing more than indicating where the heel is to the animator. We will do this by locking the degrees of freedom off.

    a.   Select the heel_jnt.

    b.   Ctrl + a to open the attribute editor

    c.   Under the "Joint" section, locate the Degrees of Freedom

    d.   Unselect all of the degrees of freedom so your joint cannot rotate.

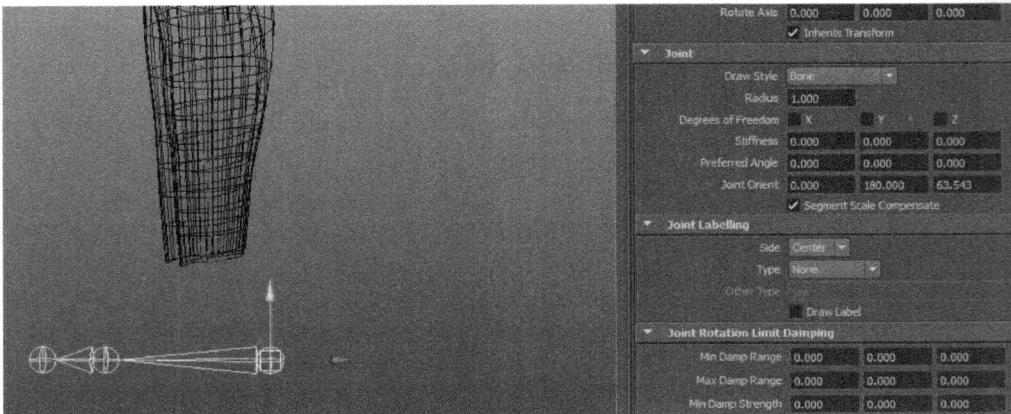

Figure 70. Degrees of freedom are controlled.

13. Now we can make the last IK handle we will require. To do so, create another handle from the ball_jnt to the toe_jnt.

    a. **Skeleton -> IK Handle Tool ▯**

    b. Choose the current solver to be ikSCsolver

    c. Turn on the "Sticky" option

    d. Click on your ball_jnt than your toe_jnt to create the ik handle

    e. Rename the handle to "toe_ikHandle"

14. You now have the ik handles in place that will move all the appropriate parts. However, moving them by hand individually can be a headache. On top of that, it is also challenging to make them zero out easily. One way around this is to group your joints. The issue with that however, is there is no nice way of selecting a group in the viewport without complicating things and using selection handles. Instead, we will create circles and use these to drive the joints. You could also draw your own curve if you prefer.

    a. **Create -> NURBS Primitives -> Circle**

    b. Move and rotate the circle so that it is centered around the ball_jnt of the foot

    c. **Modify -> Freeze Transformations** to zero the circle's transforms

    d. Rename your circle to "Ball"

15. Now that you have your circle around the ball of the foot, we can start putting the hierarchy together. Start by parenting the ankle_ikHandle to the Ball. This new circle called "Ball" will be our first controller and will allow you to roll up on to your toes, such as what happens when you stand on "tippy toes".

   a. Select ball_ikHandle

   b. Shift select Ball (the circle you just made)

   c. p (for parent)

16. Next, we will make the controller for your toe. This will allow you to rotate the toe independently of the rest of the foot, such as when you "raise your toes". Create another circle for your controller:

   a. **Create -> NURBS Primitives -> Circle**

   b. Move and rotate the circle so that it is centered around the ball_jnt of the foot

   c. Alter your circles size and shape so that it looks different from the first controller you made. This will make your life far easier when you are animating.

   d. **Modify -> Freeze Transformations** to zero the circle's transforms

   e. Rename your circle to "Toe"

17. Now that you have your circle around the ball of the foot, continue putting the hierarchy together. Start by parenting the toe_ikHandle to the Toe.

    a. Select toe_ikHandle

    b. Shift select Toe (the circle you just made)

    c. p (for parent)

18. Next, we will make the controller for your ankle. This will allow you to rotate the entire foot around. Create another circle for your controller:

    a. Create -> NURBS Primitives -> Circle

    b. Move and rotate the circle so that it is centered around the ankle_jnt of the foot

    c. **Modify -> Freeze Transformations** to zero the circle's transforms

    d. Rename your circle to "Ankle"

19. Now that you have your circle around the ball of the foot, we can clean up the hierarchy even more. Start by parenting the ball_ikHandle to the Ankle.

    a. Select ankle_ikHandle

    b. Shift select Ankle (the circle you just made)

    c. p (for parent)

20. Repeat this for the Toe and Ball to all be parented under the Ankle.

    a. Select the Toe and the Ball (holding shift)

b. Shift select Ankle last (the circle we're working with)

c. p (for parent)

d. Your hierarchy should look like the image below

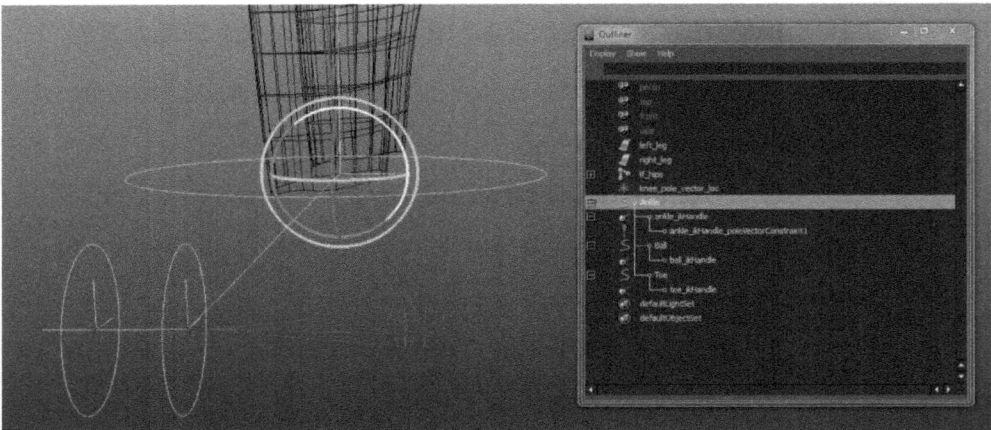

Figure 71. Foot hierarchy.

21. We are almost there, but you need two more controllers for a solid rig. The first will allow the foot to rotate off the heel. Create another circle for your controller:

a. **Create -> NURBS Primitives -> Circle**

b. Move and rotate the circle so that it is centered around the heel_jnt of the foot

  c. **Modify -> Freeze Transformations** to zero the circle's transforms

  d. Rename your circle to "Heel"

22. To clean up the hierarchy even more, we need to put everything below the Heel.

  a. Select the Ankle

  b. Shift select Heel (the circle we're working with)

  c. p (for parent)

  d. Your hierarchy should look like the image below

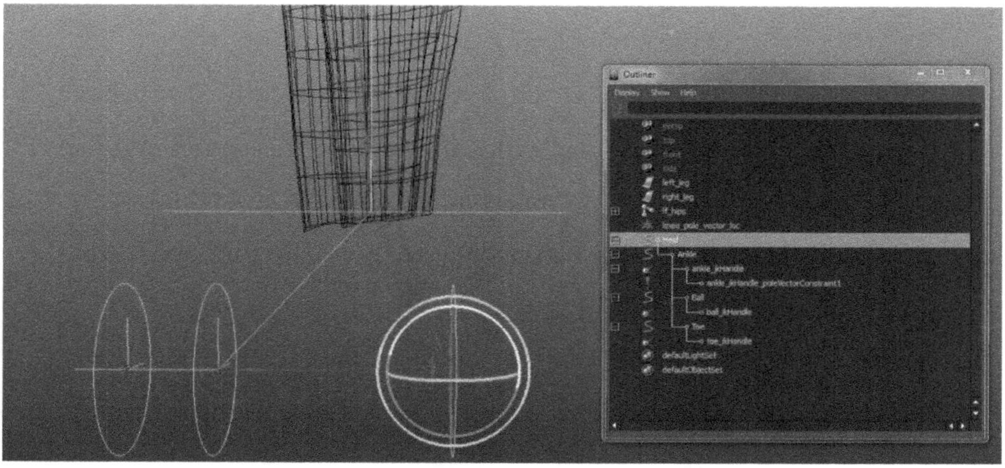

Figure 72. Heel hierarchy.

23. In addition, to make your rig even more animator friendly, the top of the hierarchy should not be the heel. That is because most people when they click on the "foot" expect to be able to move and rotate the foot from the ankle. So, let us create one more controller for the "foot" that will

allow you to rotate the entire foot around. Create another circle for your controller:

    a. **Create -> NURBS Primitives -> Circle**

    b. Move and rotate the circle so that it is centered around the ankle_jnt of the foot

    c. Alter your circles size and shape so that it looks different from the ankle controller you made. This will make your life far easier when you are animating.

    d. **Modify -> Freeze Transformations** to zero the circle's transforms

    e. Rename your circle to "Foot" (usually if you have two legs, you will want to name this something like lf_foot or rt_foot).

24. To clean up the hierarchy, we need to put everything below the Foot.

    a. Select the Heel

    b. Shift select Foot (the circle we're working with)

    c. p (for parent)

    d. Your hierarchy should look like the image below

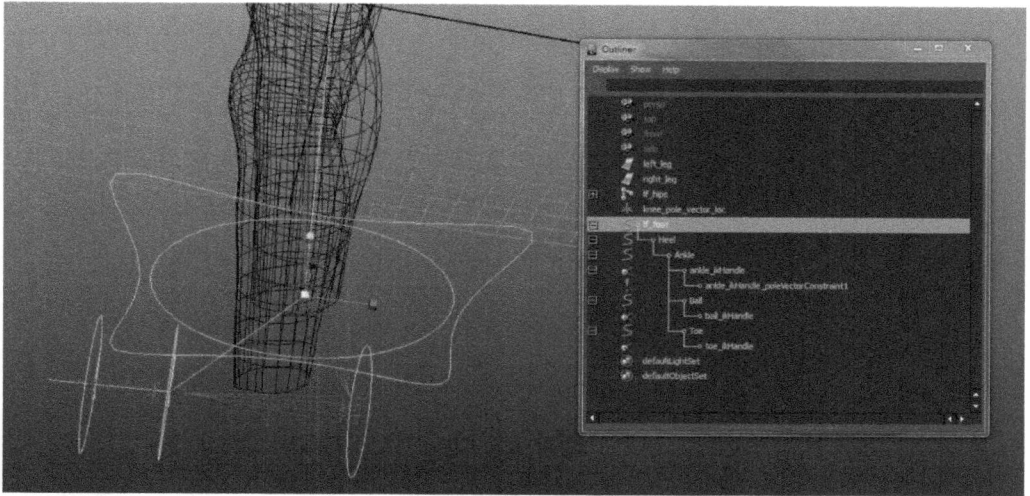

Figure 73. Foot control hierarchy.

25. The final step is some housekeeping. This means hiding things the animation team does not need to see, and locking items that should not be moved.

   a. Hide all of your ik handles by selecting them and running:

      i. **Display -> Hide -> Hide Selection** (or you can hit Control + h)

   b. Lock and Hide all of the rotates and scales on your pole vector locator by

      i. selecting it,

      ii. then shift clicking on the channels in the channel box.

iii. Finally right click and choose **Lock and Hide Selected**

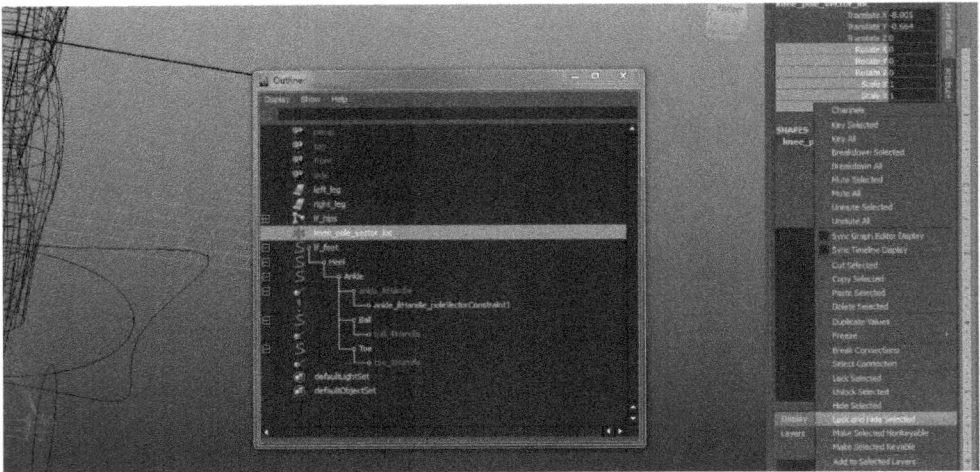

Figure 74. Lock and hide selected.

c. Similarly, lock and hide all the translates and scales for your joints

d. Lock and hide all the translates and scales for your Toe and Ball

e. You can also lock and hide the scales from your Heel, Ankle and Foot

26. Play with your rig and test out your handiwork!

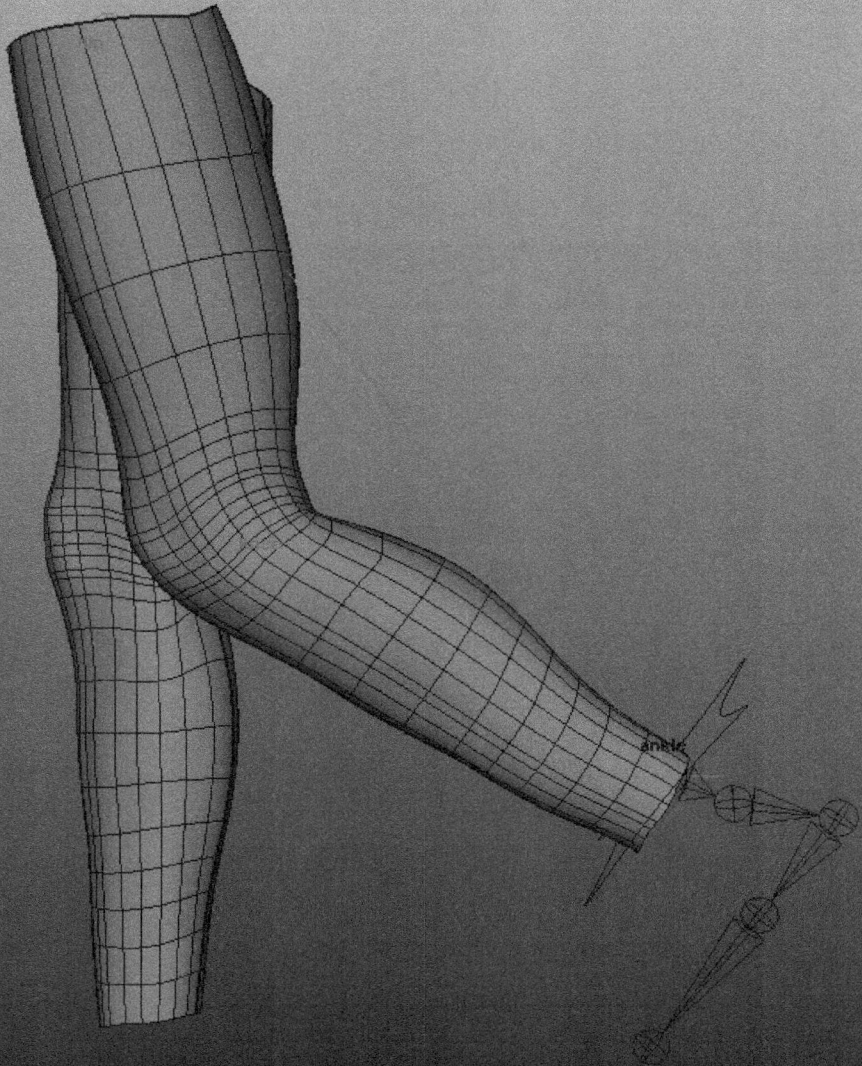

Figure 75. Animating with your new foot and leg.

Pole Vectors

A pole vector allows us to tell the IK RP solver that we want it pointed in a specific direction. Period. There is no guessing, but it always points in a specific direction. It is for this limiting reason that it is actually termed a constraint within Maya. It is actually quite simple to create.

Tutorial: Pole Vectors

1. Create your arm, name it, and create the IK RP Handle as you have done previously.

Figure 76. IK RP dialogue.

2. Create a locator.

   a. Create -> Locator

3. Move the locator to the elbow by making use of the snap tool.

4. Click on transform (or hit the w key).

5. Click on the snap to point button.

Figure 77. Snap to Point.

6. Middle mouse click and drag on the elbow. Your locator will snap into place automatically.

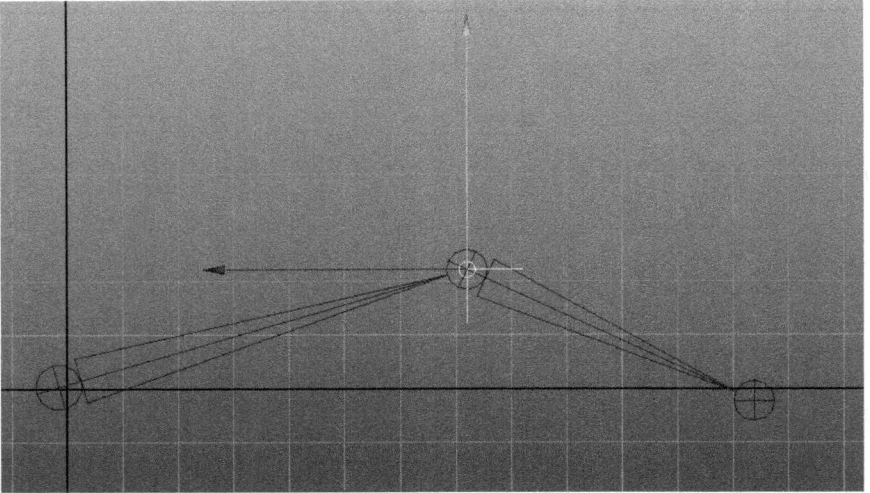

Figure 78. Locator at elbow.

7. Turn off the snap to point button and move the locator back, behind the elbow.

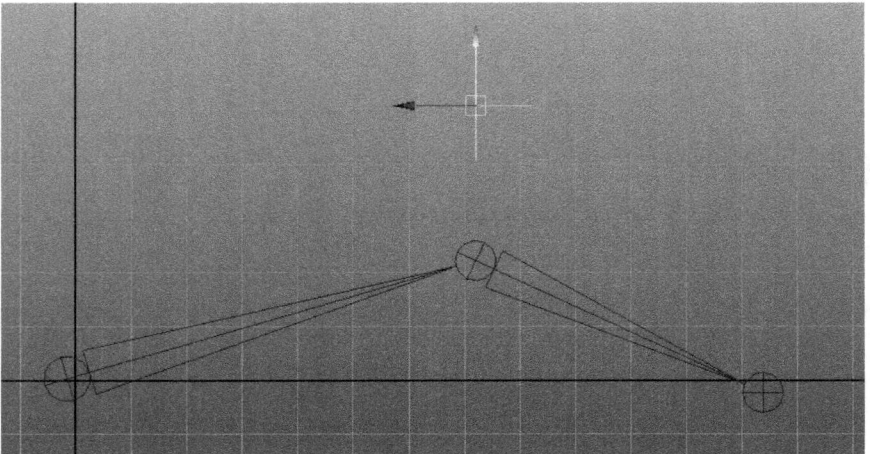

Figure 79. Locator in position.

8. Name the locator "elbow_pole_loc".

9. Select the locator, hold shift and select the IK RP Handle.

10. Create the pole vector constraint:

    a. **Constraint -> Pole Vector**

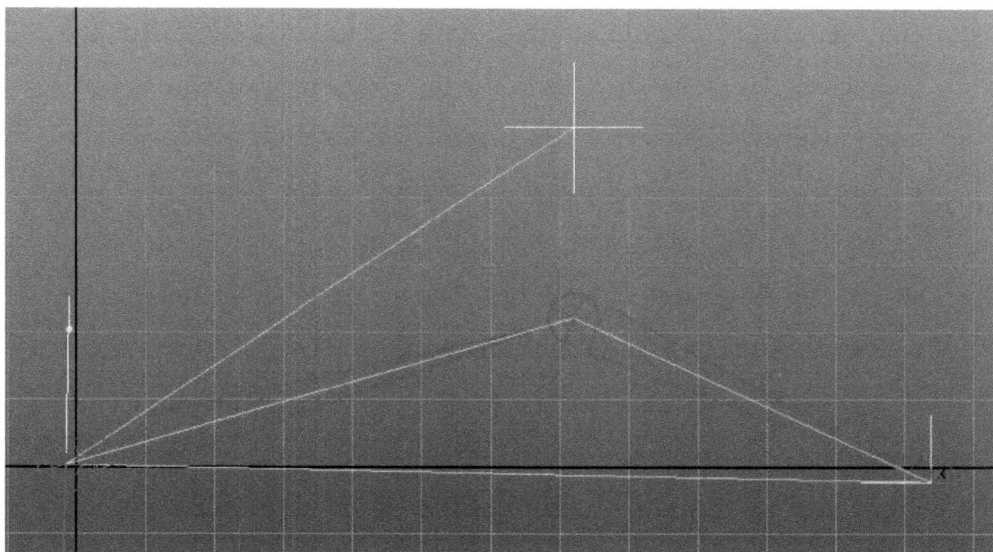

Figure 80. Pole vector created.

11. Move the locator around and watch your elbow always point at it.

This pole vector will now be where our elbow is always pointed. It is for this reason that any number of different parenting schemas can be suggested. If you leave it outside of your hierarchy, the elbows are easy to control since they always point to exactly where you left your pole vector locator. Of course, this requires that the animator "bring them along for the ride manually", or animate these pole vectors to move with the character. This can cause issues if the character starts in a scene and moves well away from the origin. It is for this reason, that the locators are often parented to something in the hierarchy. You should talk this over with the animation team to decide upon where the best spot should be. The point of consideration of course, is that the locators will follow their parents. Therefore, if you were to parent the locator to the ribs for example and your character was to twist at the hips, it may cause unwanted animation in the elbows that would then need to be counter animated. The typical setup has the locators parented to the top-level controller, often called the root. This allows them to come along for the ride when the character is moved by the root node, but still have the locators stay out of the way. Again, this is a subjective item, since some people prefer the locators to be parented to the collarbone or clavicle, so that the locators are always easy to access.

Another thing to bear in mind is that a locator is just being used for ease. The pole vector can in fact be constrained to any transform. A locator is typically used since it will not render and is not a concern if it is left visible when the scene goes out to render. Another good transform choice could be a curve (you can draw any shape you want!) or a joint. Joints are nice since they make more visual sense when parented to the skeleton, but be warned that they can also cause confusion for people later when binding or animating. This leads us nicely in to the next section, as we debate using different items to help control the rig.

Controls

Now that we have covered the basics, you should be able to start creating your skeletons. Once you have created it, the next step in rigging is to make it easier to move the skeleton around. We have already talked about IK systems, but how do you make the skeleton easy to select? This is where controls come in to play. In today's industry, the animator needs to work quickly and speeding their selection of the skeleton can play a great part in this.

There are different ways to tackle this problem. You can create fancy graphical user interfaces (GUI's) that depict your skeleton with pictures and buttons. Clicking on your button for your elbow would then select the proper bone for the elbow.

One major advantage of using a GUI is that you can incorporate the buttons in such a way that they can do practically anything. They can run a simple command to select a bone or a complex command to call custom procedures. The GUI requires using Maya's embedded scripting languages, MEL or Python. This scripting can be trivial or sometimes quite in depth, dependent on how advanced the GUI is required to be. While setting up a GUI is beyond the scope of this book, we will cover how to create your own custom GUI's in our following books in the series.

Another strategy that can be employed is using your shelf to create selection sets as buttons. This can be a great way for the beginner to learn a little MEL and to set up their rudimentary GUI of sorts. The shelf can also be easily shared amongst the animation team and quickly speed up the whole team. In following series, we will discuss how to create network shareable shelves. The following tutorial will explain how to create a shelf button for quickly selecting things.

Tutorial: Create Custom Selection Buttons on Your Shelf

1. Open your script editor by hitting the icon in the bottom right of your application.

Figure 81. Script editor icon.

2. Clear the contents of the script editor by using the icon:

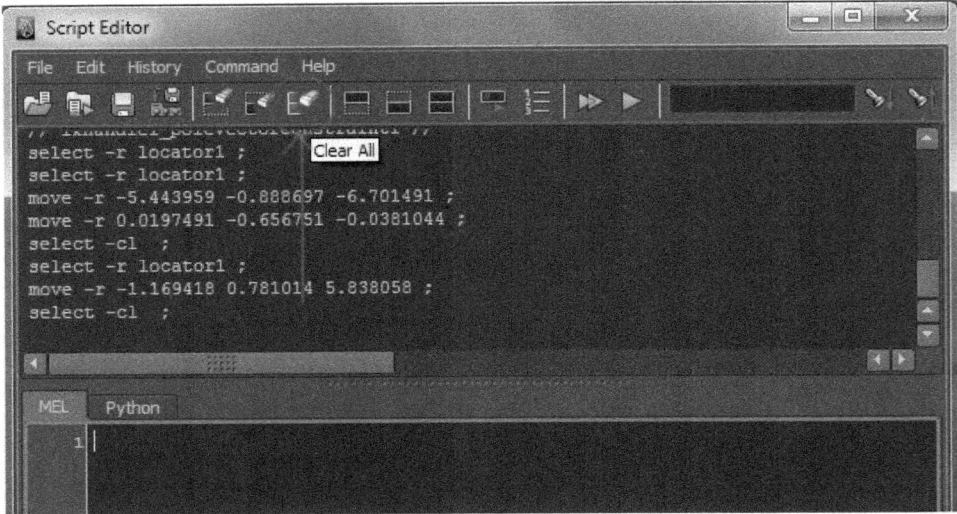

Figure 82. Clear all in script editor.

3. Deselect everything by clicking in a blank area in your viewport.

4. Now, select the joints you wish to be selected as part of your selection set. In our example, I am selecting all the finger joints of a hand.

5. Notice in the script editor that it will show the last commands. You can highlight this text and make advantage of it. Highlight the text and copy/paste it into the bottom of the script editor.

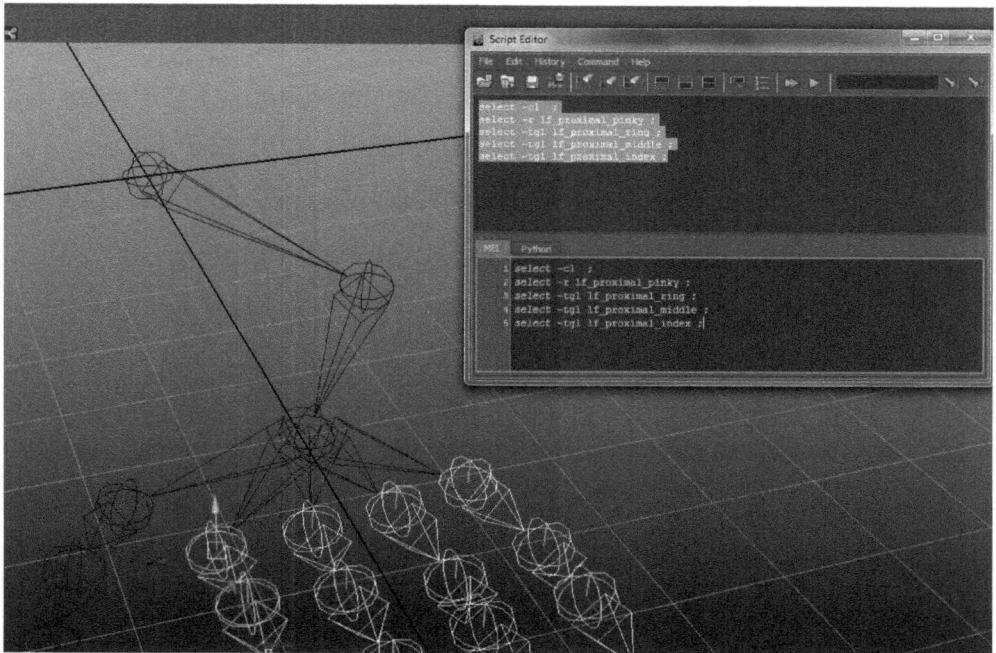

Figure 83. Select your script.

6. Ensure you clear your selection prior to running it. Ensure the first line in your new "script" is this by typing it in if you need it:

    a. `select -cl;`

7. In order for us to test the script, let's first select something different. Click on the elbow to select it.

8. Next, highlight all of the text in the bottom of the script editor and hit the numerical enter key. If you are on a keyboard that does not have one, you can likely hit ctrl + enter. By highlighting the text in the script editor, Maya will not automatically delete the text once you have executed the script.

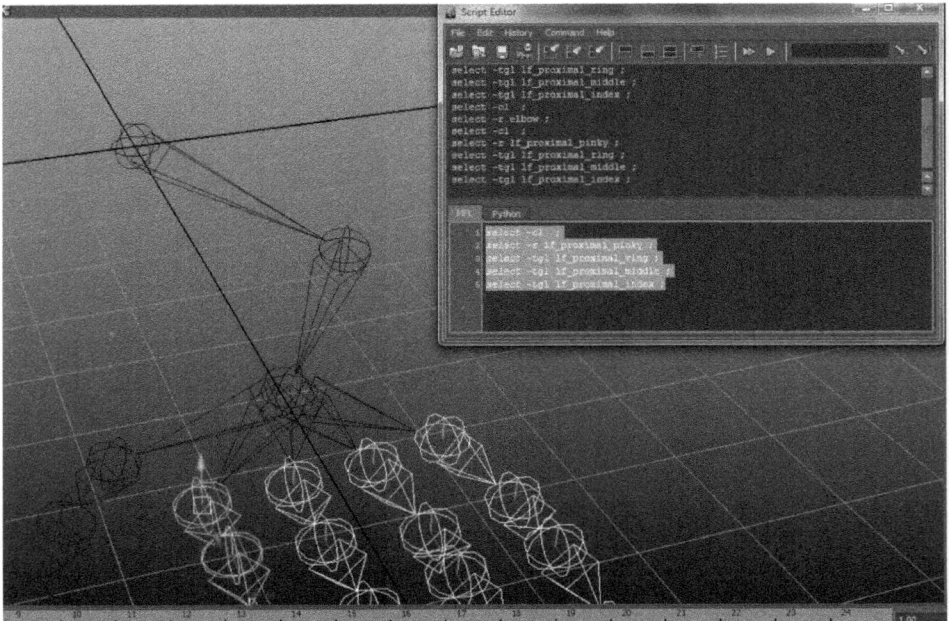

Figure 84. Highlight before running your script.

9. The joints you wanted selected should now be selected. If the results are what you are after, highlight the text once again in the bottom of the script editor.

10. Middle mouse drag this highlighted text onto your shelf. You should now have your very own icon on the shelf to select your joints. In our case, my new button selects my fingers.

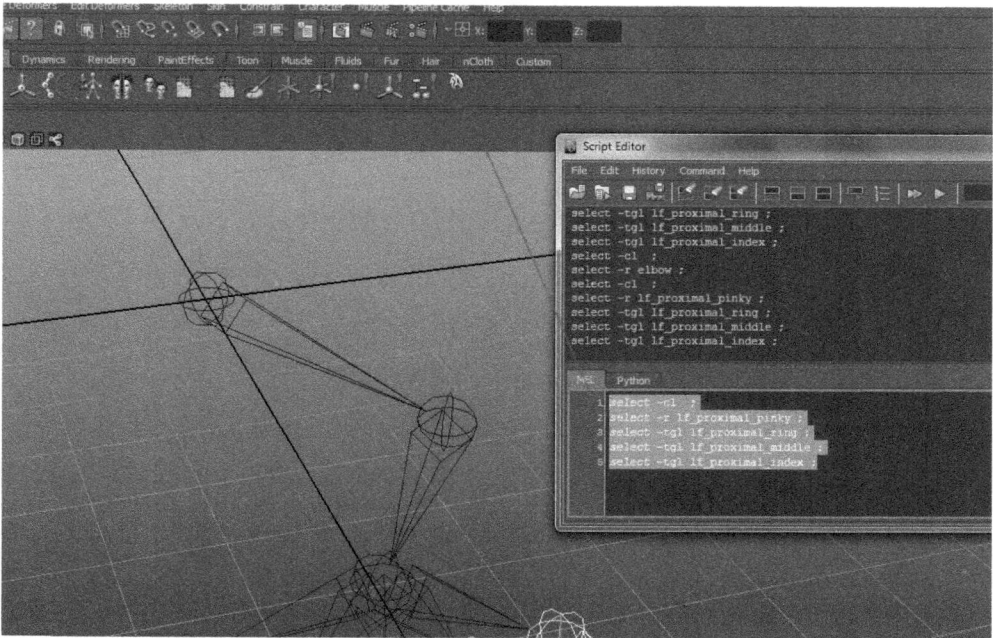

Figure 85. Middle mouse drag to create a shelf button.

Setting up several buttons like this can make your animation go a lot faster. It is often a good practice to not only make buttons for selecting joints, but also for posing your joints in positions that you use often such as "fist" or "thumbs up", etc. You can use the exact same process; just make sure you also copy the lines that have the "setAttr" command in them too. We will go more in to depth with MEL and interfaces in the next book in the series.

Beyond setting up your GUI's and shelves, a good rig should have some control system to let the animators know what pieces they should select and play with, and what pieces are not really meant to move. Later on when we discuss helper joints, the fact that not all joints are really meant to be played with will become even more apparent. This control system is often created using control curves. Curves are a great choice because by default they do not render, they do not shade themselves in the GL viewport by default, and they have their own display type which makes them easy to toggle on and off with a simple hotkey. As we discussed in the Getting Started section at the beginning of the book, you can make use of the toggle curves hotkey to quickly show or hide your control curves without actually affecting their visibility attributes.

In order to create control curves, you can simply download the tool from the website and use it on whatever joint needs a curve.

Tutorial: Installing the Control Circle Tool

1. Download the tj_circleAtJoint.mel tool.
2. Open the script editor using the icon at the bottom right of your application.

Figure 86. Script editor icon.

3. Source the script:
    a. **File-> Source Script**
    b. Browse to and select the script

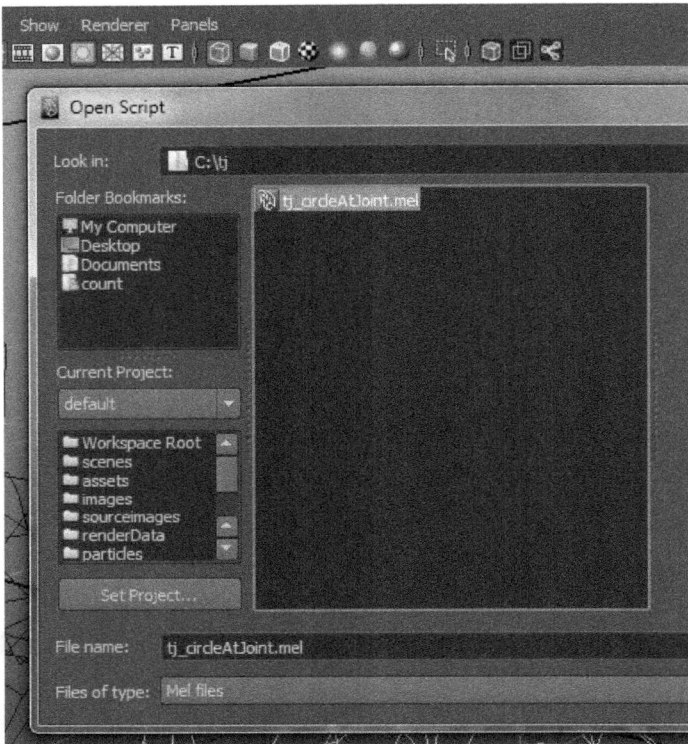

Figure 87. Source the script.

4. Once you have sourced the script, simply run the command by typing the command. You will notice that in newer versions of Maya, the command will turn cyan as soon as you finish typing it, indicating that Maya understands the script is now a command Maya can run:

   a. `tj_circleAtJoint`

Figure 88. Run the script.

    b. hit numerical enter.

5. What is simpler though is to make a shelf button. Copy these lines into your script editor and update the path according to where you saved the file:

    a. `Source`
       `"c://misc//downloads//tj//tj_circleAtJ`
       `ointTool.mel";`

    b. `tj_circleAtJoint;`

6. Highlight the text in the script editor and middle mouse drag the text onto your shelf. You will now have a button that will make the circles at any selected joint(s).

Whatever joint you want the animators to control should get a curve. A good practice is to make the curves different colours and different shapes. While doing so, your curves should also be easy to grab, so that means bigger than the surface that will be bound to the skeleton.

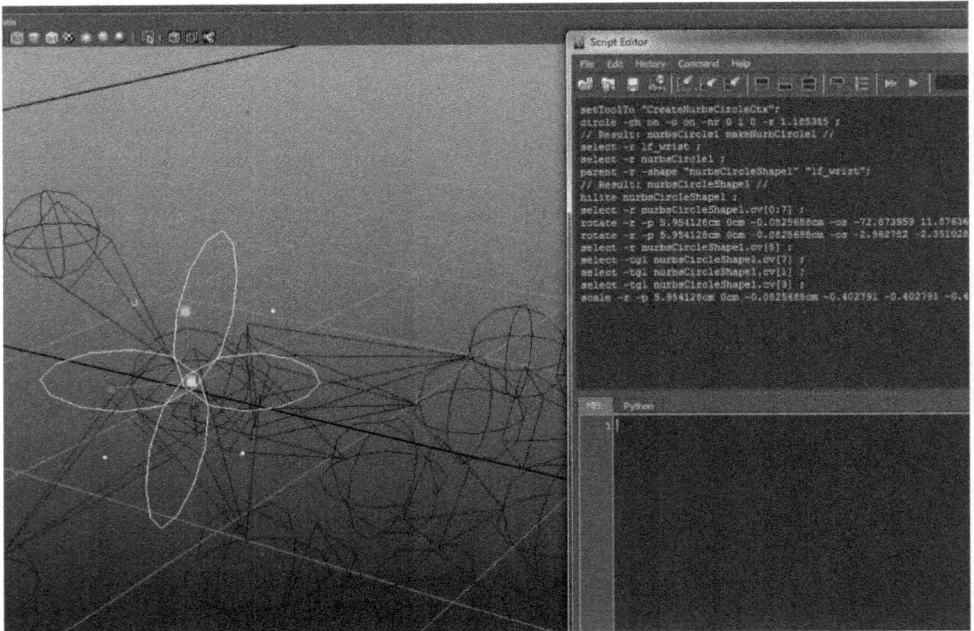

Figure 89. Changing a circle control into a fun shape.

The tool works in such a way that we take advantage of the method in which selection precision works within Maya. When you create an object within Maya, it typically comes with a shape node and a transform node. The shape node is what is actually drawn on the screen, while the transform node holds all the transform values such as scale, rotate, translate, etc. Thus, when you draw a selection box in the GL viewport, you are actually drawing a box over the shape node. Maya knows this is the case, and automatically selects the transform for that shape node because the assumption is you really want the transform selected and not to select the shape node itself. Knowing this, we can take advantage of the fact that the joints within Maya actually do not have a shape node of their own. This means we can attach a shape node to it, say one of a curve, and give the joint our own "icon" or shape node to select. When we draw a box in the viewport over the curve shape node, Maya will automatically determine we want to select the shape node's transform and will thus select the joint for us.

Tutorial: Creating Joint Shape Nodes

1. Create your joints.
2. Create a circle
   a. **Create -> NURBS Primitives -> Circle**
3. Now you can parent the circle's shape node onto your joint using some basic MEL. Open your script editor.

4. Run the command (altering the text to match your joint naming)

    a. `parent -r -shape "nurbsCircleShape1" "myJoint";`

5. Select the circle in component (blue) mode by hitting F8.

6. Move the circle to the correct position, scaling it and making it in to a fun shape.

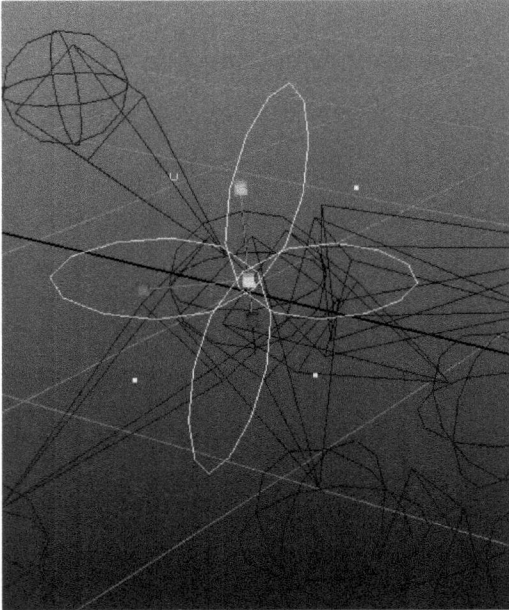

Figure 90. Controls don't always need to be a circle.

7. Make sure to clean up your scene by opening your outliner and deleting the now empty transform that was left over.

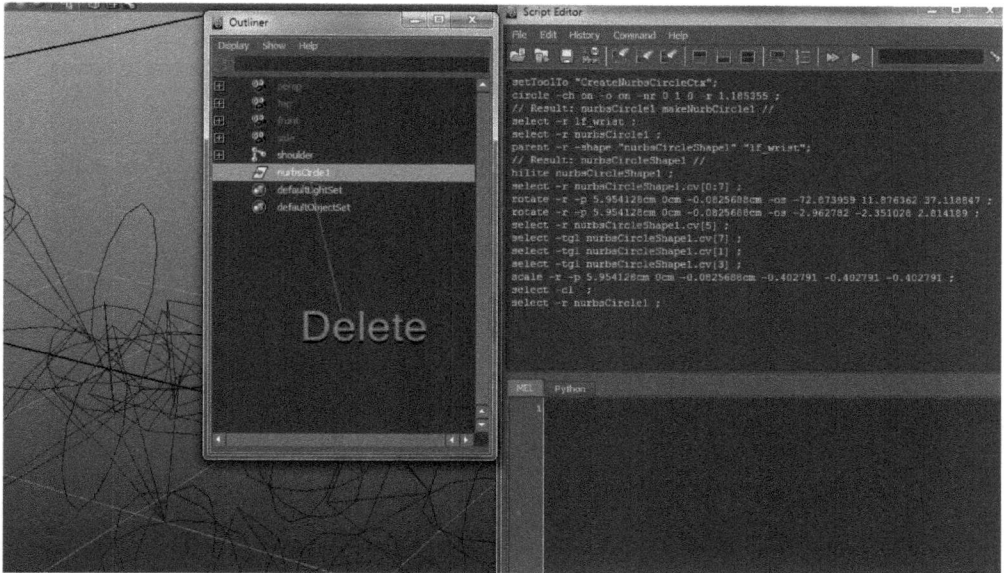

Figure 91. Delete empty transforms.

Another method that can be used is to make use of selection handles. Selection handles are a built in icon that each item gets free from Maya. These handles show up as little plus signs as depicted in the following figure.

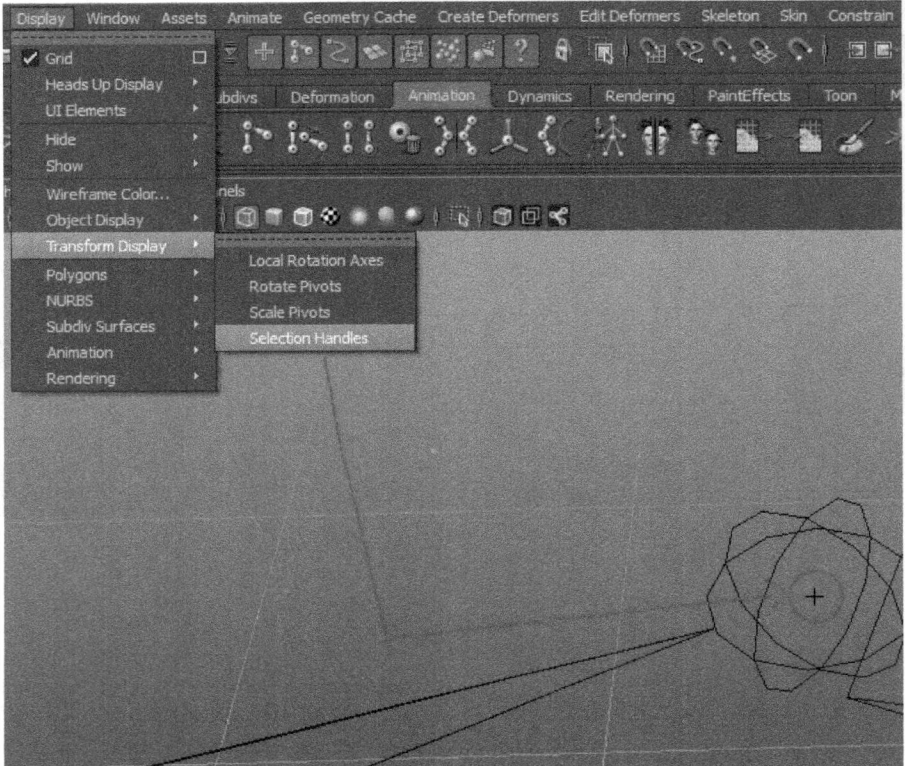

Figure 92. Showing a selection handle.

The selection handle can be small to see, and they always stay the same size no matter the zoom level. A technique used to make these icons more visible is explained in the following tutorial. This technique makes use of a larger curve that is templated out. Templating something within Maya allows the object to remain visible but makes the object become unselectable. While this method does work, it is more elegant to use the shape node methodology as outlined earlier.

Tutorial: Template a Curve for A Custom Icon

1. Create your joints and select one that you wish to have a selection handle for.

2. Display the selection handle for the joint:

   a. **Display -> Transform Display -> Selection Handles**

3. Move the selection handle out in to a more convenient place by selecting the joint and entering component (blue) mode by hitting:

   a. F8

   b. Turn off all selections by clicking on the arrow icon and selecting All Components Off

Figure 93. All components off.

c.   Turn on Selection Handles

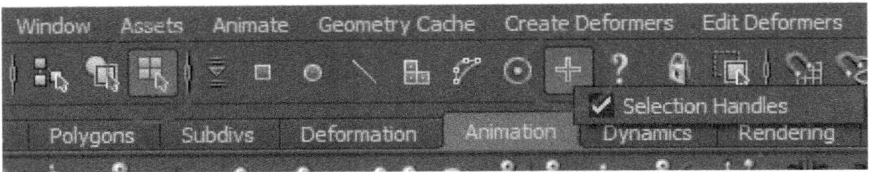

Figure 94. Right click and turn on selection handles.

4.   Select the selection handle and move it to a better place.

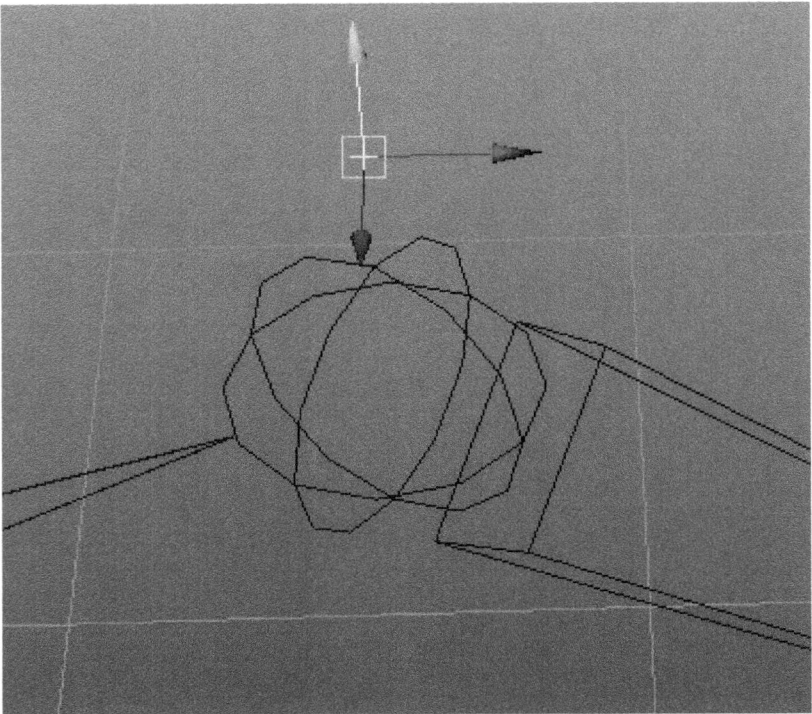

Figure 95. Move the selection handle so it's easier to select.

5. Enter object mode and create a curve that is a nice icon.

    a. F8 (to go back to object (green) mode)

    b. **Create -> Pencil Curve Tool**

    c. Draw a nice icon. As soon as you lift up from your
        left click, the tool will complete, so make sure you
        hold down the mouse button until you are done.

6. Move the curve to be centered around the selection handle

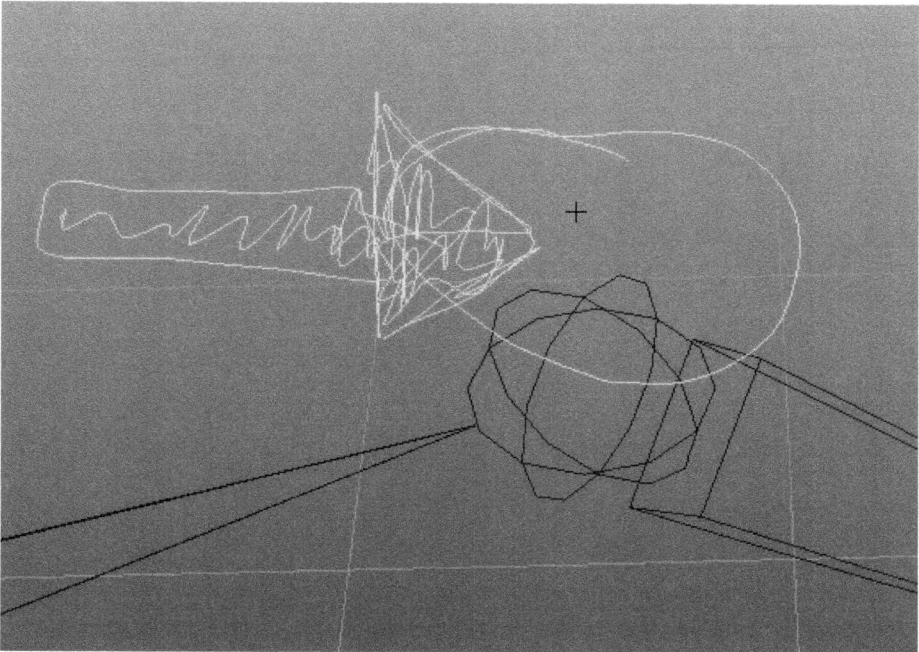

Figure 96. Draw your own custom icon.

7. Parent your curve to the joint by:

    a. Select the curve,

    b. Hold shift and select the joint too

    c. p

8. Template the curve to make it unselectable by:

    a. Select the curve.

    b. Open the attribute editor by hitting ctrl + a.

    c. Expand the Object Display portion under the shape node.

    d. Click on "Template"

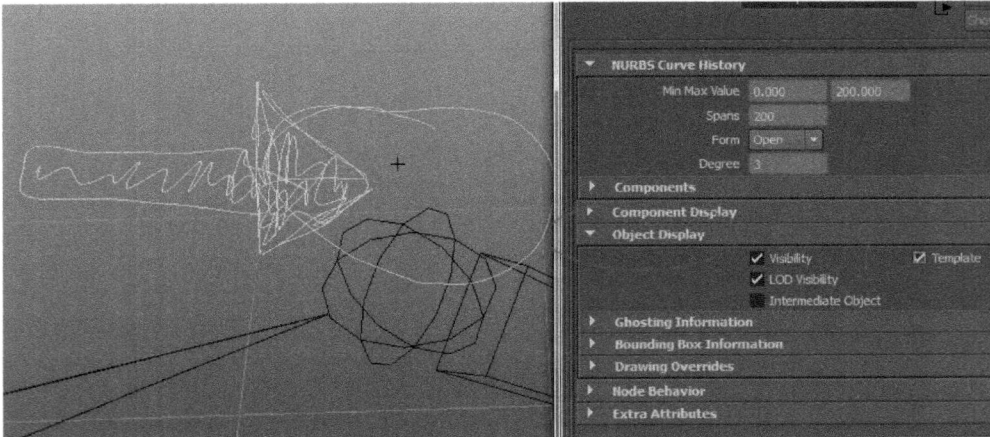

Figure 97. Turn on template in the attribute editor.

Once your curve is templated, it is unselectable. When the user drags a box around the curve to select it, we will actually now trick them and instead will select whatever was in their selection box, which is the selection handle. This is a sneaky way to get people to select the joint, and while it works, is not necessarily as clean as the parenting of the shape node technique described above. One note, templates by default are grey and harder too see. You may want to adjust your colour preferences if you are using this technique, but I would suggest using the curve technique first described instead.

Custom Attributes

When we start creating controls, the next natural step is to create attributes with your own names. The standard "translate X" or "rotate Y" aren't going to mean much when you want to connect up a "curl fist" or a "smile". Remember how in the foot rig tutorial we built our own attribute called "roll"? Let us review the process.

Creating your own attributes within Maya is indeed a straightforward process. First, you select your object, and then make use of the add attribute command:

Modify -> Add Attribute...

This will bring up an editor that allows you to create your attributes. Your long name can be anything you want, such as "fist". There are 6 types of attributes you can create:

Vector:

This attribute handles 3 sets of float values all together. An example would be "translate". The vector is broken in to 3 sets of data: x, y, and z.

Float:

This numeric attribute allows a decimal place. An example of a float value is 0.01. Most of your attributes you will create will likely be floats.

Integer:

This numeric attribute does NOT allow a decimal, such as 10 or 2. While this does allow you to clamp down the precision, you will most likely not make use of integer attributes often.

Boolean:

This is afan attribute that can be either on or off, like a toggle switch such as a light switch. This can be quite handy for attributes that can be hooked up to turning on or off items, such as a smooth node. Mathematically speaking, on is equal to 1 and off is equal to 0, a fact that can be used in expressions.

Booleans are also great for distinguishing between groups of attributes. For example, if you are creating a number of finger controls on your wrist controller, it can be a good idea to have something saying "these are finger controls" to make it clearer for the animators. The following image shows the Boolean attribute used to distinguish between muscles and tendons. It is a good idea to lock your channel too, which turns the attribute grey in the channel box and provides another visual cue.

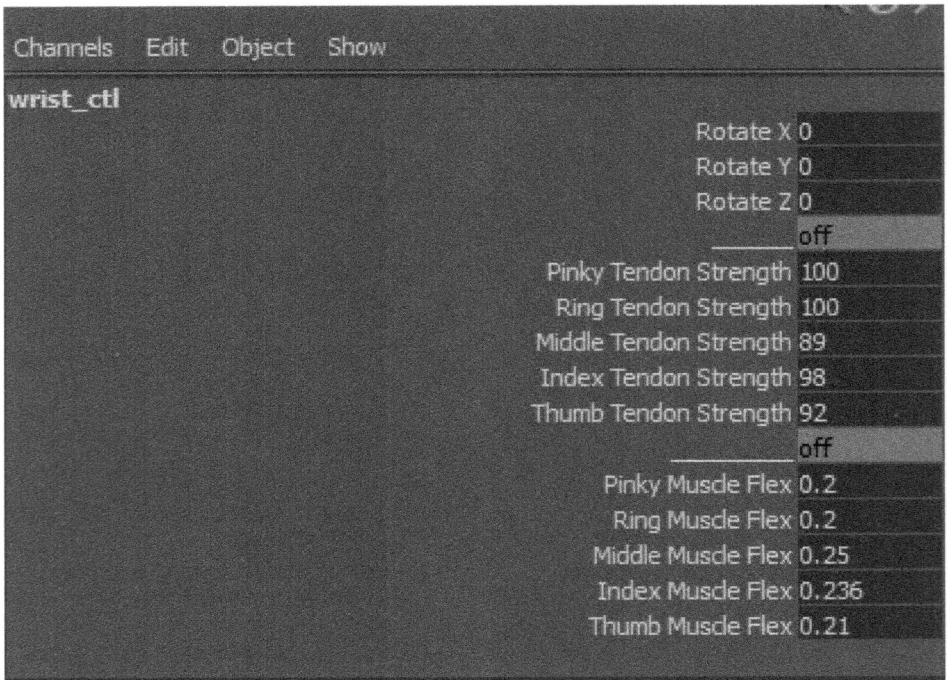

Figure 98. Using attributes to delineate.

String:

This attribute type is what holds a description or text. You most likely will not make use of this type often either. An example of a string would be "my text entry".

Enum:

An enumerated (enum) attribute type is a type that allows you to create a list of entries in a pull down list. This can be quite useful for your rigs to have custom settings that the animator can choose. The enum is constructed in such a way that the animator simply sees the pull down list, much like a menu. Each item on the list corresponds to an index number and thus allows you to make use of programming methods that merely care about which item in the list was selected and not necessarily need to know what the string description of that item was. In other words, you can write an expression that simply cares that item 2 was selected, and not that item 2 means "turn hair preview off" to the user.

Rotate Z	0
	off
Pinky Tendon Strength	100
Ring Tendon Strength	100
Middle Tendon Strength	89
Index Tendon Strength	98
Thumb Tendon Strength	92
	off
Pinky Muscle Flex	0.2
Ring Muscle Flex	0.2
Middle Muscle Flex	0.25
Index Muscle Flex	0.236
Thumb Muscle Flex	0.21
Animation Hair Control	Turn Hair P...
	Turn Hair Preview Off
	Hair Fast Preview
	Hair Medium Detail
	Hair Full Sim Detail

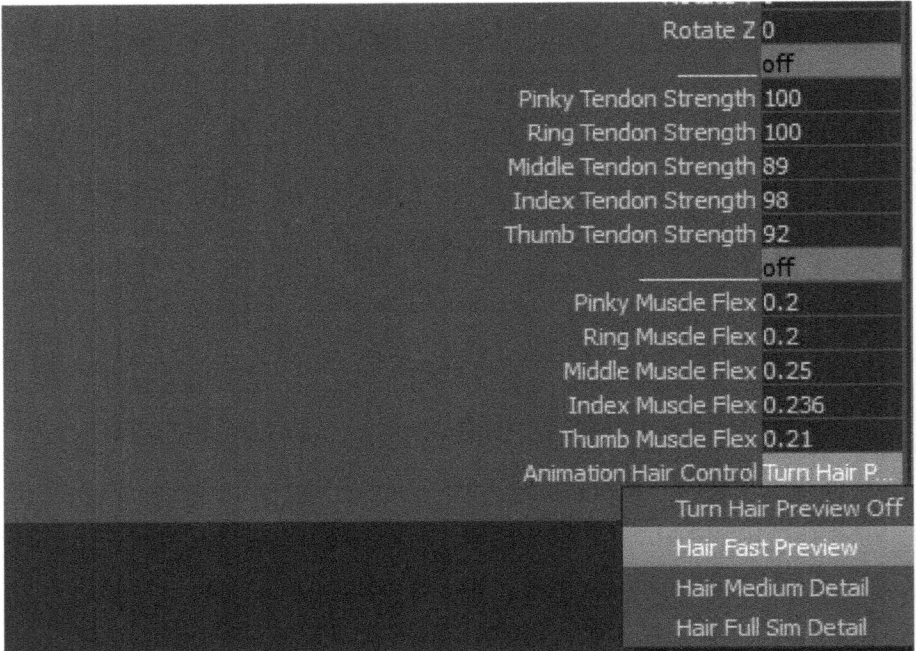

Figure 99. Custom attributes for hair controls.

Once you have chosen your attribute type, there are a few other options to make note of. The minimum/maximum fields will help you limit the range that your attribute can be modified to, and the default is as equally straightforward. A good guideline when creating attributes is to set your maximum to go a little beyond what you think you will need. Take for instance a blend shape. These typically range from a zero to one range, so when creating your attribute you may want to set your minimum to zero, your maximum to two, and your default to zero. Doing so will allow the animators to push the values a little if they need to, but still lock them down to a range that should not cause too many problems. It is rare that you can predict the exact range every time for everything the animation may require.

Having chosen your attribute types, and your ranges, you can then hit the Add button. Doing so will create your attribute as expected.

Armed with this knowledge, we can now proceed to make our own attributes that make sense for our own rigs. The following tutorial will walk you through how to create some new attributes for hand controls.

Tutorial: Make Custom Attributes

1. Create the hand joints and make a circle controller around the wrist using the techniques previously described.
2. Select the circle.
3. If this circle is just for our attributes, we can clean up the channel box a bit. Select all of the attributes in the channel box.
4. Right click on the channel box and select:
    a. Right Click on Channel Box -> Lock and Hide Selected
5. Now let us add our own attributes. Use the command:

a. Modify -> Add Attribute

6. In this case, let us make some attributes to control the fingers. These will need to be numbers with a decimal place, so let us create a float attribute:

    a. Choose float, enter a name ("index curl" in our example), and give the attribute default, min and max values.

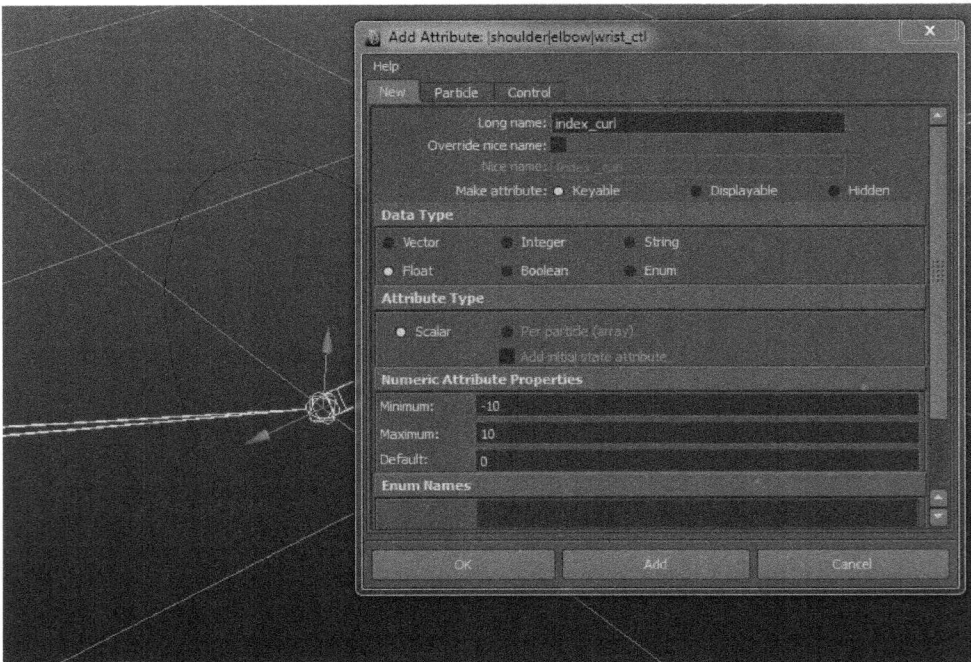

Figure 100. Index curl attribute.

    b. Repeat and add curl attributes for each finger

7. If you would like to add separators in the channel box, a good practice is to make use of the Boolean and to name it with a number of underscores

    a. Modify -> Add Attribute

    b. Select Boolean, give the long name of "_____" and press ok.

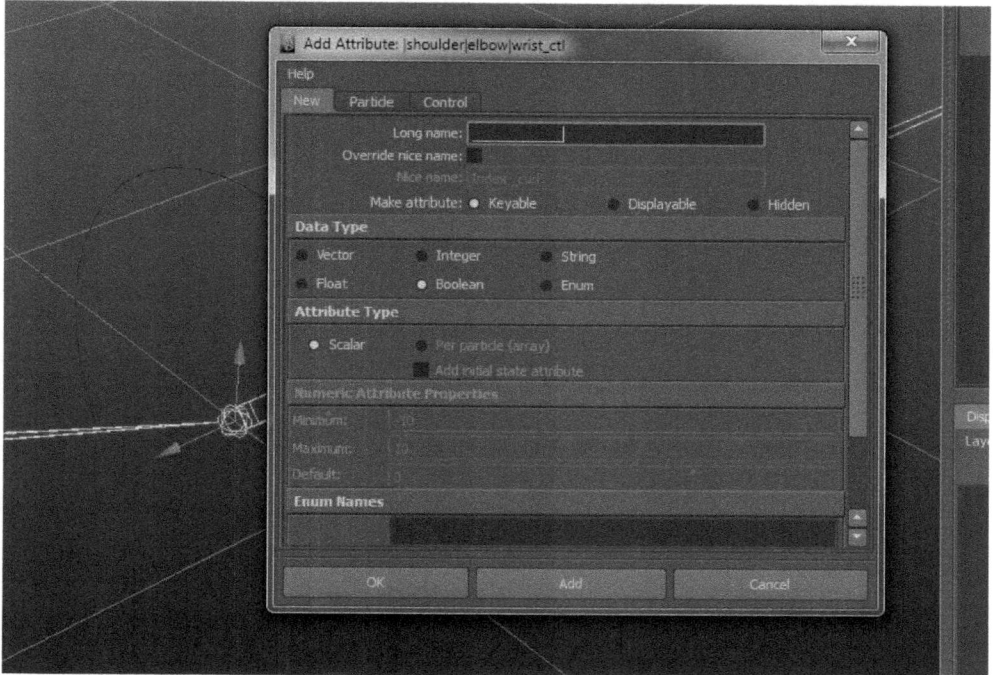

Figure 101. Create a attribute to act as a separator.

8. Now you can select this attribute and lock it in the channel box.

    a. Select the "_____" attribute in the channel box.

    b. Right Click in Channel Box -> Lock Selected

9. Add some additional attributes for other options like "make fist, point, thumbs up", etc.

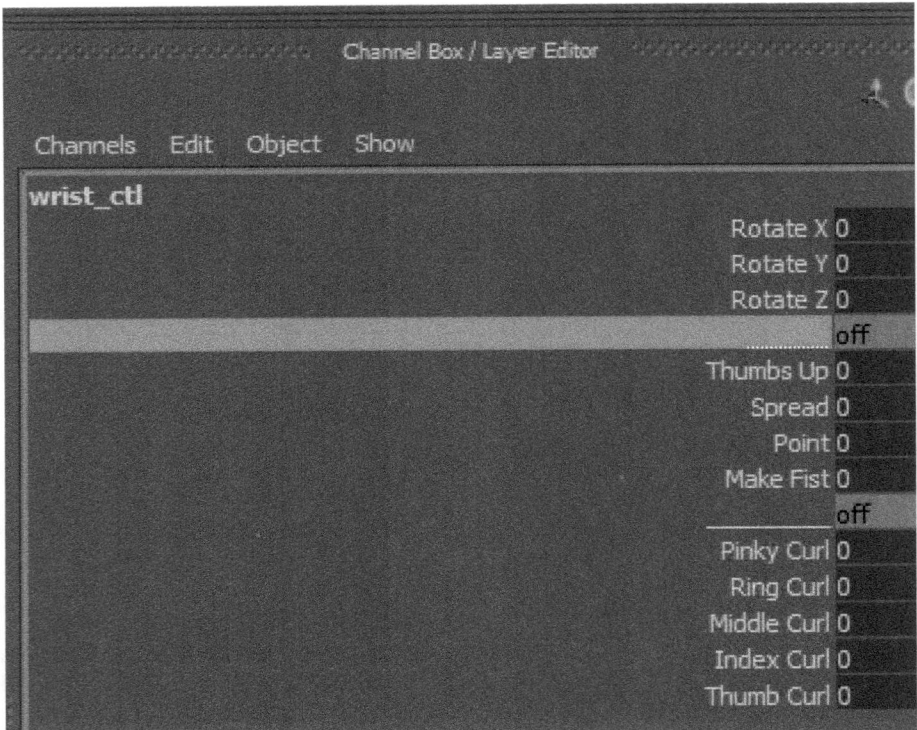

Figure 102. Locking the attribute makes it a visual separator.

In the next few sections, we will describe how to make use of these new attributes to make your hand actually do what they describe easily. You can use attributes to do many things, from curling your fingers to making a fist. Note how the separator makes it easier to distinguish quickly one section of controls from the next. This is a good practice to put a little order and cleanliness to your controls and will make your animation that much easier.

Direct Connections

There will be many times in your character setups where you will have one object that you wish to control another object. This can be easily accomplished with a direct connection. The direct connection essentially tells Maya that one node's values will be replacing another node's values. It is as simple as that, and connecting things together is quite easy to do. Simply open the connection editor:

Window -> General Editors -> Connection Editor

Once this is open, you can load your item on the left and find the attribute you wish to connect. Notice the top button is showing "From -> To"

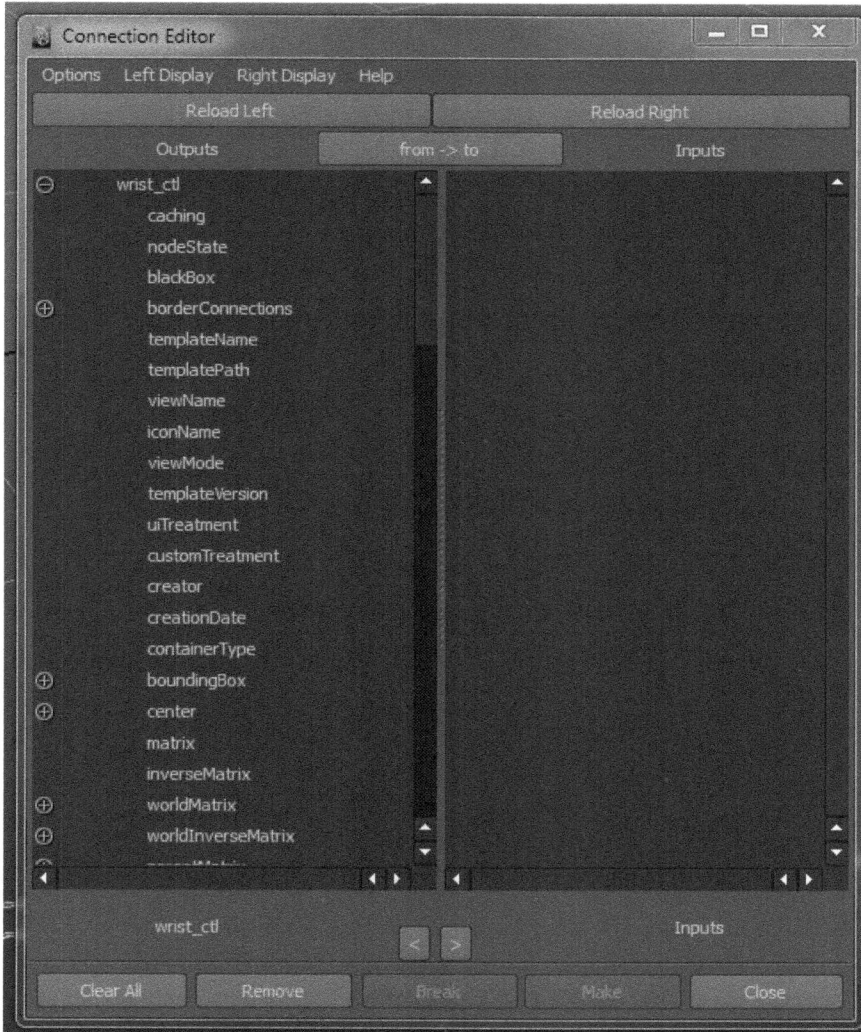

Figure 103. Connection editor.

This indicates that the attribute that is selected on the left will drive the attribute selected on the right. Select your second object, hit the "reload" button on the top, and select your attribute(s) to drive. Yes, you may have noted that you can select one or more than one attributes. The following example shows how to connect one object to another and replicate the behavior of a point constraint. Of course, we are merely connecting the translation values and it is important to note that the pivot values do not change so this is not a true point constraint.

Tutorial: Make a Direct Connection that Acts Like a Point Constraint

1. Create a ball:
   a. **Create -> NURBS Surfaces -> Sphere**
2. Create a cube too:
   a. **Create -> Polygon Primitive -> Cube**
3. Let us connect the cube to the ball so it will go wherever the ball goes.
   a. Select the cube.
4. Open the connection editor by using the command:
   a. **Window -> General Editors -> Connection Editor**

5. The cube was selected when you first opened the connection editor, so it will automatically be on the left side already. With the cube selected, hit the reload right button. The cube will be the "to" object, so check that the middle button says From -> To

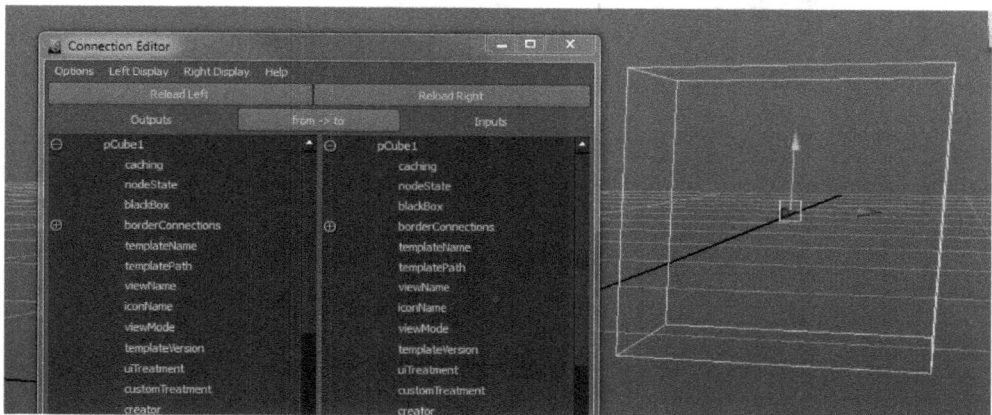

Figure 104. Connection editor.

6. Select the ball and click the "reload left" button.

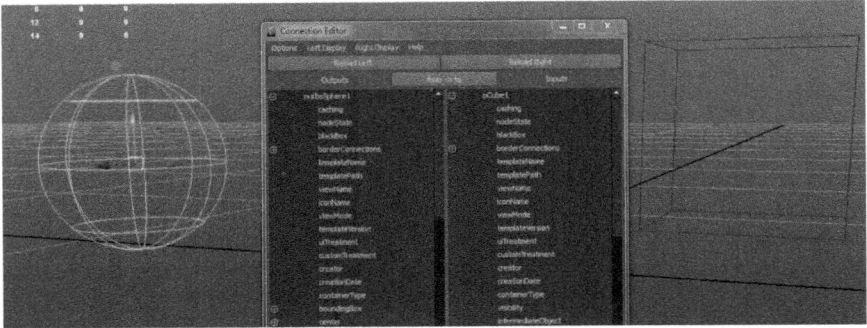

Figure 105. Ball loaded into connection editor.

7. Scroll down, expand the translate section and select the translateX attribute on the left side and then select the translateX attribute on the right side as well.

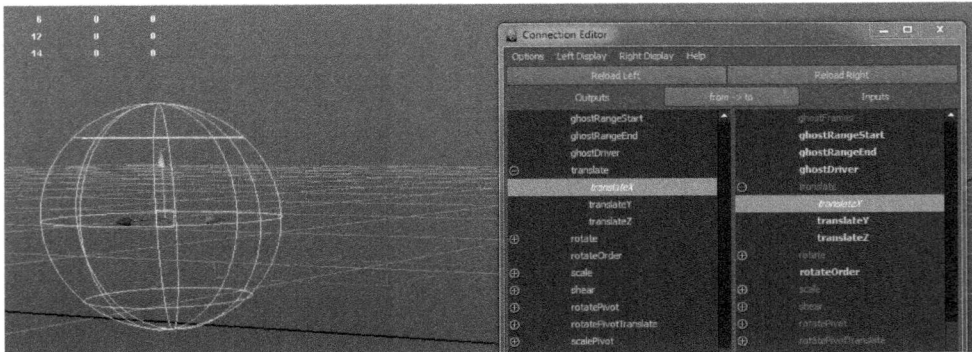

Figure 106. Connect the translate X attributes.

8. Repeat this process for translate y and z. This will connect each individual translate attribute from the ball to the cube. You will see the cube has moved directly on top of the ball.

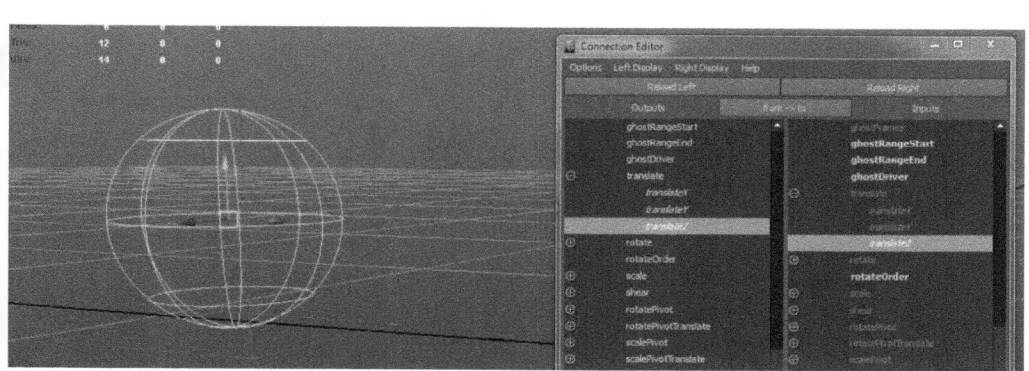

Figure 107. The cube snaps to the ball.

9. Now moving the ball will move the cube, it will behave very much like the point constraints we made use of earlier.

You can of course use the connection editor to link up almost any attribute to any other attribute. This is a great way to also link one attribute up to many attributes. In other words, you could link up several items to be all driven by one and save yourself the work of animating each individually. For example, you could set all the scales of your buildings in a city to a master scale control to quickly make the city get bigger or smaller.

One good tip to remember in using your connection editor is that any custom attributes you have made will appear always at the bottom of the list. Knowing this can definitely save you some time in searching for them!

Expressions

Expressions are a mathematical way of getting stuff done within Maya. They can be as simple as a direct relationship, where one item is exactly the same as another; or they can be extremely complex where a number of things happen when certain conditions are met and others happen when different conditions are met. For example, the direct connection example above of a pseudo-point constraint could be replaced with a simple expression that connected the translations of the two objects. Let us walk through how to do just that.

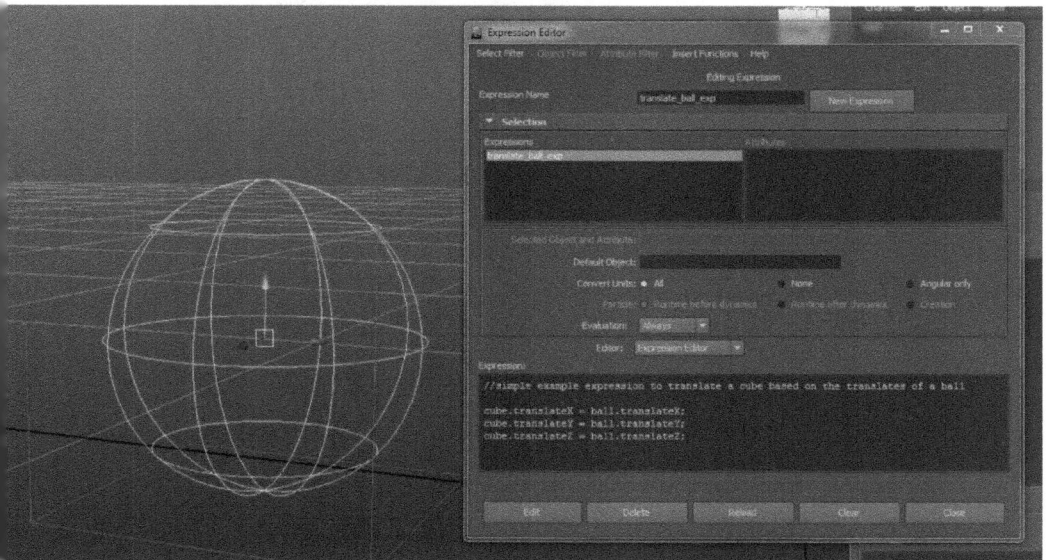

Figure 108. Simple expression.

To create an expression, you need to open your expression editor:

Window -> Animation Editors -> Expression Editor

The first step is to always name your expression. Once you have named your expression, you will also want to turn your select filter to "by name".

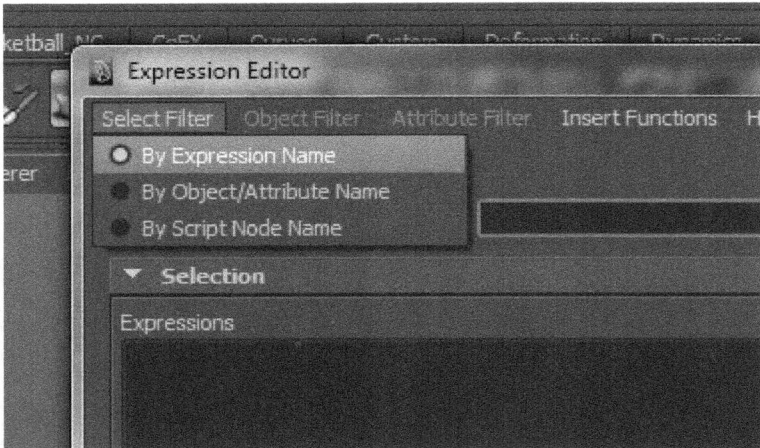

Figure 109. Selection filter.

The expression editor is by default filtered to "by object". This means that when you select an object and open the expression editor; all the associated expressions are shown first. This can useful if you have many expressions in your scene, but there is also a catch. This filter is always active, and so when you deselect the object, or select something else, the expression editor will update. While this sounds trivial, it can result in you losing your work. So, the key take away here is to always name your expression FIRST and then filter by name. It is also a good idea to explain what you are doing in your expression using a few comments. Doing so will allow you to remember what the intentions were months later, as well as anyone else who works on your scene. So, the first steps you always do when creating an expression should be to give it a name and to quickly enter some comments as to what it is for. Create the expression immediately (with only comments as your "expression") and then go about doing the actual math. This will ensure you never lose your work. The ability to leave comments is a definite advantage of using expressions and you should make use of that. This is explained in the tutorial below.

Tutorial: Make a Simple Expression To Squash a Ball

1. This tutorial will link the scale attributes up so that your ball will automatically squash and stretch. First, let us start by making a ball:

    a. **Create -> NURBS Surface -> Sphere**

    b. Rename your object to be called "ball".

2. Let us connect the scale attributes so that when it scales taller in the y axis, it preserves its' volume by getting smaller in x and z. Open the expression editor:

a. Window -> Animation Editors -> Expression Editor

3. Make sure you have the filter to "by name" as discussed above. Give it a new name, like "ball_squash_exp" in the name field. Once that is done, the very first step to any expression is to give it some comments and a description. Type:

   a. //a simple expression to add squash and stretch

   b. // by (put your name here), (and the date too)

4. The next line will link up the scale in x to be driven by the scale in y. Since we want it to be the exact opposite, we can write a simple inverse expression by dividing y by one:

   a. ball.scaleX = 1 / ball.scaleY;

5. Do the same for the z axis as well:

   a. ball.scaleZ = 1 / ball.scaleY;

6. Now hit the "create" button in the expression editor.

7. Try scaling the ball in y in your scene. You will notice now
   that the ball will stretch and squash quite nicely.

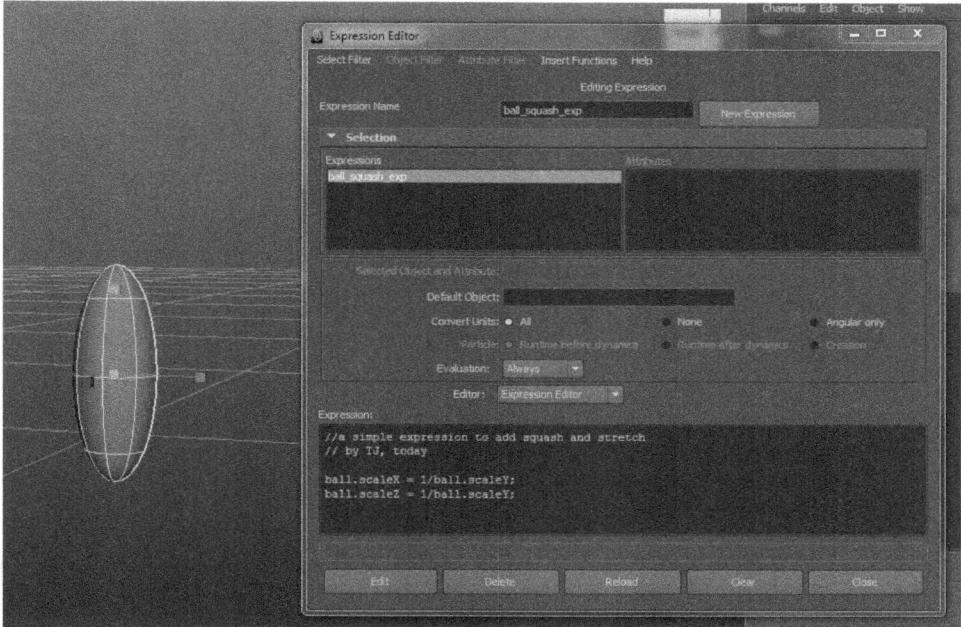

Figure 110. Squash ball expression.

While expressions can be simple, the real power of expressions can be seen when they are crafted to solve certain problems that would be more difficult and time consuming to animate by hand. Take for instance your forearm. There is a twisting motion that happens with the radius and ulna twisting over each other as you rotate your wrist. To solve this with your deformations, it can be easiest to spread the twist out over several joints. We will discuss the deformations portion in great detail in the following chapters, but an expression can help us here with the dissipation of the twist. For an easy example, perhaps we have 3 joints that will handle the wrist rotation, and will spin with a weighted scenario. In other words, the middle of the 3 joints would spin 50% of the rotation of the wrist, and 50% of the rotation of the elbow. The

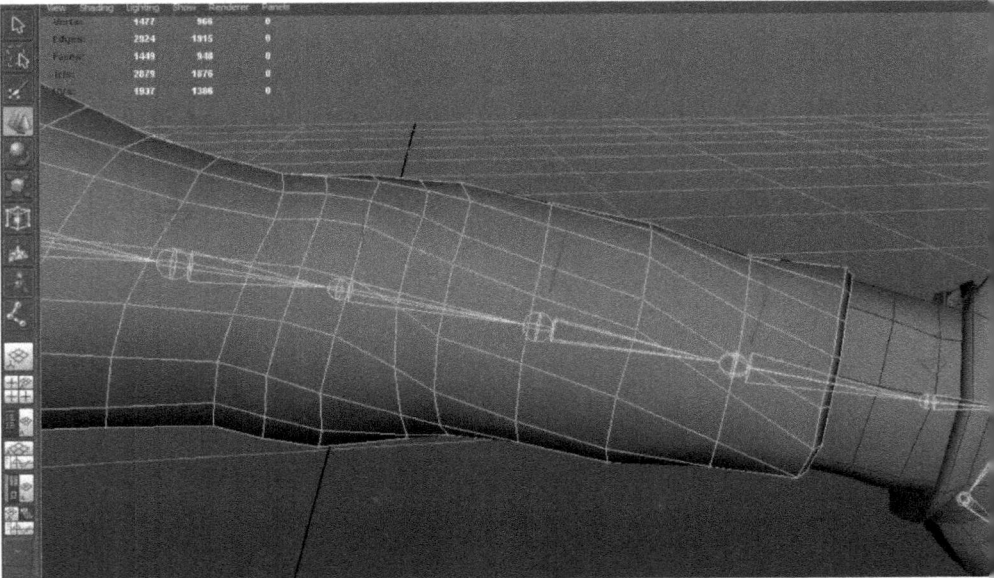

Figure 111. Twist expression.

joint higher up the arm would be 25% wrist and 75% elbow, and the joint lower down the arm would be the opposite.

This can be solved in a variety of ways within Maya, but for our purposes, a simple expression is best. The following tutorial explains how to do this.

Tutorial: Wrist Rotations

1. Create a simple arm with a shoulder, elbow, and wrist.

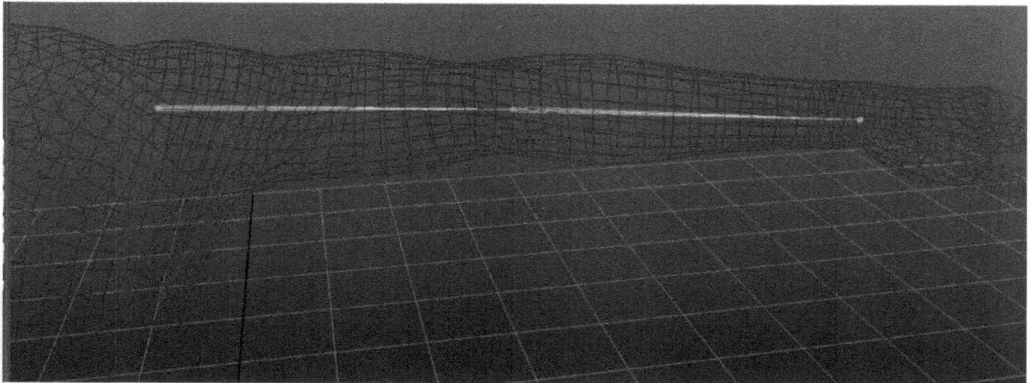

Figure 112. A simple arm.

2. Now draw a joint a little up from the wrist and hit enter. Position it accurately and play with the radius value until the joint is easy to see. In our example, we needed to adjust the radius to 2.

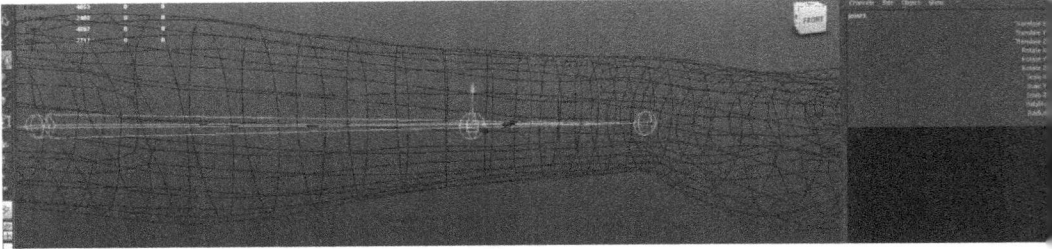

Figure 113. Adjust the radius.

3. Repeat this twice to match the three joints that are shown in the image. Note that they are not parented to anything yet. It can be simpler to duplicate the first joint rather than drawing it with the skeleton tool. Try this by selecting the first joint and hitting ctrl + d.

4. Name these joints "forearm_twist_01_jnt", "forearm_twist_02_jnt", and "forearm_twist_03_jnt". Take the time to correct the local rotation axis if required so they point in the proper direction.

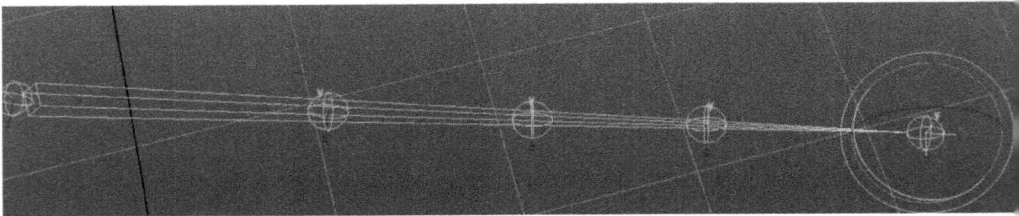

Figure 114. LRA's are fixed.

5. Now, parent each of these joints to the elbow.

a. Select "forearm_twist_01_jnt", then hold shift and select the elbow. Hit p.

b. Select "forearm_twist_02_jnt", then hold shift and select the elbow. Hit p.

c. Select "forearm_twist_03_jnt", then hold shift and select the elbow. Hit p.

6. Since the bone in your forearm stays a constant length, having each of these parented to the elbow will always result in them being aligned down the bone properly no matter how the arm moves.

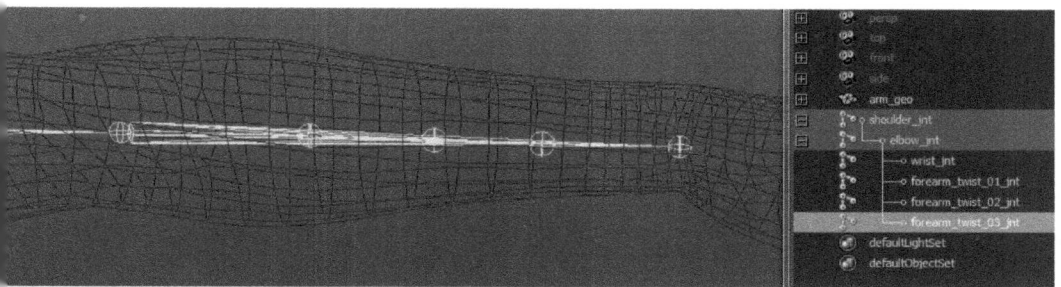

Figure 115. The joints are parented.

7. Let us make an expression that carries the rotation down the arm.

a. **Window -> Animation Editor -> Expression Editor**

8. Ensure the name filter is on, and give the new expression a name like "wrist_rotation_exp".

9. Enter some description:

```
// this expression will stagger the
wrist rotation over several forearm
twist joints

// by (your name), (date)
```

10. Now, as described above we need to stagger the rotation over the several joints. Your expression should then look something like this:

```
//the first bone gets 75%

forearm_twist_01_jnt.rotateX =
wrist.rotateX * 0.75;

forearm_twist_01_jnt.rotateY =
wrist.rotateY * 0.75;

forearm_twist_01_jnt.rotateZ =
wrist.rotateZ * 0.75;

//the second bone gets 50%

forearm_twist_02_jnt.rotateX =
wrist.rotateX * 0.50;
```

```
    forearm_twist_02_jnt.rotateY =
wrist.rotateY * 0.50;

    forearm_twist_02_jnt.rotateZ =
wrist.rotateZ * 0.50;

    //the last bone gets 25%

    forearm_twist_03_jnt.rotateX =
wrist.rotateX * 0.25;

    forearm_twist_03_jnt.rotateY =
wrist.rotateY * 0.25;

    forearm_twist_03_jnt.rotateZ =
wrist.rotateZ * 0.25;
```

16. Hit the create button to create your expression. Note, if

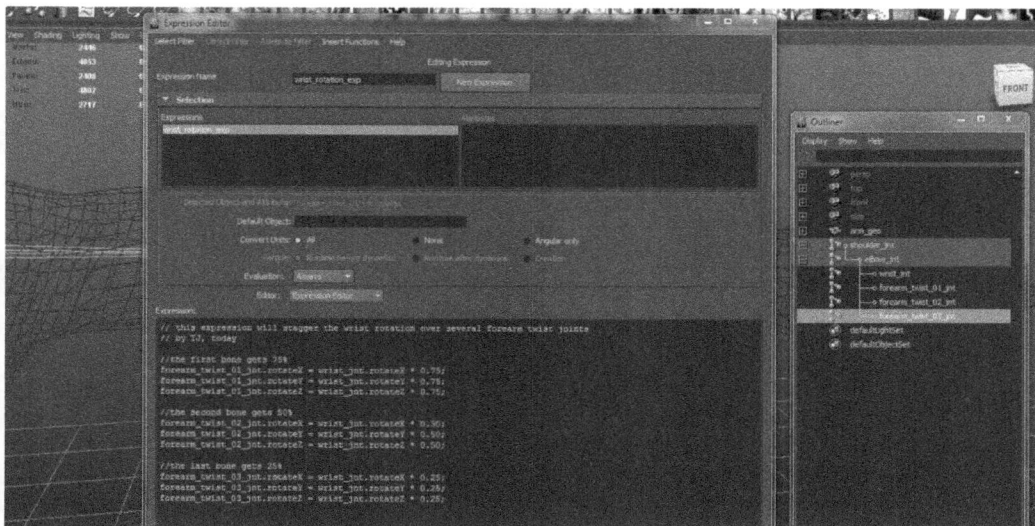

Figure 116. Expression is created.

you have already hit create, you will instead have to hit edit.

Now, rotating the wrist bone will rotate the bones and let them twist in a staggered fashion. You will quickly realize though that we need to edit the expression since these bones only really twist in one direction, and not all three. Try opening your expression editor and deleting the lines you do not need yourself. Do not forget to hit the edit button. ☺ You should end up with an expression like:

```
//the first bone gets 75%

forearm_twist_01_jnt.rotateZ =
wrist.rotateZ * 0.75;

//the second bone gets 50%

forearm_twist_02_jnt.rotateZ =
wrist.rotateZ * 0.50;

//the last bone gets 25%

forearm_twist_03_jnt.rotateZ =
wrist.rotateZ * 0.25;
```

Even with default weights, the example file shows how effective this simple expression can be.

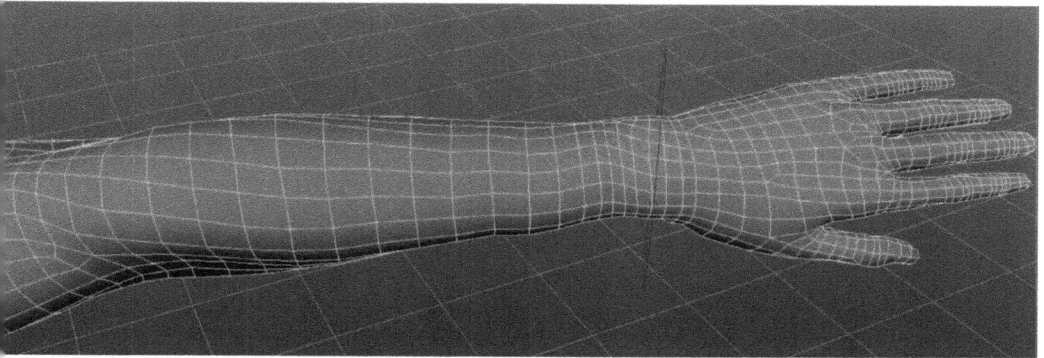

Figure 117. Rough bind showing twist.

Example File: 3_arm_twist_01_model.ma

Example File: 4_arm_twist_02_base_joints.ma

Example File: 5_arm_twist_03_twists_drawn.ma

Example File: 6_arm_twist_04_twist_exp_added.ma

While this certainly is not the most complex use of an expression, I am sure you can quickly see the advantages of only having to rotate the wrist and several other bones all rotate properly because of that. Once you start to use expressions, you will start to see all sorts of areas to try them out. Maybe the car tires need automatic rotation, or perhaps you want to add a sine wave in to a blowing grass scenario. You can also make use of conditions in expressions. Take for example the tendons in the back of your hand. If you make a fist, and raise just your index finger to point outwards, you will notice the tendon on the back of your hand that drives your index finger has formed an S shape. However, if you raise your middle finger with the index, this time pointing a "V", you will notice your index finger tendon is now straight. In fact, any time the two go up together, the tendon is straight. This is because of how the two tendons are physically bound in an anatomical sense.

You can write an expression that would toggle on the proper motion based on these two conditions. This is done using an If/else paradigm. In the following tutorial, you will learn how to create a conditional expression.

Tutorial: Write a Condition (If/Else) Expression

1. This tutorial will demonstrate how you can make one bone rotate according to another, but only if the first one "hits" the second. Start by drawing two joint pairs to match the image below.

2. Name your first joint "master_jnt" and the second joint "driven_jnt".

3. Play with your joints to understand your rotational relationship. In our drawing, the first pair can rotate for 15 degrees before they "hit" the other joint pair.

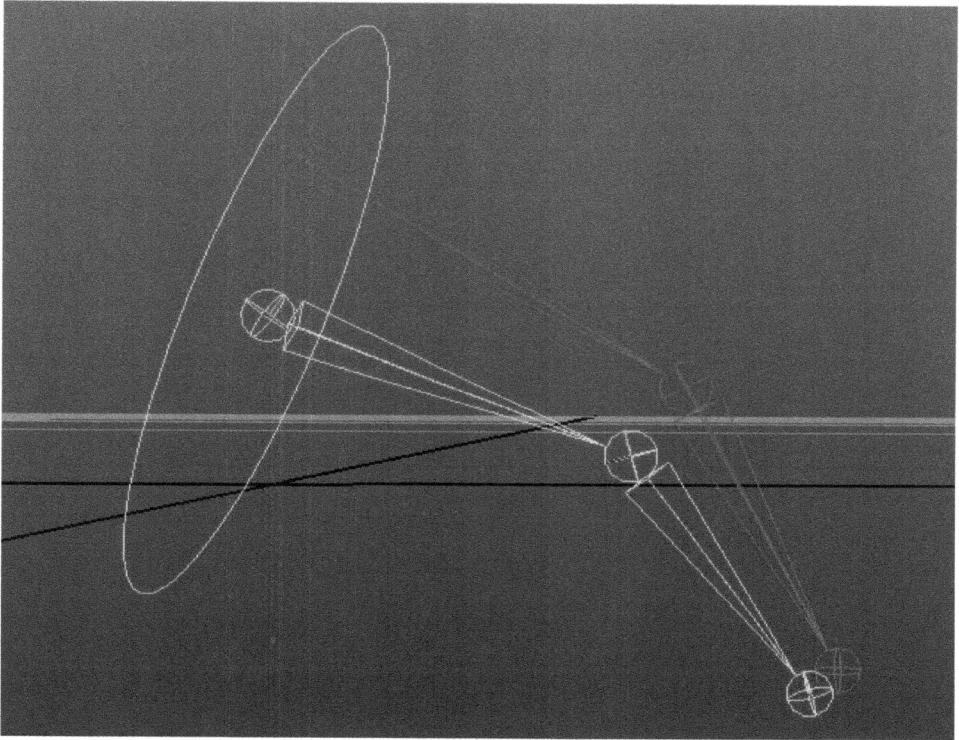

Figure 118. 15 degrees hits the other joint.

4. Let us make an expression to represent this. Make sure to

give it a name such as "driven_rotation_exp".

```
//this expression demonstrates if/else
statements

// the driven joints will move out of
the way to match the master joints

// by (your name), (date)

if (master_jnt.rotateZ >= 15)

    {

    //the joint is past 15, so make sure
to move out of the way

    driven_jnt.rotateZ =
master_jnt.rotateZ - 15;

    }

    else

    {

    //the master joint is less than 15,
so stay still

    driven_jnt.rotateZ = 0;
```

}

    a. Hit the create button.

After you create your expression, try rotating your master joints on the z axis. You should have the one pair staying still until your master joint gets to 15 degrees. Then, as you continue past 15, your driven joint will start moving as well. This premise can be used in rigging for something like a skirt. Picture the leg moving towards the skirt. Your skirt should stay stationary until the leg hits it, and then after that the skirt should match the motion of the leg. This is a great way of getting some "cloth dynamics" for "free" and works really well!

Example File: 07_joint_expression_example.ma

Set Driven Keys

There are times of course when creating an expression can seem daunting or involve too much complex math for you. Let us face it; sadly, not everyone enjoys writing a lot of heavy mathematical scenarios. This is when our friend, the set driven key, can come in to play. The set driven key is a way to make one attribute drive another. Here, unlike a direct connection, you are allowed to create a more complex relationship where things can change over time and this is the real advantage of the set driven key. You can come back later of course and edit your graphs associated with your set driven key to change this relationship. However, it is important to know that this is one area of disadvantage for the set driven key. Editing the graphs associated with your set driven keys can become complex, and often editing an expression can be the simpler of the two routes, especially if you are inheriting the work from someone else. After all, the set driven keys do not normally come with comments explaining exactly what each step is doing.

The easiest way to open your set driven key editor is by using the channel box right click menu. Select an attribute in the channel box, click on edit at the top of the channel box, and then set driven key.

(Channel Box Top Menu) -> Edit -> Set Driven Key…

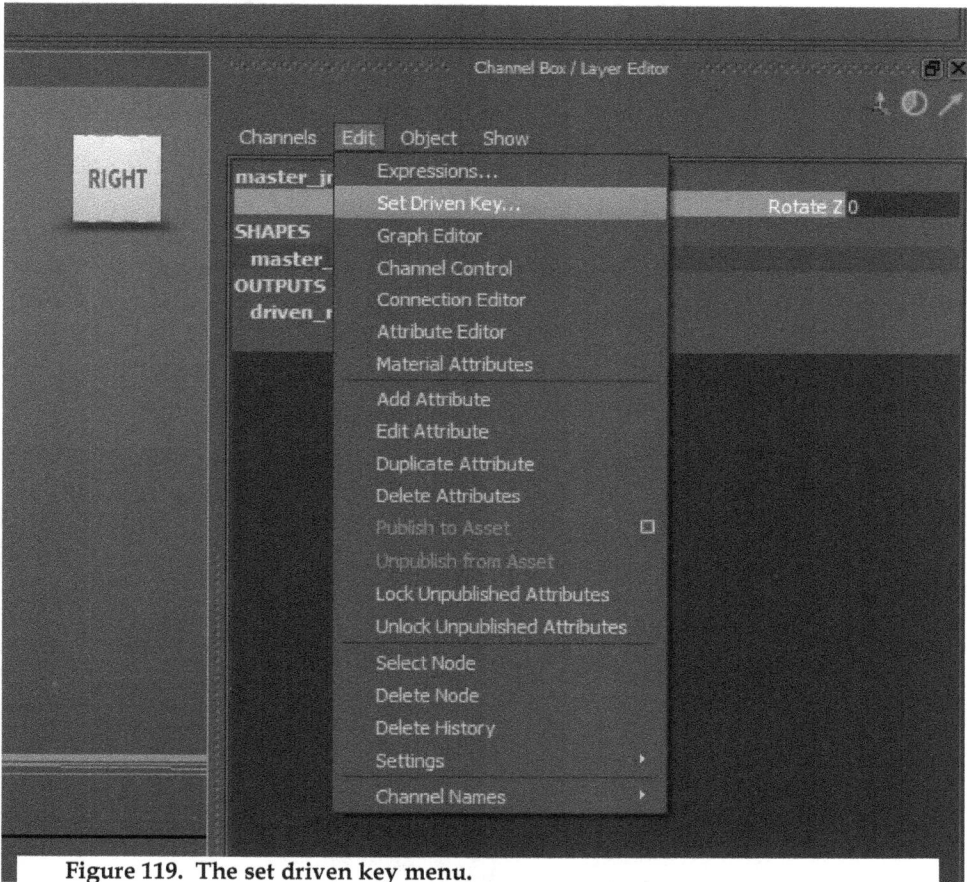

Figure 119. The set driven key menu.

In the following tutorial, we make use of our own attributes to curl our fingers into a fist.

Tutorial: Set Driven Key for Creating A Fist

1. Create your finger joints and a wrist controller as outlined in previous tutorials.

2. Add a "fist" float attribute to your controller as outlined in the previous tutorials as well with a minimum of 0 and a maximum of 10.

3. Set your fist attribute to 0, and your finger rotations to 0 as well.

4. Select all of your finger joints.

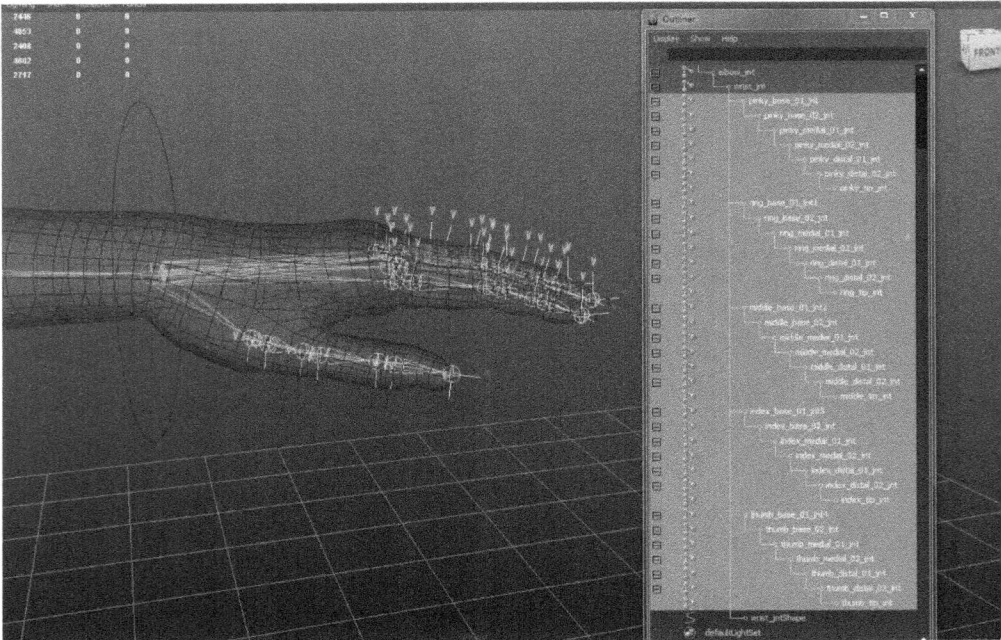

Figure 120. Select the fingers.

5. Select your first finger joint's rotation z in the channel box, then open the set driven key command:

   a. **Animate -> Set Driven Key -> Set ...**

Figure 121. Set driven key.

   b. With your Rotate Z axis selected, click the "load driven" button. This will bring the joint information into the lower half of the window.

   c. Select all the joints under the driven portion of the window, and then select Rotate Z. This will tell Maya that all of your joints rotate Z attribute is what we want to drive.

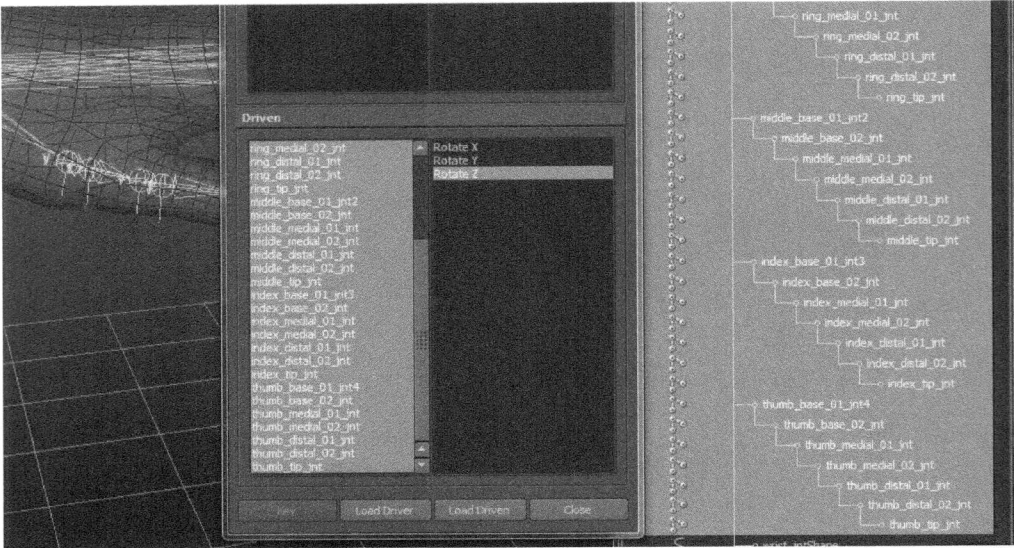

Figure 122. Select all joints for rotate Z.

d. Select your control with the fist attribute and click the "load driver" button.

e. Select the fist attribute in the window.

f. Click the "key" button. This will set the key at 0 for the pair of attributes: fist and rotate Z for every joint selected.

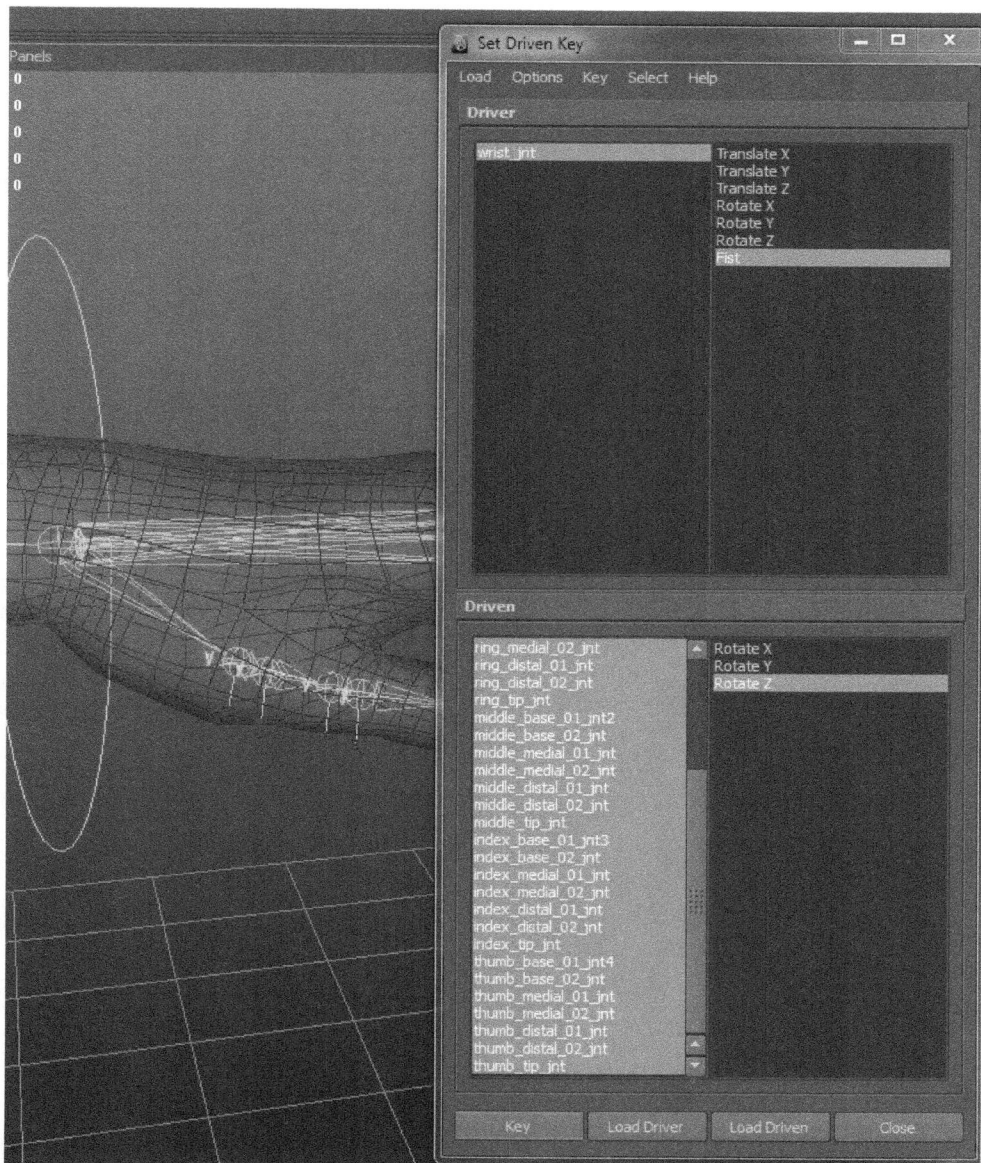

Figure 123. Set driven key window.

g. Set the attribute for your fist to 10.

h. Now pose your fist by rotating the joints until you have a fist you are happy with.

i. Bring up your set driven key window and the first joint's rotate z attribute. Click "key" to save the new fist position at the value of 10 for your fist.

Once you have done this for each joint, you can now select your control. Clicking on the "fist" attribute in the channel box and middle mouse dragging back and forth will have your hand going from an open hand at 0 to a fist at 10.

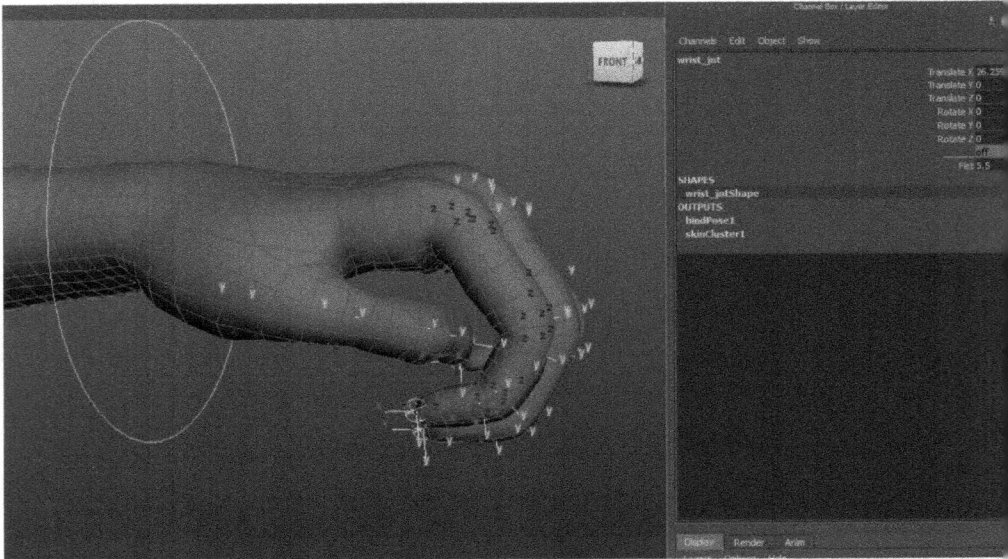

Figure 124. Changing the attribute animates the hand.

Example File: 08_set_driven_fist_01_base_joints.ma

Example File: 09_set_driven_fist_02_attr_added.ma

Example File: 10_set_driven_fist_03_key_created.ma

You can see how a complex animation can easily be driven by one attribute. Notice how only the z axis animation was saved. This was because we explicitly picked only the z axis. You can easily control exactly what axis is driven via this method.

Much like expressions, set driven keys can be simple or quite complex. You can even stagger the animation so that the thumb rotates more slowly than the fingers in order to close on them on the outside of the fist. By setting intermediate keys, this is accomplished. Experiment by setting a key for your thumb when the Fist attribute is at 5. In our main setup tutorial, you will learn how to use set driven keys to make a foot roll and move automatically through the various poses associated with a walk cycle.

Other Things to Consider in Architecture

There are a few more things we should make note of before moving on to creating your rigs and looking at deformations. Your rigging practices should always encompass the underlying theme of scene cleanliness and intuitiveness. In other words, anyone should be able to open your scene and immediately know what is going on and what controls do what. Creating control curves and custom attributes in a clean fashion can go a long way to helping this, as outlined above. You should also consider carefully grouping your objects and naming all of your nodes in a consistent fashion. Prefixing your label of items lf_ for left and rt_ for right is a good first step, but everything should be named in a consistent fashion. The best naming convention is one that is understandable and ALWAYS followed on every node, in every scene.

To make things even quicker to understand, items that should not be moved or touched can be "locked down". This can be as simple as locking the attributes and often one wants to hide them from even being seen. The following tutorial explains how to do that, and it is a relatively straightforward process. Doing so will now reduce the visual clutter for each object as they are selected. After all, if an object only needs to rotate, why should you show the translates, scales and visibility or allow the animators to have the option of touching things that may break your rig?

Tutorial: Lock and Hide Attributes

1. Create a ball as outlined in the previous tutorials.
2. Select in the channel box all the attributes but the rotates and run the command:
   a. **Right Click in Channel Box -> Lock and Hide Selected**

As your skills develop, you will want to start writing simple MEL scripts that can help you lock and hide attributes to speed this process up.

As we mentioned above, your attributes should be "frozen" as well, using "Freeze Transformations". This will allow your rigs to be moved back to a default pose in a very quick and intuitive fashion.

So, in summary, prior to moving on to deformations ensure your rigs:

- Properly positioned.
- Have a clean scene hierarchy.
- Follow a consistent naming convention.
- Have been frozen or zeroed out.

- Have been locked down and simplified as much as possible.

- Have easy to understand controls (bonus points for using colours)

Rigging Architecture Summary

After finishing the above section, you have covered all the basics for the first half of the domain of character setup, which is often referred to as your motion systems. You should now be able to create your own motion system for your characters and make it an elegant one that is a joy to animate.

Deformation

Introduction

So far, we have spent all our time talking about creating ways to move stuff around and all the building blocks necessary to create these methodologies. Now we can start to focus on how things actually look as they move around. When we speak of deformations, we are talking about how the models are pushed,

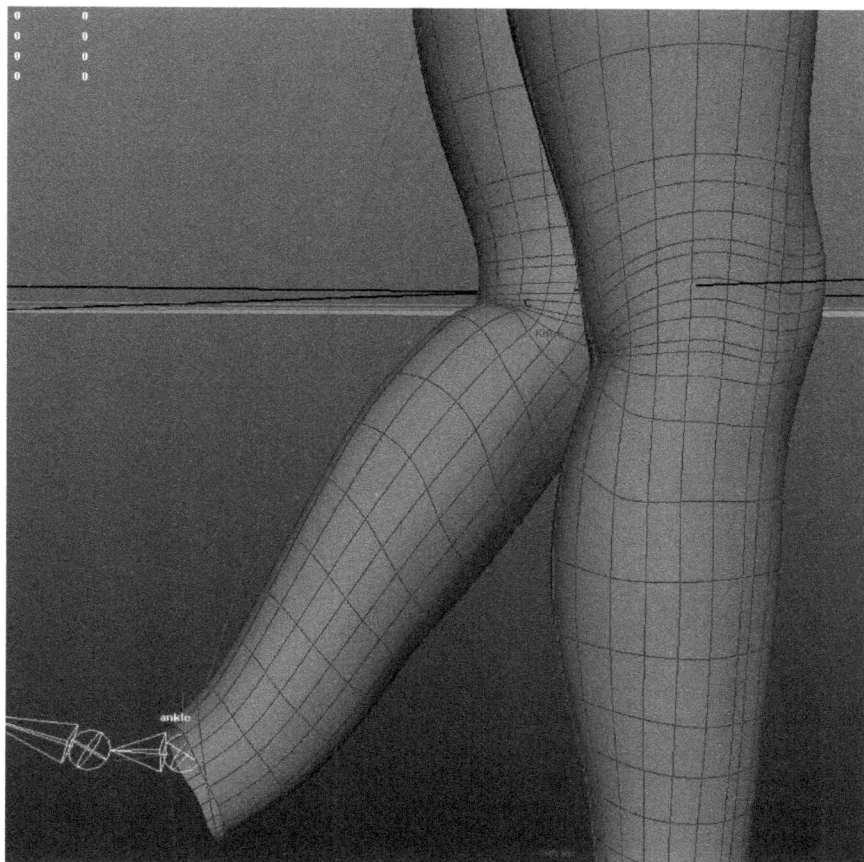

Figure 125. Legs bending.

bent, and how they change in shape. That means the object starts out as one shape and is bent or moved into another shape. For example, when you bend your leg, the way the model should move or deform is much different than if you are merely translating a hard object around like a lamp.

While the concept of a model deforming is trivial, deforming the model well can be a complex and vexing challenge that is an art form unto itself. In fact, several major studios will break the task in to those who can deform characters well and those who can setup their movement systems well.

The second half of this book is devoted to helping you get your model not only deforming, but deforming well. As your skills grow, you will want to add in layers of complexity and expand far beyond just these basic building blocks. We will cover these more extensively in future books in the series.

By the time you finish this section, you will be knowledgeable in all areas of deformation, from rigid binding to painting clusters. We will cover all the basic building blocks you need to make your models and characters deform well in a believable fashion.

Example File: 11_leg_01_joints.ma

Example File: 12_leg_02_setup.ma

Example File: 13_leg_03_experiment_with_

muscles_from_advanced_rigging_book.ma

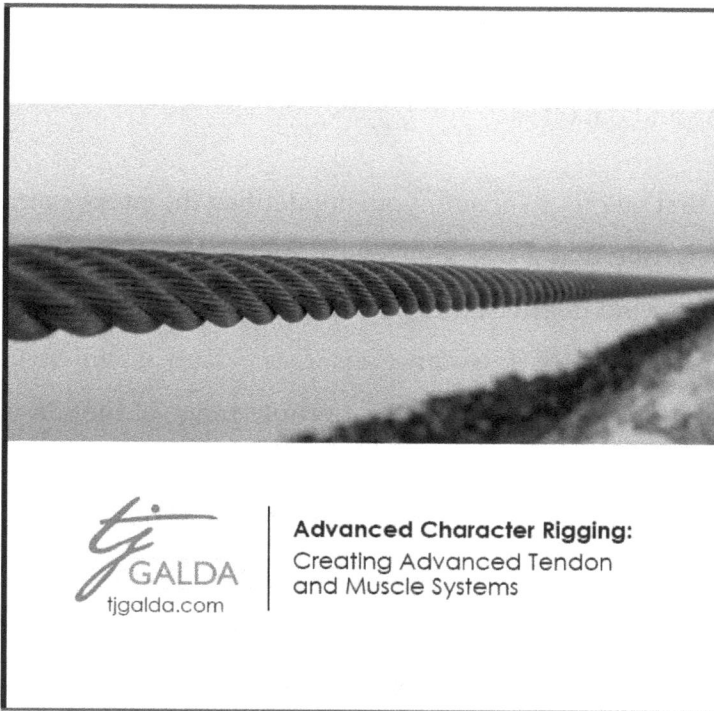

Figure 126. Cover of advanced book.

Preparing Your Model for Deformations

Before we start covering the various areas of the deformation system, we should take a minute to talk about getting prepared for doing so. Your deformations will only be as good as your modeling and data flow.

The first step is to ensure your model has the proper amount of data. While doing this well will take practice, you should be aware that your model needs more data in areas where it will bend, and should be less dense in areas where it will not. By controlling this, you will allow for a proper range of motion while keeping the model deforming quickly. The denser, or heavier, the model is, the slower the overall system will be. Areas where your model will bend will need more data for the computer to move around when it bends. For example, putting in more information around the knee in your leg is good, while taking some out of the shin is also a good idea.

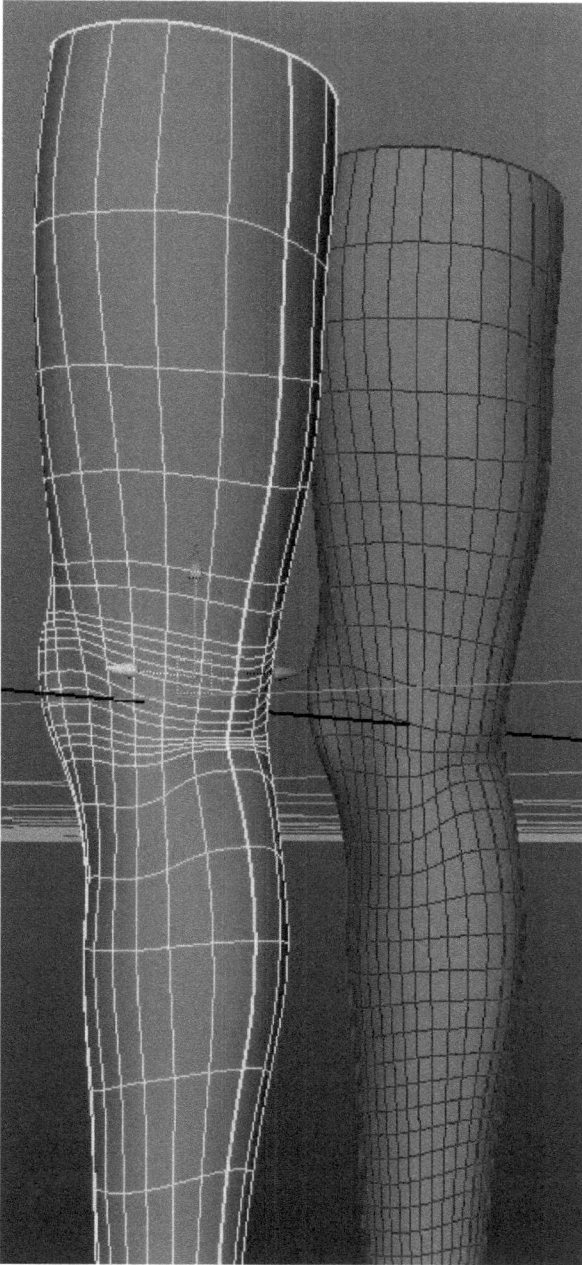

You can clearly see that you can put information where you need it and remove it where you don't and maintain an effective silhouette.

As this is not meant to be a modeling book, we will leave the topic there. Just remember, every single vertex in your model will have to be accounted for during deformation whether you need it or not.

Figure 127. Good leg and bad leg.

This directly impacts not only your animation and rendering speeds, but also how much work you must do in setting up your deformations, so taking as much OUT as you can is a good idea.

Double Transformations and Considerations

When you first start working with deformations, you will indubitably run across a phenomenon known as "double transformations". This happens when an object ends up moving twice as far as you are expecting it too and is typically the result of a deformation motion and parenting inherited motion combining. In other words, the parent of your object is telling the object to move to a position. Then, by bending the controls, the controls are deforming the object to a position. If either happened in isolation, the result would be fine. However, when they happen at the same time, they are summed together, or are additive. The result is that the end position of the object is twice what you have expected.

Thus, it is important that you are very careful when setting up your hierarchies. Any objects that are to be deformed should NOT be parented to the joints or rigs that will move them. For example, if we are deforming the leg, the leg should be in a separate group from the skeleton, as depicted in the figure.

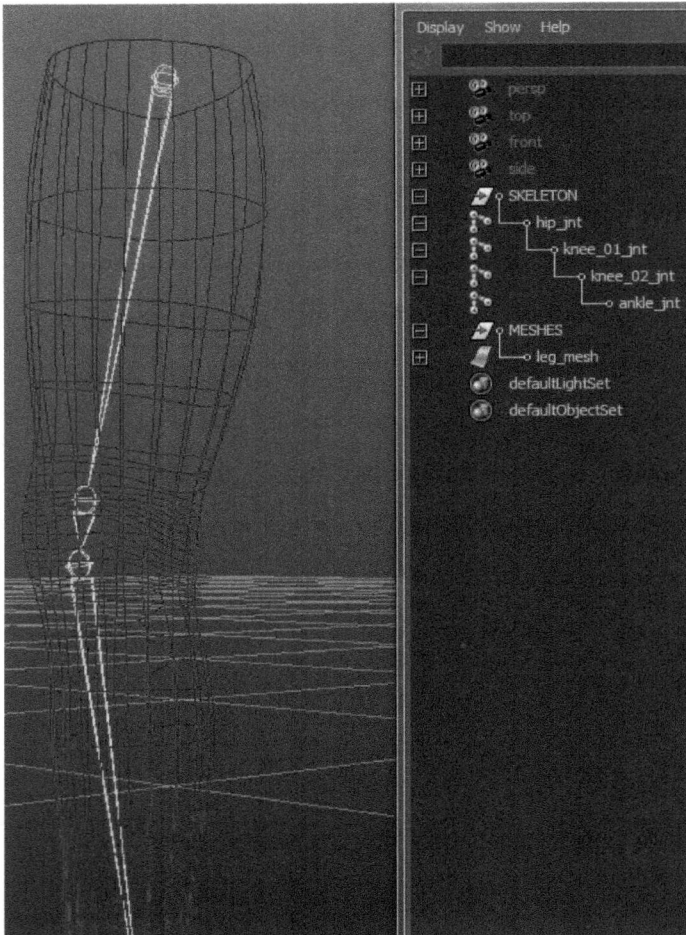

Figure 128. Leg parenting.

Later on, we will discuss how several deformations will happen and compete in a "deformation order". For now, be careful to treat any object that will be deformed as one that should not be moved unless by those deformations. Thus they should be not parented into your skeleton or to your controls but rather put in their own group. Often this group is called "history" since construction history can often create double transformations if parented in the wrong spot.

Tutorial: Parenting Your Objects Properly

1. Create a simple arm with a shoulder, elbow, and wrist.

2. Create a tube to be the arm:

   a. **Create -> NURBS Surface -> Cylinder**

   b. Move and scale the cylinder into the right position.

3. Select all of your joints and the cylinder then bind the object:

   a. **Skin -> Smooth Bind**

   b. We will describe the smooth bind in more detail later, for now the default values will be fine.

4. After the tube has been bound, try bending the elbow. The tube should move much like an arm. Try selecting the shoulder and transforming it around the scene, the tube should come along for the ride.

5. Now, let us break the rig by parenting the tube to the elbow.

   a. Select the tube, then hold shift and select the elbow.

   b. P

6. Try moving the shoulder again. This time, the tube will move away from the arm. This is because of the double transformations. The parent relationship of the elbow says to the tube "move!" but the tube is also bound to the joints. This binding also says "move!" and so the tube ends up moving "twice" or has "double transformations".

7. Hit undo (z) to get back to the original state of the tube in the right position.

8. Create an empty group:

   a. Select nothing by clicking out in your scene.

   b. Ctrl + g

   c. Name this group "history".

9. Parent the tube to the history group:

   a. Select the tube, then the "history" group holding shift.

   b. p

10. Now try transforming the shoulder around. Once again, the tube should move properly around the scene, without double transformations.

This sense of a history group is important. Note that the tube does not double transform if it is not parented to the joints. But, you will want to have your geometry parented to something in order to have a clean hierarchy and avoid a messy scene. A history group is a good way of putting all of your geometry together. As long as it is not parented to your joints or controllers, you will avoid the double transformations and yet still keep everything together neatly.

Clusters

Clusters have been around since the inception of Maya. These great little guys are nothing more than a way to group a selection of points. To make a cluster, you simply select the control vertices or vertices you want in your cluster, and use the command:

Deform -> Create Cluster

That is all there is to it. By doing so, you will have created a cluster that you can then move around and force your geometry to deform at your will. Clusters can be used in advanced techniques or simple ones, and are always there when you need a group.

Tutorial: Create A Cluster To Move Points

1. Create a ball.
2. Enter the component (blue) mode and select some of the vertices.
3. Now create a cluster using the command:
   a. **Create Deformers -> Cluster**
4. Move around the cluster and you will see the points you had selected move as well.

If you would like to have even more control with your cluster, you can select your object itself and run the same command. This time, instead of a group of vertices, your entire object is now part of the cluster. You can further control your precision by painting your cluster weights. This will allow you to paint an area or map of exactly how your cluster should work.

We will cover painting weights in much detail later on in the section. The only difference between painting weights for your smooth bound skin and a cluster is that cluster weights are either in the cluster or not. That means that in this scenario, smoothing your weights is your friend. These are covered in more detail later, but remember for now that smoothing a cluster is actually a GOOD thing and will not result in having the weights mysteriously assigned to something else automatically. This is outlined in the tutorial below.

Tutorial: Creating a Cluster and Painting Control

1. This time, we will create a cluster that you control by painting. Create your ball again.
2. Select the ball in the object (green) mode.
3. Create a cluster using the command:
   a. **Create Deformers -> Cluster**
4. Select the ball and paint the cluster weights by:
   a. **Edit Deformers -> Paint Cluster Weights Tool []**

5. When painting the weights, the amount of influence ranges from 0 to 100%, which also corresponds to the colour value from black to white. Try replacing the weights to zero by using the replace option, the value of 0, and hitting flood.

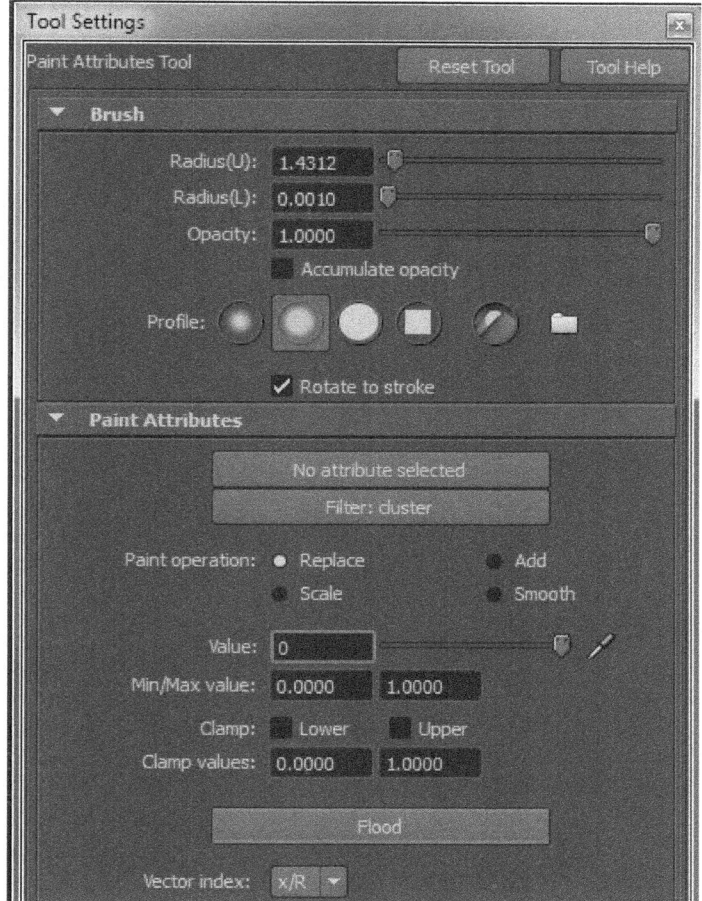

Figure 129. Cluster Painting Tool.

6. Now paint in an area to control. Select a value of 1, choose
    add and paint using the left mouse button on the object.

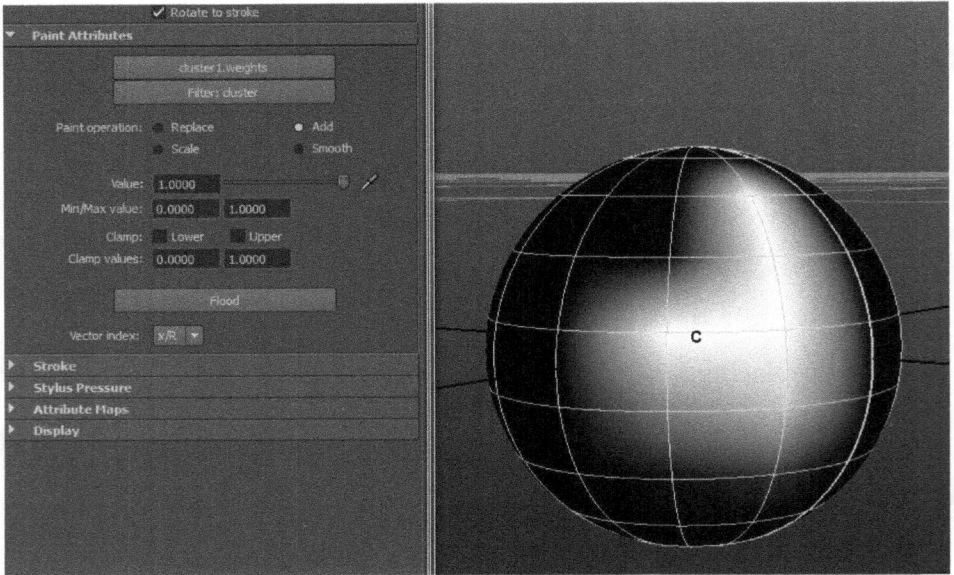

Figure 130. Painting a cluster.

We will describe the painting nuances in the next section, so
for now move the cluster handle around and notice that only the
area that you painted will move around.

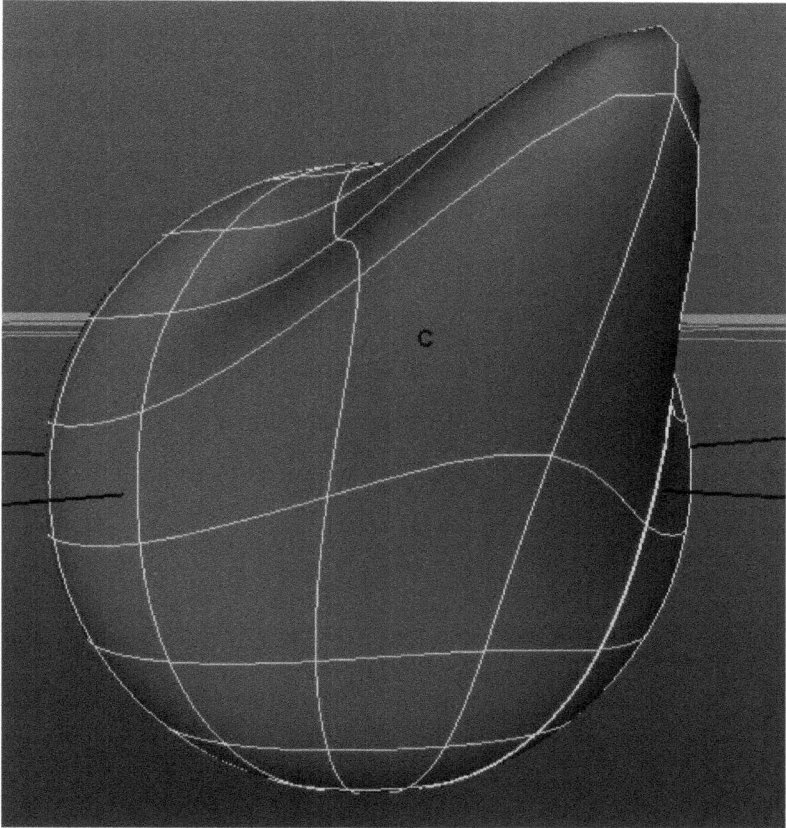

Figure 131. Pulling the cluster.

Now let us talk more about painting and what weights actually are.

Weights and Envelopes

When we are referring to weights, we are referring to essentially a weighted percentage. Typically, weights range from a value of zero to one (if normalized). Normalizing your weights will take your existing range and force the range to be a true percentage, and thus a zero to one range. A weight of 100% is thus 1, and a weight of 0% is thus 0. To further visualize this, Maya allows one to paint their weights and shows the percentage in a grayscale fashion. That renders a weight of 0 (0%) as absolute black and a weight of 1 (100%) as pure white. This means a weight of 0.5 (50%) will be 50% grey.

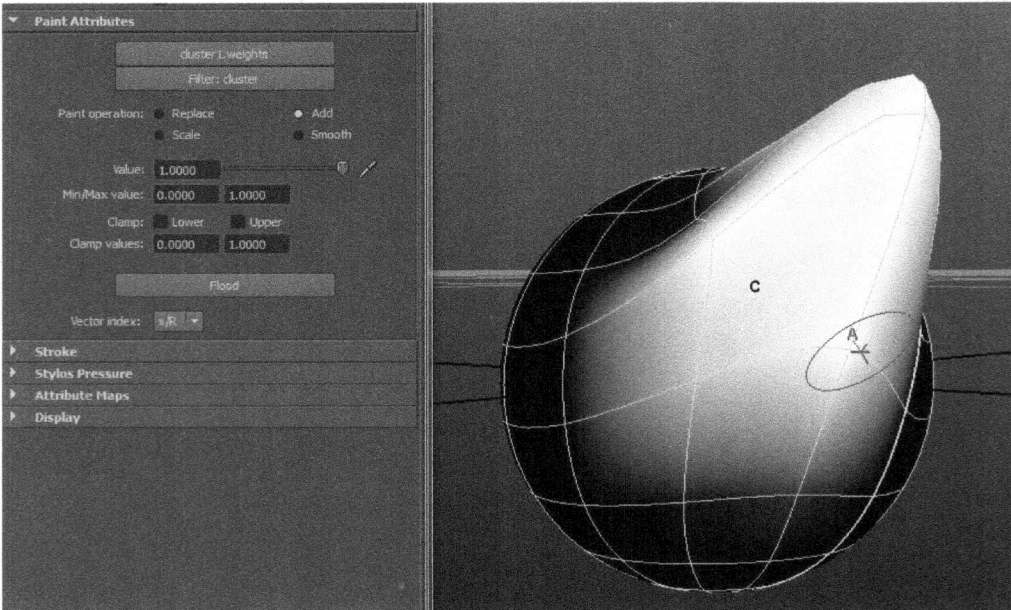

Figure 132. Painted cluster.

A group of vertices that are weighted have their weight information stored in a weight map. Each vertex in your weight map must have a percentage of the weight assigned to it, and the entire list of vertices with their associated value is called a weight list.

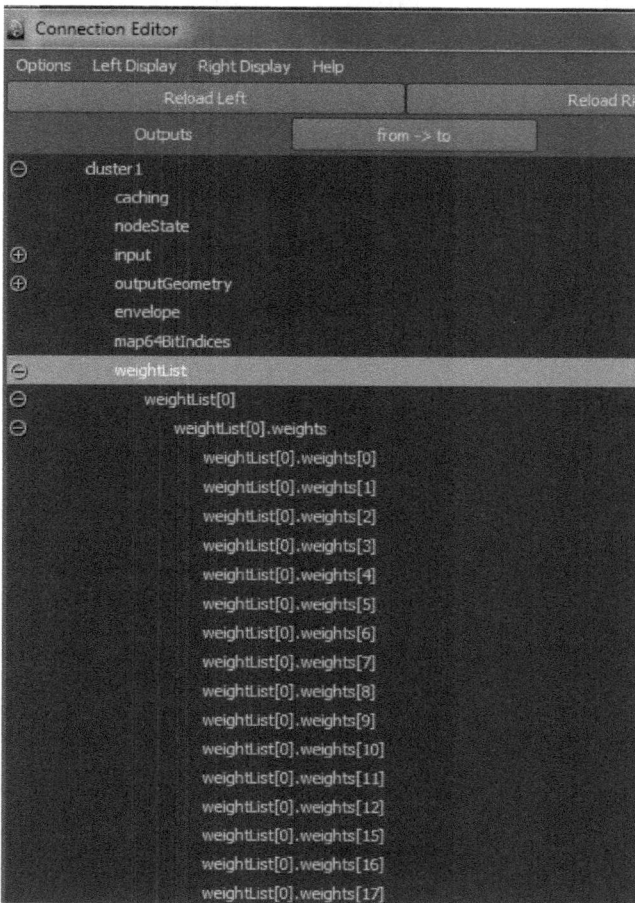

Figure 133. Weight list.

Envelopes are a way of describing the effect that a deformer has on an object. The envelope can have a range from zero to one in which to reflect the percentage of control that is has. In other words, a deformer with an envelope of 1 is fully controlling the deformation of the object. This allows you to dial up or down how much deformation any particular deformer is creating. The typical default value of an envelope is 1, which means it is fully engaged.

Let us look at envelopes and weight lists as if they were in a stage lighting setup. One could think of the envelope of each deformer as essentially a "master dimmer switch" and the individual weights as "individual dimmer switches". This means that if the weights are painted, we can dial up or down their effect by merely controlling the envelope value. The individual vertices have individual control or dimmers, but all of them are also controlled by the master dimmer switch or envelope.

Tutorial: Envelopes and Clusters

1. Create a cluster that you control by painting. Create your ball again.
2. Select the ball in the object (green) mode.
3. Create a cluster using the command:
   a. **Create Deformers -> Cluster**
4. Select the ball and paint the cluster weights by:

a. Edit Deformers -> Paint Cluster Weights Tool []

5. Replace the weights to zero by using the replace option, the value of 0, and hitting flood.

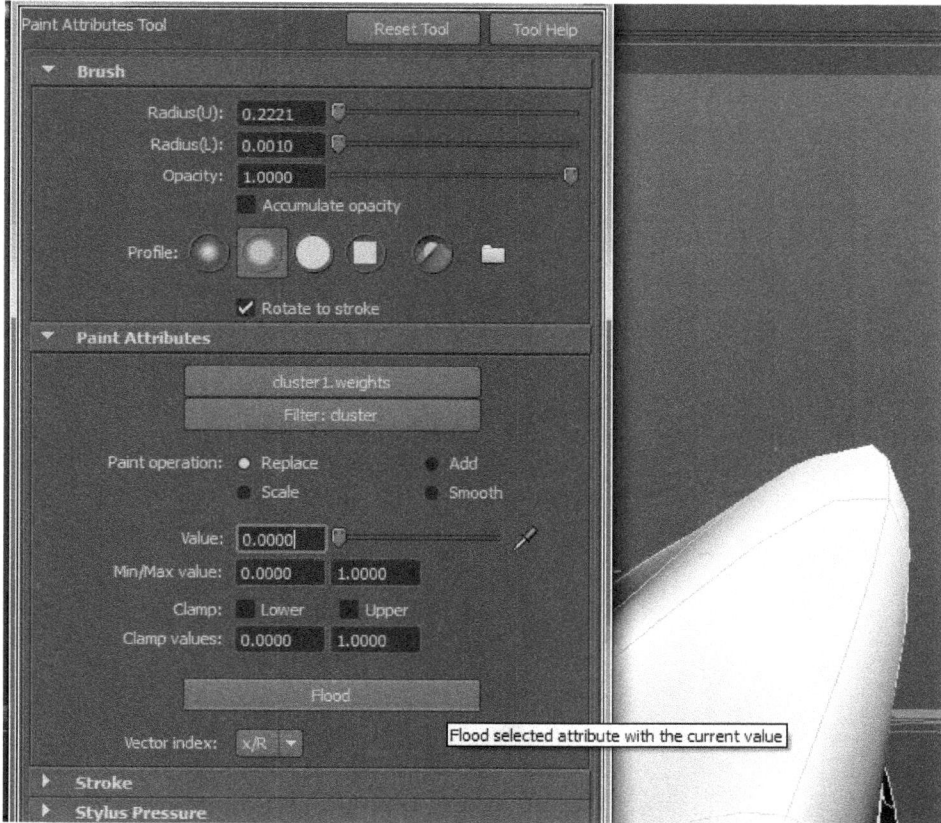

Figure 134. Cluster options.

6. Now paint in an area to control. Select a value of 1, choose add and paint using the left mouse button on the object.

7. Close the painting window and move your cluster so you have a bulge deformation in your ball.

8. Select the cluster handle and click on the cluster handle in the channel box.

9. Select the weight attribute in the channel box and middle mouse drag in the view port. Watch the amount of bulge dial up and down depending on the amount of envelope.

We will come back to weighting in our skinning discussions, but we should first cover some other basic deformers before we get in to the more complex ones. Let us leave painting weights for now and cover some basic deformers.

Lattice

A lattice is also known as a "free form deformer" (FFD). This FFD, or lattice, is a way of creating an object around your model that will then deform your model based upon the closest point associations.

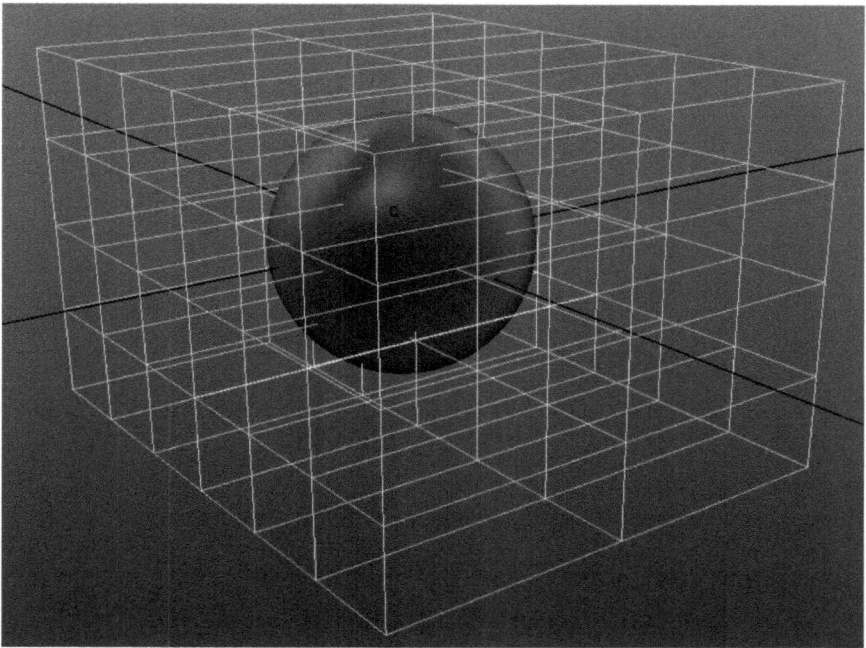

Figure 135. Creating a lattice.

In other words, when you create a lattice, you will get a box around your object. To do so, simply select your object and run the command:

Create Deformers -> Lattice

Pulling on the vertices of the box will also pull on your object, with a falloff happening as the points of your object get further away from the point on the lattice.

Tutorial: Create a Lattice

1. Create a ball.
2. Select the ball and create a lattice to deform it:
   a. **Create Deformers -> Lattice**
3. Select the lattice points in the component (blue) mode and move them around.
4. Delete your lattice, and watch the shape return back to the original ball shape.
5. Select the ball again and create another lattice.
   a. **Create Deformers -> Lattice**
6. Select the lattice and change the amount of divisions of the lattice to see the level of detail increase.
7. Enter component (blue) mode and edit your lattice shape. Notice that the more divisions, the more precise your

deformations have become. However, it also takes more effort to get a large smooth shape as well.

Once you have created your lattice and played around with them, you will notice that you can change the level of detail by playing with the settings under divisions. Increasing the division count will increase your ability to pull very specific areas.

Upon completing your modeling changes, you can "bake in" the changes, or keep the results as part of the overall model, by deleting your construction history. Simply select your object and run the command:

Edit -> Delete By Type -> History

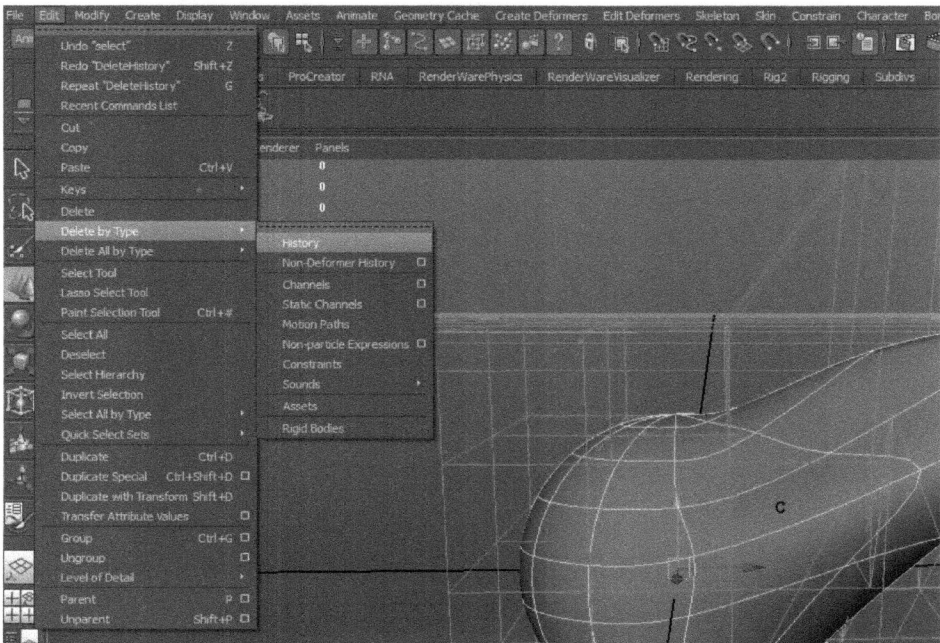

Figure 136. Delete history.

This will delete all the construction history for your selected objects, so be careful when you choose to run the command. However, in this tutorial, the result is a model that we have changed by using a lattice and keeps the results. This can be a great method for modeling complex shapes.

Tutorial: Use a Lattice and Delete History

1. Create a ball.
2. Create a lattice as discussed previously.

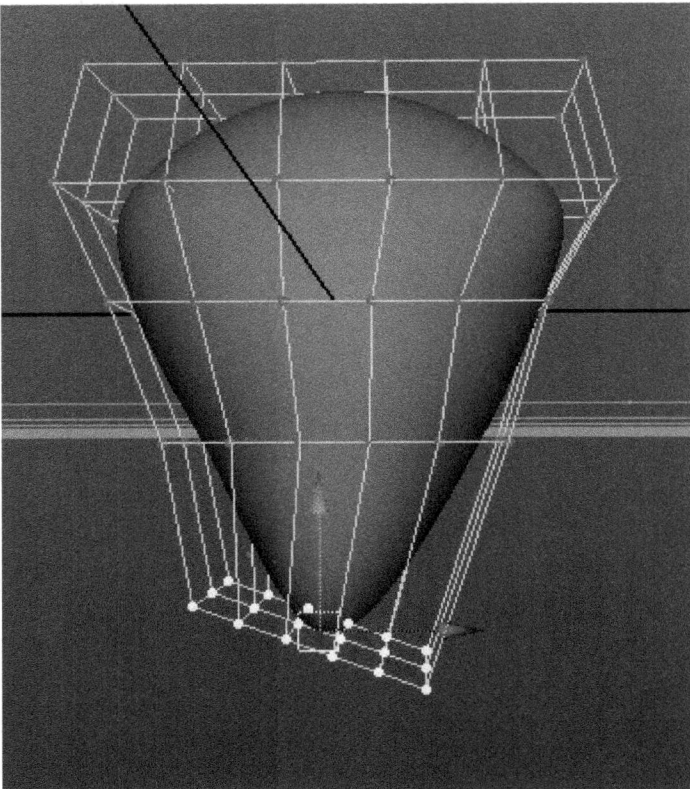

Figure 137. Tear shape made by a lattice.

3. Edit your lattice to make the ball into a tear drop shape

4. Select the ball.

5. Delete the history to keep the new shape, using the command:

   a. **Edit -> Delete By Type -> History**

Lattices can be useful far beyond just helping you to model. The nature of a lattice is dependent on the settings you have chosen, but by default, the relationship is set up to be one of closest points. In other words, moving your object through the lattice will cause your object to deform differently because as the object moves so too does the closest point at any given spot in relation to the stationary lattice. This can be quite useful for making your objects squeeze or grow and having that effect animate. In our tutorial, we show our model squeezing through a small hole and emerging on the other side, which is all accomplished by simply having it move through the lattice.

Tutorial: Squeeze a Fish Through a Hole

1. Create a simple model. In our case I made a rough fish shaped model out of a polygon sphere.

2. In order to have the lattice work as the model passes through something, we need to attach the object to a

motion path. Before doing so, make sure you have frozen your transformations on your model in order to make the axis flow work better. Deleting your history is also a good idea. Select your model and:

   a. **Modify -> Freeze Transformations**

   b. **Edit -> Delete All By Type -> History**

3. Draw a curve for your fish to swim along. In our example, it was easiest to switch to the top view and use the pencil tool:

   a. **Hotbox -> Click and Hold in the Center -> Top**

   b. **Create -> Pencil Curve Tool**

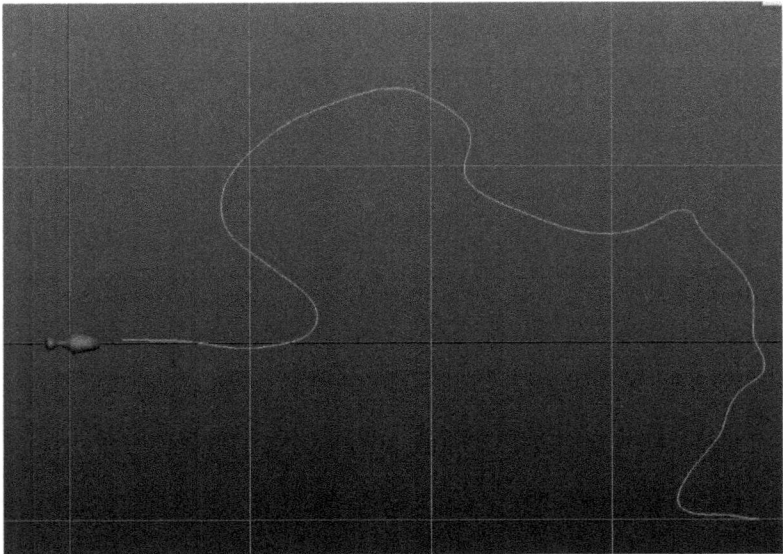

Figure 138. Drawing a path for the fish.

4. Attach your fish to the curve using the motion path tool:

    a. Select your fish then your curve.

    b. Animate -> Motion Paths -> Attach to Motion Paths []

    c. Using the options, specify the front and up axis. In our example, the fish's front axis was x and the fishes up axis was y.

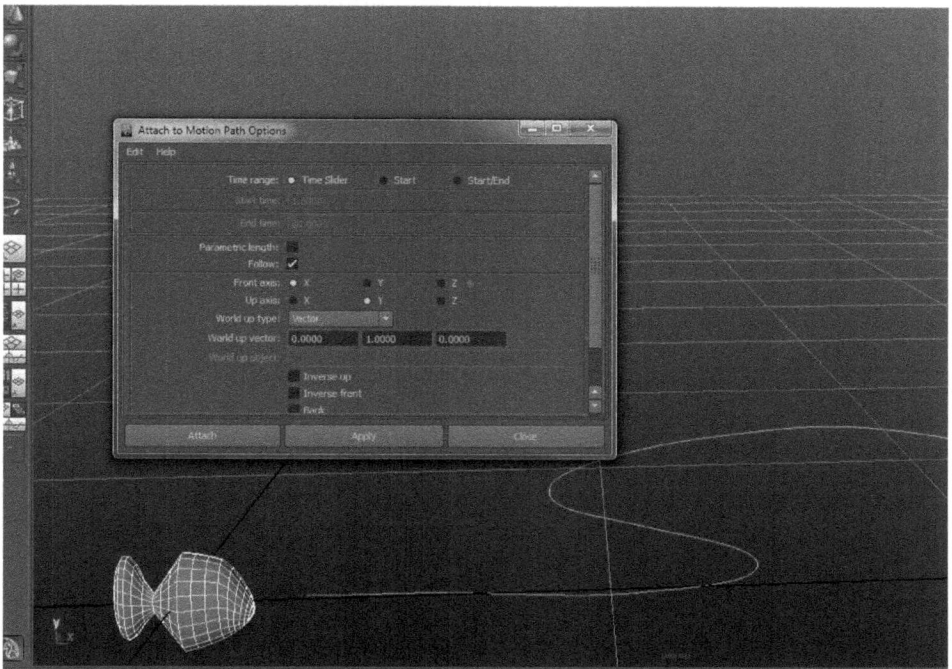

Figure 139. Fish up axis.

     i. Also, ensure the "bank" option is turned on.

5. You will notice the fish may be pointing with the wrong end up. Click on "motionPath1" in the channel box and use the different twist attributes to rotate the fish properly. In our example, the side twist needs to be set to 90. The alternative is to break the connection of the proper rotation axis and rotate that axis. In our example, we can accomplish the same thing by breaking the connection of rotate Z and changing the value to 90.

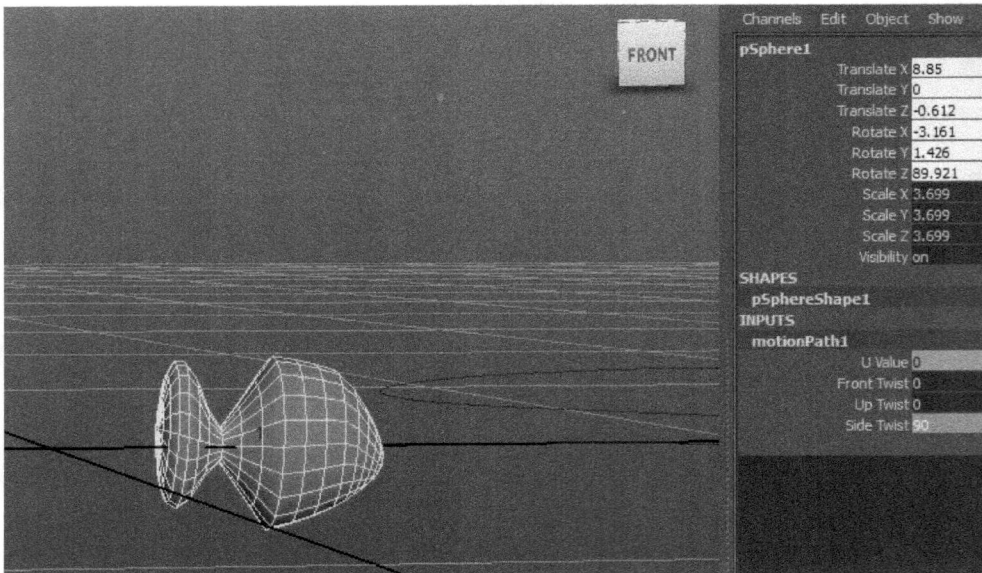

Figure 140. Adjusting the side twist.

6. While the twist and changing the rotation values are valid methods, the best way to ensure your fish is moving with the right direction as up is to ensure you first freeze the transformations of the fish before attaching and then use the world up type as "vector" in the options. Try this again but this time first select your fish and:

   a. **Modify -> Freeze Transformations**

   b. Use the world up type "vector" option

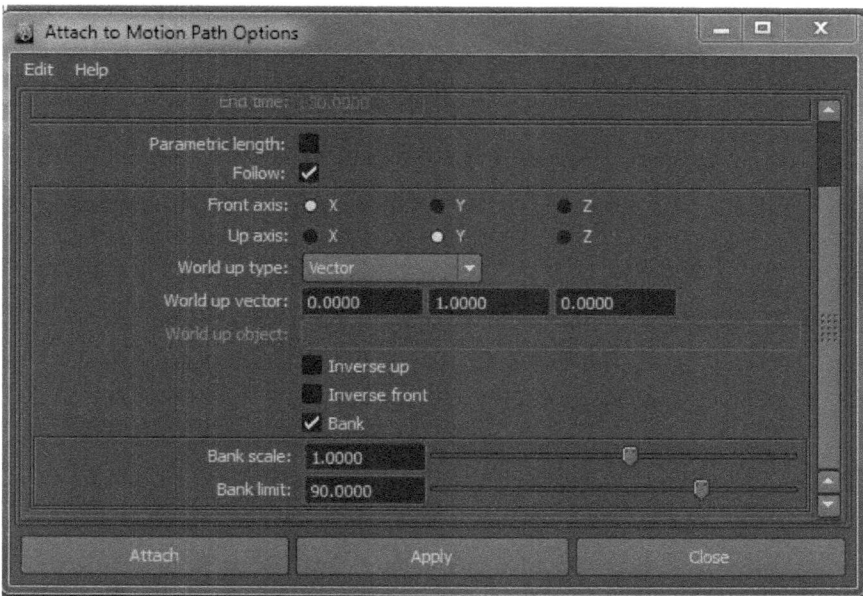

Figure 141. Choosing the vector option.

7. Scrub the time slider and you will notice that your fish will move along the curve.

8. Select your fish after you've watched him "swim" along the curve, and create your lattice along the curve using the flow path tool:

   a. **Animate -> Motion Paths -> Flow Path Object []**

      i. In our case, you would like to see a lattice along the curve, so select lattice around curve in the options

      ii. Having more detail in the lattice will be helpful, so select a higher number for the "divisions front". In our example, I have chosen 40, 4 and 4 divisions.

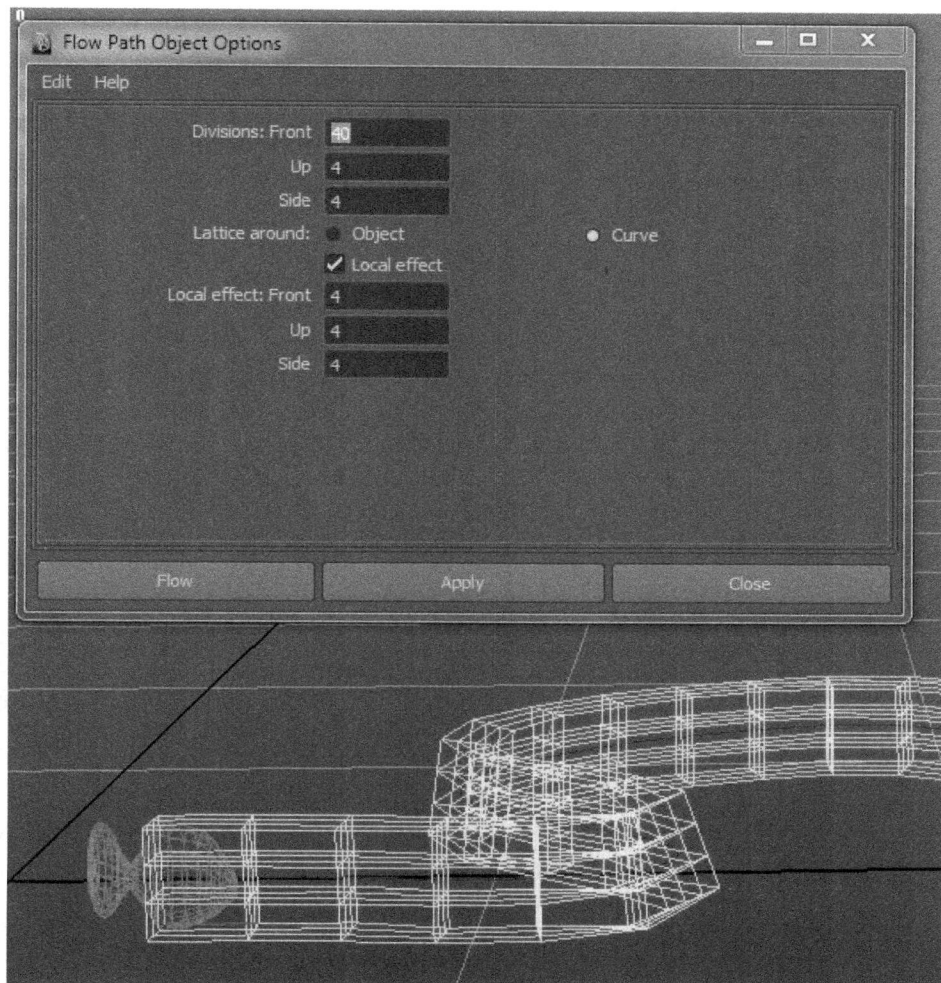

Figure 142. Lattice Options.

9. You can now edit your lattice to have the desired squishing (or twisting or any deforming) affect that you wish. To make this easier than just editing points, it is wise to select a row of points and create a cluster as depicted in this image:

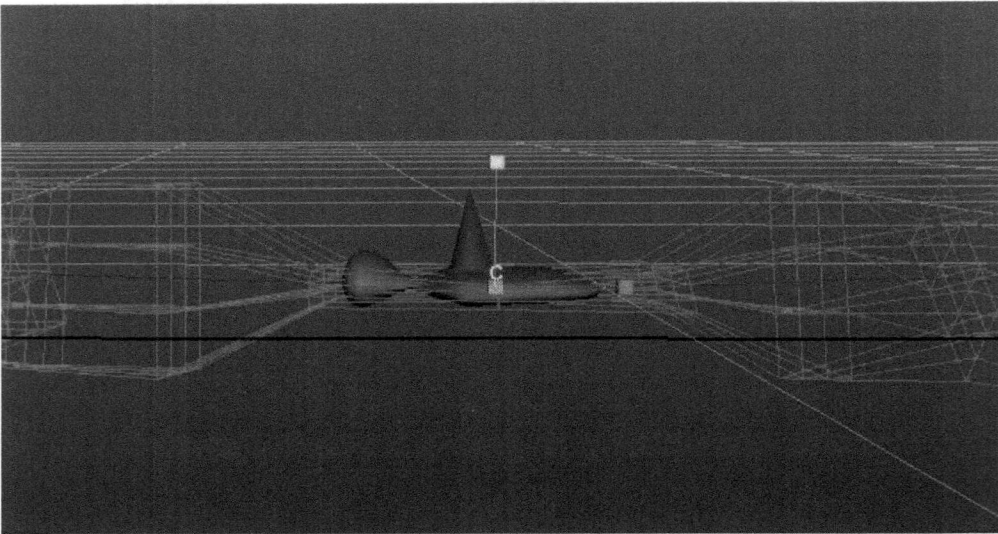

Figure 143. Clusters can squish the lattice easily.

Example File: 14_fish_motion_path_01_rough_fish.ma

Example File: 15_fish_motion_path_02_fish_animates.ma

Example File: 16_fish_motion_path_03_fish_lattice.ma

We can also make use of the ideas of expressions that we covered earlier, and the lattice itself as a way to grow objects. In a very rudimentary example of a muscle, the tutorial below shows how to use the lattice as more than just a modeling technique. I say rudimentary because this muscle is merely growing and not sliding around under the skin like true muscles would.

Tutorial: Make an Arm Muscle Using A Lattice and An Expression

1. Create a simple arm skeleton with a shoulder, elbow, and wrist.
2. Create a simple arm geometry by modeling a tube in to position. Ensure you have several divisions/isoparms near where the bicep should be.

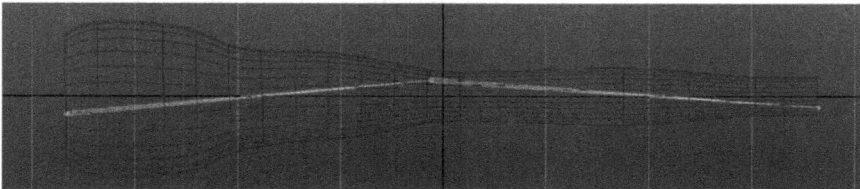

Figure 144. Very basic arm.

3. Select the vertices around the bicep area in the component mode

4. Create a lattice to drive these vertices:

   a. **Create Deformers -> Lattice**

5. Ensure you have enough divisions, in our example we changed the divisions to 8, 5 and 8

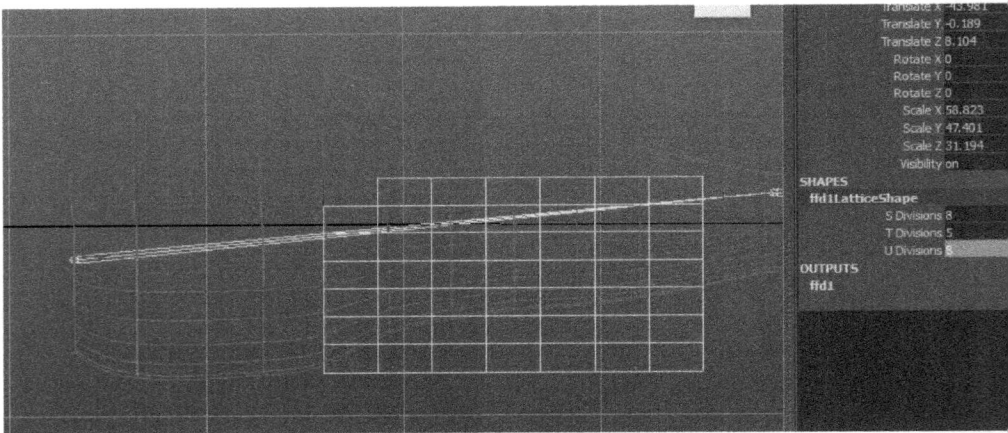

Figure 145. Adding more divisions.

6. Select your lattice and move the pivot point to where the muscle would flex by hitting insert and translating the pivot point to the proper location. Test your choice by scaling the lattice and viewing the results.

7. Once you're happy with the location and scaling, make sure to freeze the transformations on your lattice.

    a. **Modify -> Freeze Transformations**

8. Now let us write an expression to flex the muscle based on the elbow bend. Open the expression editor:

    a. **Window -> Animation Editors -> Expression Editor**

9. Write a simple expression to scale the lattice called "bicep_muscle_exp":

    a. `//this expression will bulge the bicep`

    b. `// by (your name), (date)`

    c. `Lattice.scaleZ = 1 + (elbow.rotateZ / 90);`

This simple expression will cause the scale to grow as the elbow bends. The end result is a very basic bicep muscle bulge.

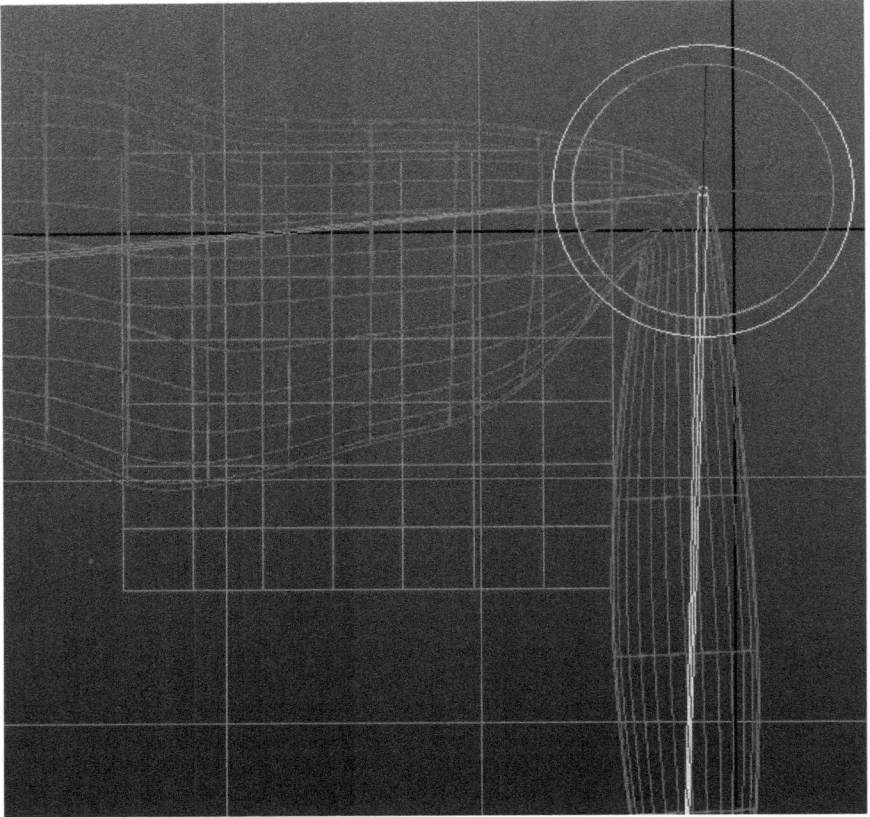

Figure 146. Basic flex.

Experiment with your mathematical expression to dial in the scale factor a little more precisely. Next, try repeating the process using a cluster and a set-driven key instead of the lattice and expression. You will get the same results, but you will also become more familiar with the basic building blocks. The goal is to understand how each of them work so that as you progress you can decide for yourself what to use where and not have to rely on a tutorial.

Both clusters and lattices have different strengths. Clusters are light and simple but therein lays their power. Lattices are far easier to visualize, but also can be a bit more complex to determine things like what to hide or show the animation team, how or where to parent them, etcetera.

Blend Shapes

Blend shapes, or morph targets, are a deformation technique that relies on modeling. In this technique, one sculpts the end position of how the model should look. This is most often used for facial rigging, and a series of models or targets, are created to simulate the various poses that a face can get in to. In our example, we keep this quite simple, but these blend shapes can get quite complex and are not restricted to just the face.

Blend shapes are a very good way for the beginner to start out conducting expression and lip sync animation tests with. The first step is to model all the various poses you will use. You do so by simply duplicating the original or "default head" and modifying each duplicate. It is important to note that each blend shape target must have the identical topology as the original. In other words, you must duplicate the original and then can move vertices around but you cannot add or delete any data (faces, edges, etc.).

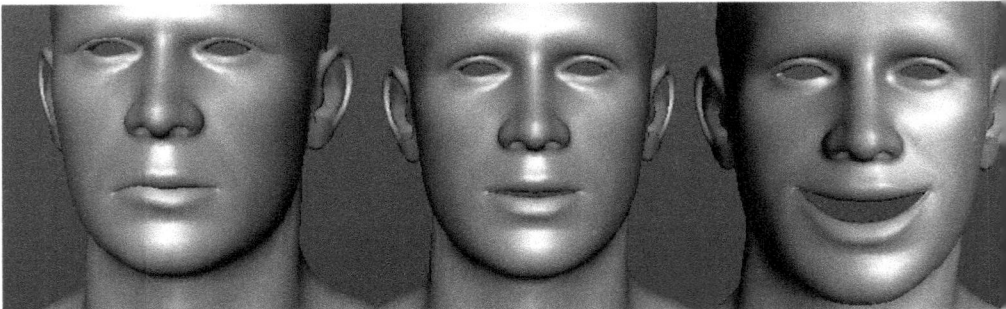

Figure 147. Different blendshapes.

Once that is complete, you merely select the objects that are the targets, and then select the default object last. After selecting your models, run the command:

Create Deformers -> Blend Shape

It is easy to see why naming conventions are so important in this example. Creating your blend shape, you will now have controllers that slide on and off and these are all named according to your objects' original names. Thus, if you have not named your objects first, your slider controls will be in turn hard to understand. The following tutorial will show you how to create your blend shapes and where to find the controls. This is yet another area that reinforces the importance of naming conventions and sticking to them as you work.

Tutorial: Blendshapes

1. Create a ball, and pull out a point to make a nose. Take a little time to model it so you have a very basic head.

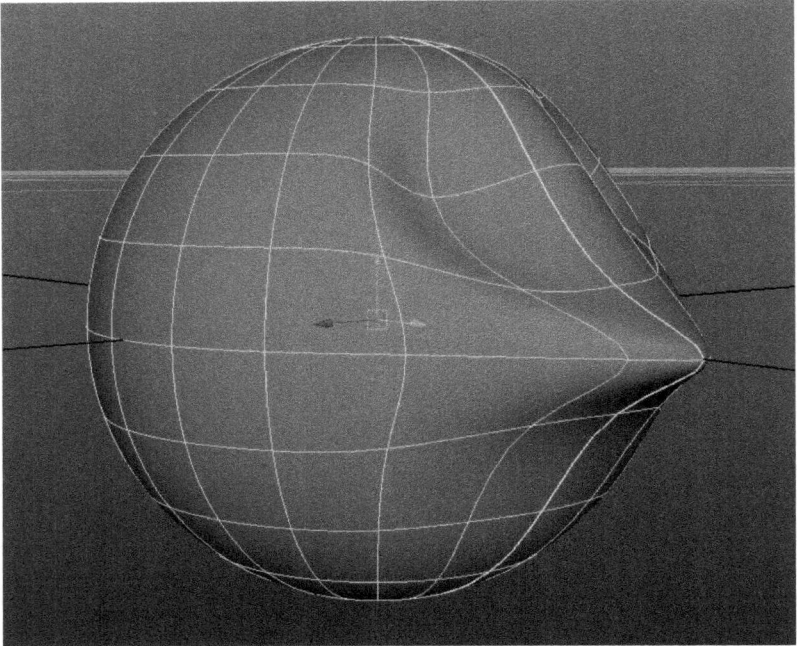

Figure 148. Very basic head.

2. Next, since your blendshape has to have the same topology, make a second identical ball:

   a. Select the ball

   b. Ctrl + d to duplicate it

3. Move the new head to the side and model your duplicate shape to have a bigger chin

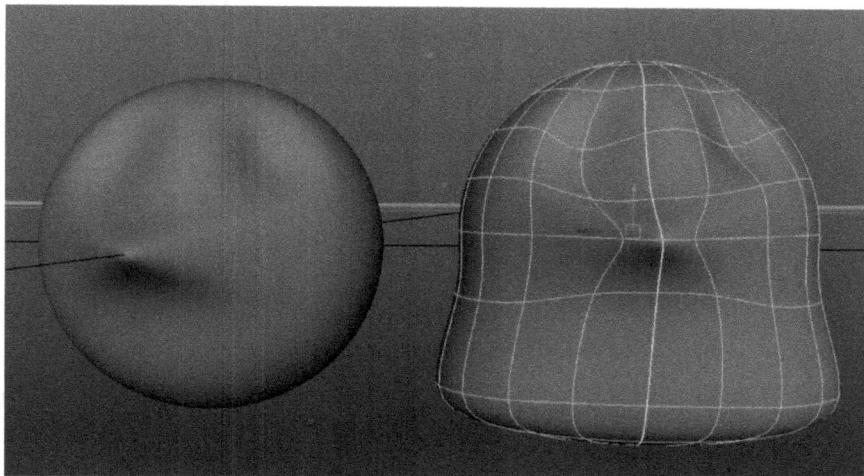

Figure 149. Different chin.

4. Duplicate the original head again and move it to the side again.

5. Model your second duplicate shape to have a bigger forehead.

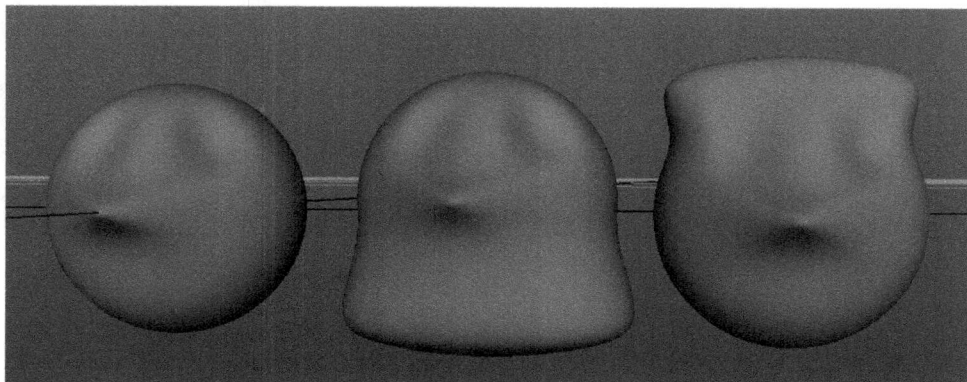

Figure 150. Bigger forehead.

6. Select the two duplicate shapes.

7. Hold shift and select the original head, so that it was selected last.

8. Create a blendshape by running the command:
   a. **Create Deformers -> Blend Shape []**
   b. Give your blendshape a name and click the create button

Once you have created your blend shapes, you can select the default head and use the channel box to get to the attributes to change it. The name you have given your blendshape will appear in the channel box, and the names of your models will appear as the attributes.

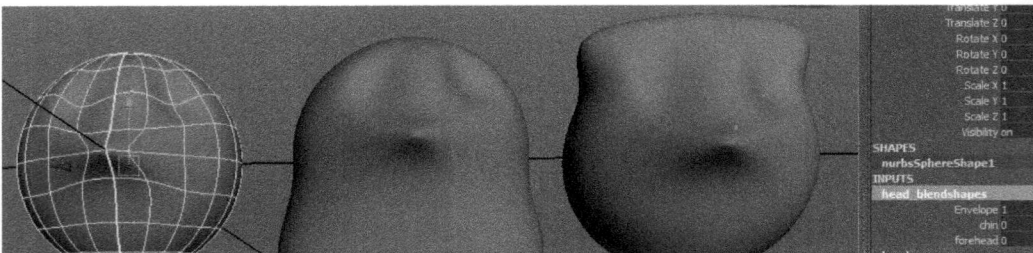

Figure 151. Blendshape attributes.

Alternatively, you can use the blend shape editor:

Window -> Animation Editors -> Blend Shape

It is important to note several things about blend shapes before we can move on. First, you will have seen that naming your objects prior to creating our blend shapes is important as the controls will be named according to your original objects.

Second, it is always a good idea to make a few extra "blanks" of the blend shape. In other words, if the model has 15 mouth shapes, I will make 20 blend shapes. 5 of those targets will be straight copies, unedited and still included in the blend shape. Doing so allows you to quickly create new targets by modeling on one of the blanks (copies) later whenever you wish. You can then allow the animator to model any whacky shapes during animation without having to recreate your blend shapes or modify your rig. Having this ability to fix problems that were unforeseen is almost always a blessing and should always be a common practice in your rigging.

Third, you can delete the models to reduce your scene size. If your blend shape targets are a dense mesh, you can easily bloat up your scene size by having 20 or 40 extra targets sitting in your scene. Blend shapes have been constructed so that once you have created the system, you can then delete the target models and the blend shape will still work. Simply select the models and delete them to do so. It is important to note that doing so will definitely reduce your scene size, but will also NOT allow you to go back and modify any of the targets to change their shapes. The deleted shapes will be stored mathematically behind the scenes. Optimizing your scene is always important, but this was particularly important a few years ago. As computing performance and storage space increases, this has become less of an issue of late. If in doubt, keep your blendshapes but if you know they are done and you are never going back then it is a good practice to delete them to save the memory.

Fourth, blend shapes are a linear transition. This means that Maya has measured the different positions between the original and the target for each vertex and will move that vertex along a direct line between the two positions. Maya literally looks at where the original point was and where the target point is and interpolates a straight line between the two points. Your weight or percentage can then be applied to determine where the vertex should be along that straight line. When you are first starting out this will not cause you much concern, but as you get further in to the nuances of movement you will need to find ways to get around this problem of a straight line. For instance, if you are using a blend shape to create blinks for your character, you may wish the geometry to slide down in an arc around the eyeball and not simply straight down. As shown in the image below, the eyelid needs to bend around the eye and not travel in a straight line to the end position. If it did travel in a straight line, the result would be the eyeball penetrating through the eyelid.

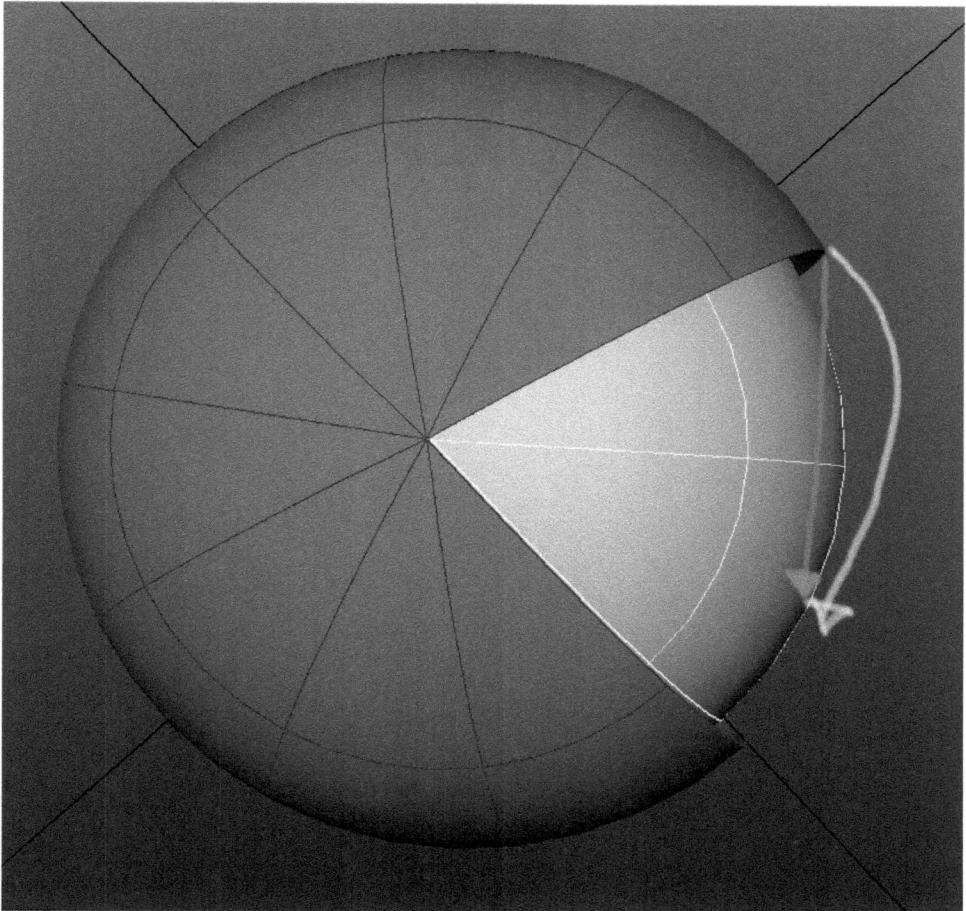

Figure 152. Eyelid needs to travel in an arc.

Creating arc paths is too complex and beyond the scope of this manual. Please see our upcoming titles to learn ways around this issue.

The keys to remember with blendshapes are to make a few extra shapes (we suggest 5 blanks) and then to delete your history when you've created your blendshape to save memory.

Rigid Binding and Edit Membership Tool

With rigid binding, we will now enter a whole new section of deformation and usually the most common one: binding. Binding generally is described as deformations that are created using a joint based system (although, in a purist sense, anything can be bound to anything). The theory behind binding is to take a default point, in this case the joints, and deform the models "bound" based on the change of positioning of the default point. In other words, the model is tied to the joint in a spatial sense and follows along wherever the joint moves to maintain that relationship, acting as if it were directly welded or "bound" to the joint.

Rigid binding is the simplest of the scenarios of binding to a joint. In rigid binding, each point is connected to the closest joint. Maya will calculate the distance between the assigned joint and the each point at the default pose. This initial positioning of your joints is referred to as the "bind pose". Once bound, each point then moves exactly the same as each joint to maintain the original distance. In rigid binding, the result is that each point moves as if welded to a steel rod that is also welded to the joint itself, much like a pin cushion. The typical binding scenario will assign each point to the closest joint, but this can be edited using a relationship editor. This relationship editor allows you to control whether the point is assigned to a particular set (in this case a group for our deformer) or not. The tool is called the edit membership tool, and can be found as:

Edit Deformers -> Edit Membership Tool

In the following tutorial, you will get to put this tool to use, but let us take a second to explain how it works. By selecting your deformer, in our case the rigid bind deformer, and then running the tool, you will get an arrow shaped cursor and all of your points on your model will light up.

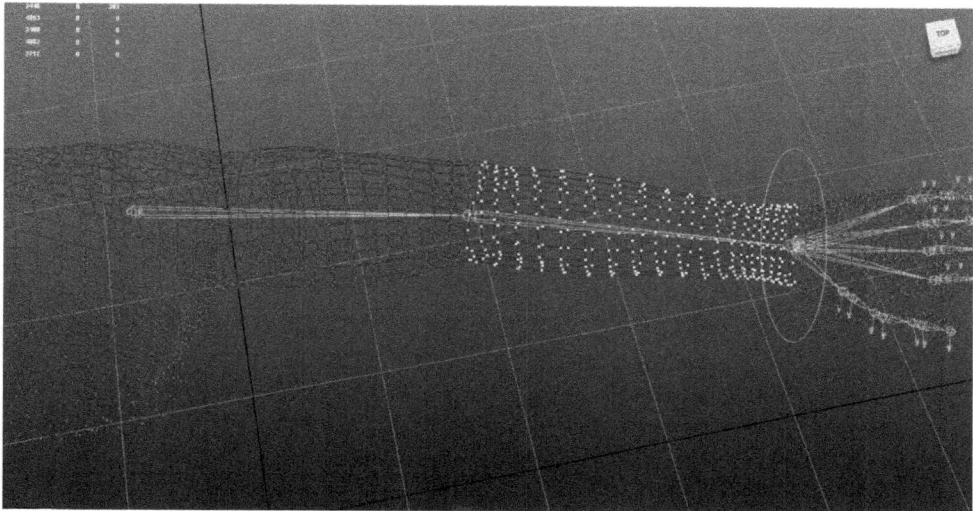

Figure 153. Edit membership.

This arrow cursor allows you to pick which vertices are in the set and which are not. If they are a reddish brown colour, they are not in the set and thus not affected. If they are a yellow colour, they are in the set and will be affected. You can add or subtract your vertices using the standard Maya keys. Holding shift and dragging a box or clicking on vertices will toggle their status (in becomes out, out becomes in). Holding shift + control and dragging a box or clicking on vertices will force the selected ones to be added, turning them yellow. Holding only control and dragging a box or clicking on vertices will force your selection to be removed, turning them reddish brown.

qThis edit membership tool is used for many deformers beyond just the rigid bind, for example to control all the non-linear deformers that we will refer to later on. Let us put these last few concepts to use in the following tutorial on rigid binding and editing your memberships.

Tutorial: Using Rigid Bind and Edit Memberships

1. Create your arm skeleton with a shoulder, elbow, and wrist.

2. Create a simple arm model using a tube and modeling it into position.

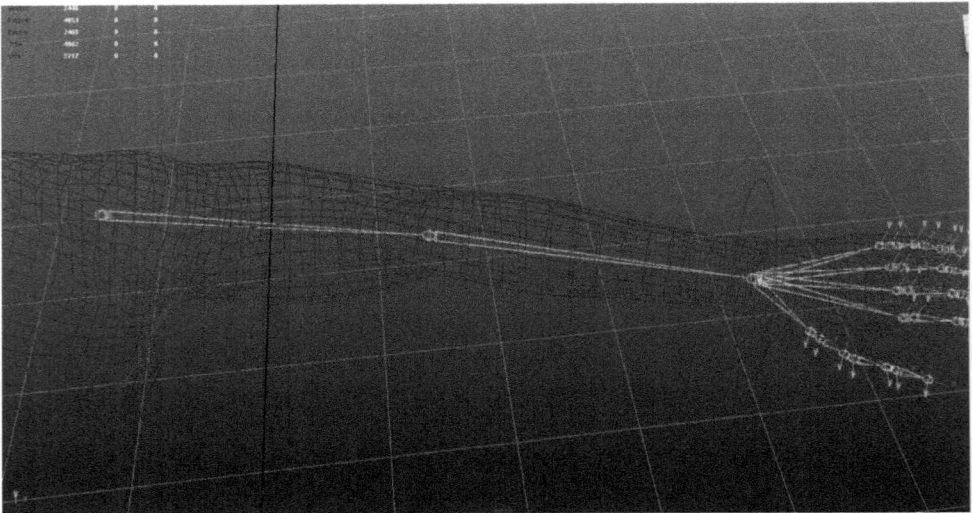

Figure 154. Basic arm.

3. Select all of your joints.

4. Hold shift and select your model.

5. Bind the arm using a rigid bind via:

   a. **Skin -> Bind Skin -> Rigid Bind []**

   b. Because you selected the joints you want to use, the bind to option should be set to "selected joints". The remainder of the default options will be fine, so hit "Bind Skin" to bind your mesh.

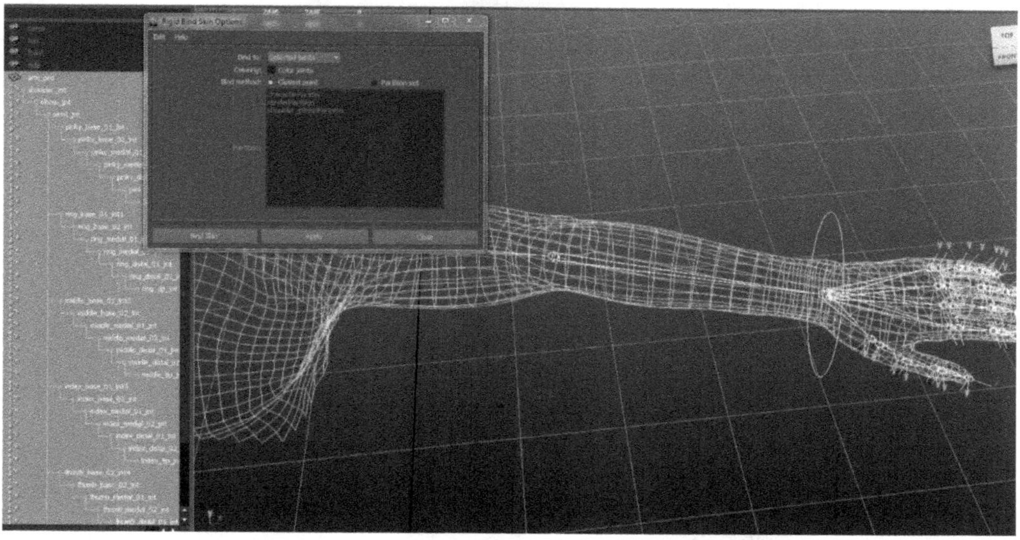

Figure 155. Binding options.

6. Try bending your arm by rotating the elbow. Notice that the deformation at the elbow is an either/or scenario where some vertices move and others simply do not. There is no overlap or multiple influences in rigid binding.

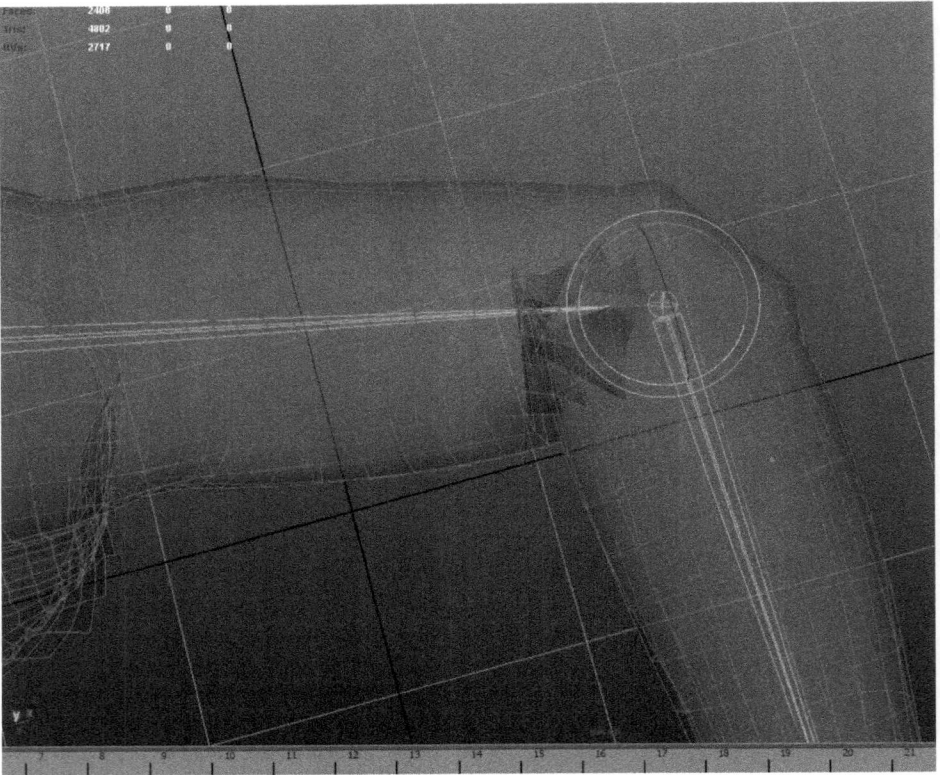

Figure 156. Rigid bind.

7. To change which vertices are impacted we will use the edit membership tool. Select your mesh and enter the tool via:

   a. **Edit Deformers -> Edit Membership Tool**

   b. Click on the joint you wish to edit

8. Click on the elbow joint and notice all of the yellow vertices which the elbow joint controls.

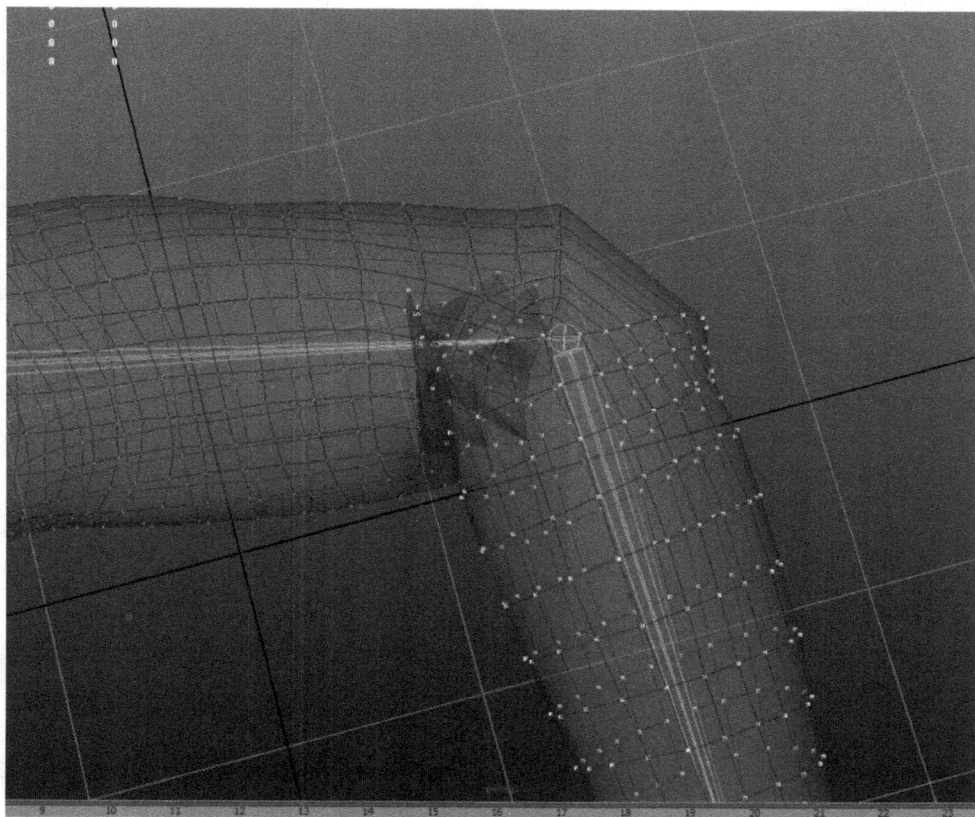

Figure 157. Select the elbow vertices.

9. Hold shift down and select additional vertices for the elbow to control in order to improve the deformation slightly.

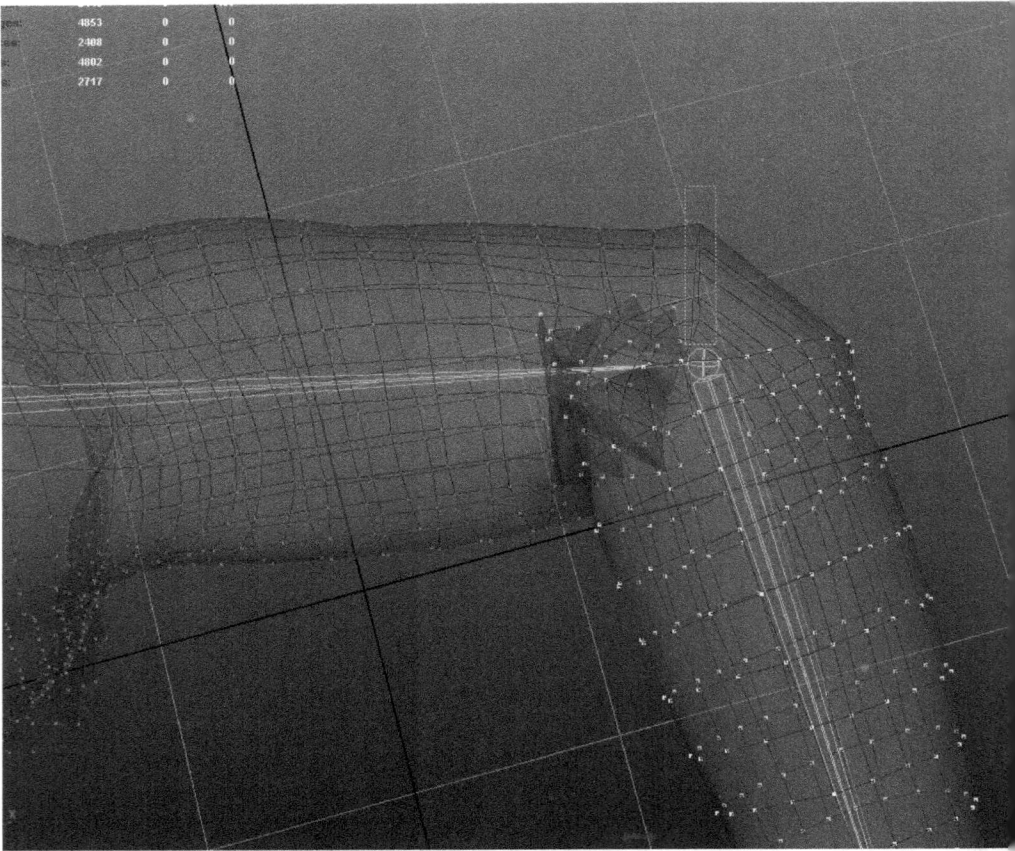

Figure 158. Adding vertices at the elbow.

10. Play around with using control and shift to add and remove vertices for better deformation.

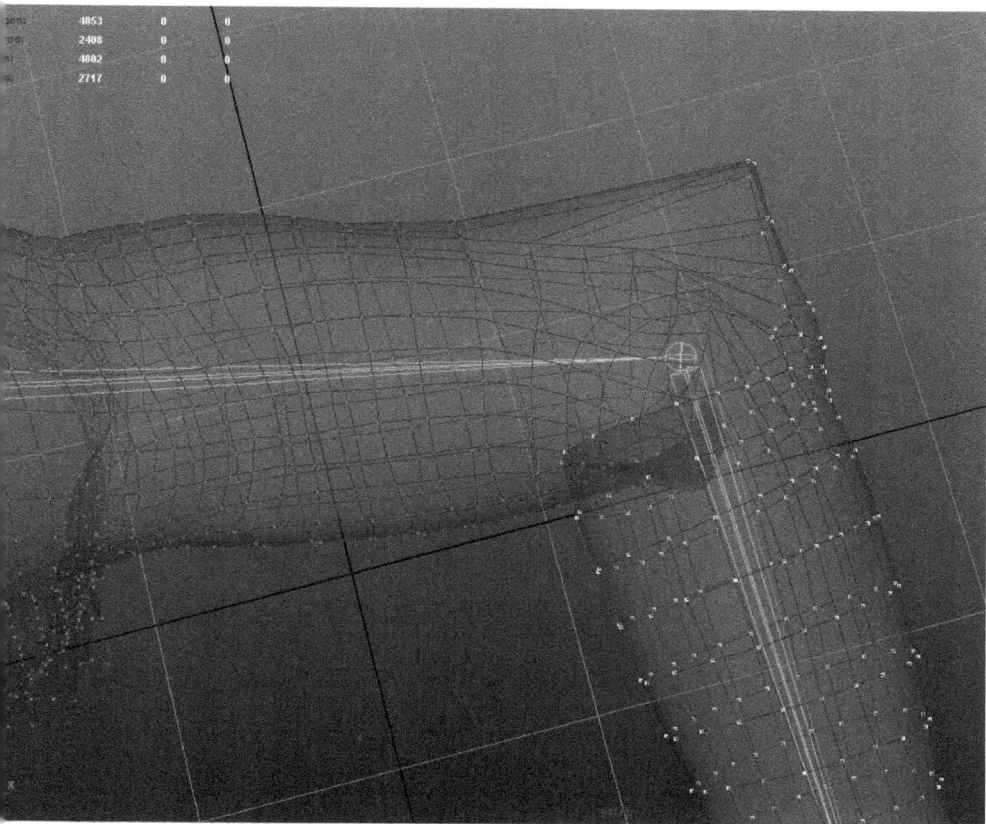

Figure 159. Better results.

Rigid binding acts in many senses as if the object was directly parented to the joints. This relationship is slightly different of course because in a rigid bind a model can be "parented" to several joints. This could also be replicated by clustering groups of vertices and then parenting the clusters to the joints. This can get confusing of course, so rigid binding was created to make it far easier. The rigid binding, while essentially the same as multiple clusters, simplifies the scenario by containing all the data of which vertex is controlled by which joint all condensed into one envelope. Each joint essentially has a cluster of control that any particular vertex is either in or out of. Each vertex is in only one joint's control, and this is a strict (or rigid) relationship.

To improve the deformation ability of a rigid bind, flexors can be added to the binding. A flexor is simply a type of lattice that will allow the user to then dial in a change via set driven keys or expressions. A good example is looking at a simple flexor to create a muscle bulge. In this example, the flexor scales and bulges based upon the elbow rotations to create a sense of the muscle bulging in the arm. The results of course are rough at best, with a one to one relationship and no skin sliding ability. You will notice that it is however similar to the lattice expression example that we showed earlier.

Tutorial: Building a Flexor for the Arm

1. Repeat the steps to creating a rigid bind for a simple arm in the tutorial above.

2. Create a flexor by using the command:

   a. **Skin -> Edit Rigid Skin -> Create Flexor ...**

   b. Use the option of flexor type: Lattice

   c. Select your shoulder joint. We will create a flexor based on the bone between the shoulder and the elbow.

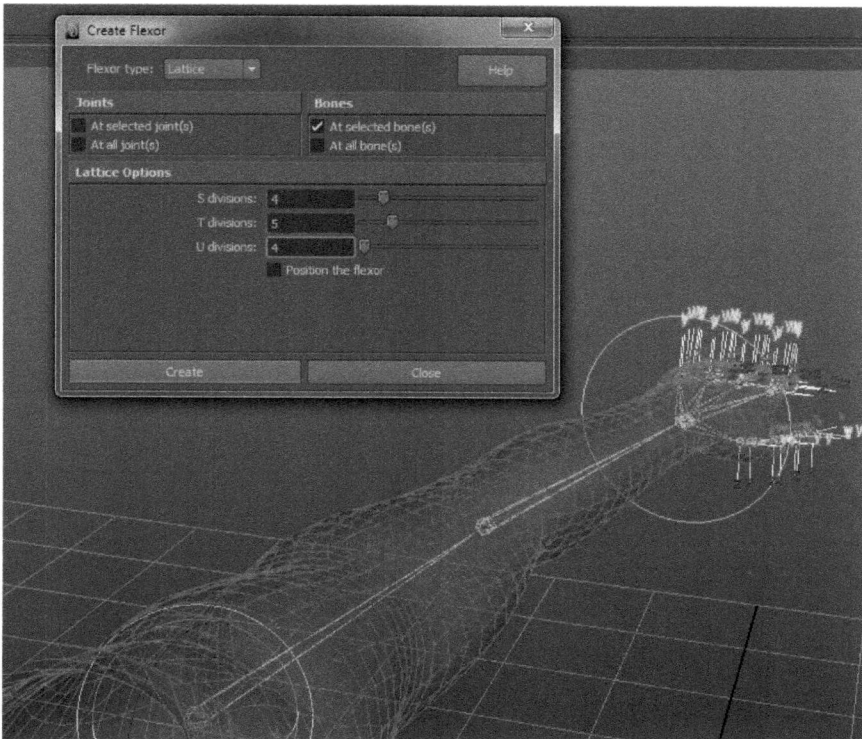

Figure 160. Flexor options.

d. Turn on "At selected bone(s)" and turn off everything else

e. Divisions should be 4, 5 and 4 as a good starting point.

f. Hit Create

3. Select the new lattice, our example was named ffd4Lattice.

4. Notice the options in the channel box below under "boneFlexor1". In our example, we have a bicep and tricep function already as attributes. Play with the values here to see your muscle flex. Our example file a value of

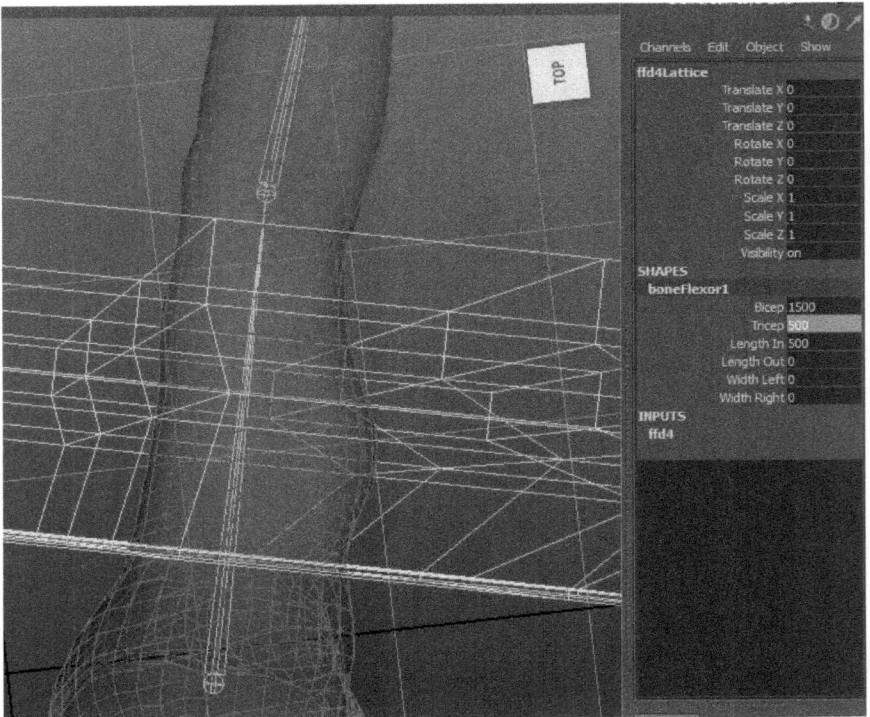

Figure 161. Bulging by changing attributes.

1500 at the Bicep and 500 at the Tricep creates a nice muscle bulge.

5. Now bend the elbow by rotating in Y. Notice that the muscle values you entered in at the rest position super inflate your flexor. You will need to adjust the values so that the maximum flexed state looks proper, which we will do using animation.

6. Use your knowledge of set driven keys to make these values animate based on the elbow rotation

   a. Select elbow joint

   b. Select rotate Y in the channel box

      i. Channel Box Menu -> Edit -> Set Driven Key

   c. Load Driver, select elbow joint and rotate Y as the driver

   d. Select the flexor lattice (ffd4Lattice in our example)

   e. Open the attribute editor

   f. Select the boneFlexor1 tab and hit select button at the bottom of the attribute editor to select this node

   g. Load Driven and choose bicep, tricep, length In and Out attributes

   h. Rotate the elbow to a flexed rotation, our example is -97

i. Play with the values of the flexor until you have a nice flex. Our values were:

    i. Bicep 100, Tricep 60, Length In 30, Length Out 40

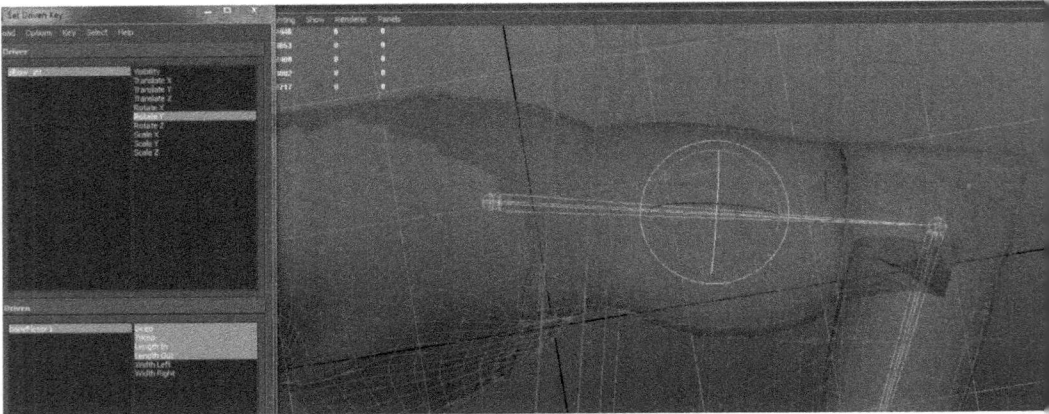

Figure 162. Set driven key to control flex.

j. Key in the set driven key tool

k. Rotate elbow back to 0 in rotate Y

l. Reset all flexor values to 0 if desired and hit key in the set driven key tool

m. Hyper-extend the elbow, our example was rotate Y of 7 degrees

n. Adjust flexor values to make the tricep flex nicely. Our values were:

    i. Bicep -200, Tricep -1000, Length In -800, Length Out -500

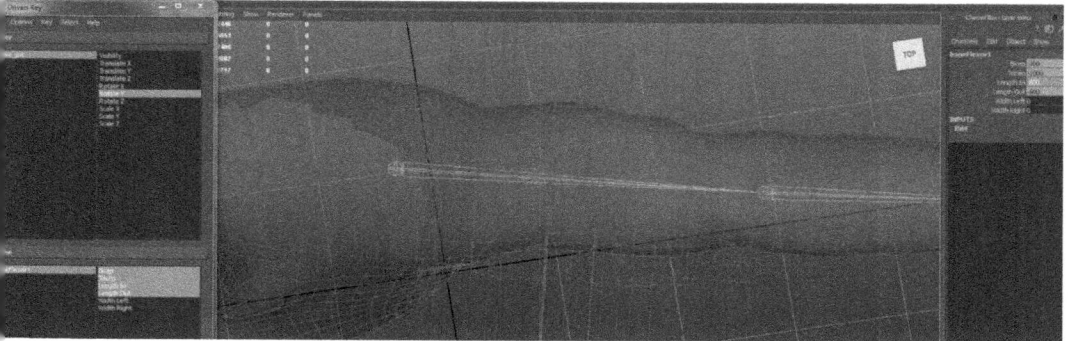

Figure 163. Tricep sized.

    o. Key in set driven key tool

    p. Test your animation by rotating the elbow back and forth. Add additional keys if required in your set driven key to tune the result.

Example File: 17_rigid_bind_01_initial_bind.ma

Example File: 18_rigid_bind_02_added_flexor.ma

Example File: 19_rigid_bind_03_flexor_driven.ma

While rigid binding has slowly become outdated and is not used often in production any more, the basic theory of how a rigid bind works, what a flexor is, and how to set all of this up is a great stepping stone for the beginner. It is especially nice in later versions of Maya where muscle groups such as biceps and triceps are added by default, making the setup process much simpler. Learning all of these concepts then brings us far more readily to our next topic, smooth binding.

Smooth Binding

Smooth binding builds upon the concept of a rigid bind. Once you have learned how the joint binding system works within Maya, learning the theory of the smooth bind is straight forward. The main difference between a smooth binding scenario and a rigid binding scenario is the amount of influence each vertex can have. In a smooth bind, each vertex can be influenced by any number of specified joints, which of course is much different than a rigid bind where each vertex is controlled by precisely one joint.

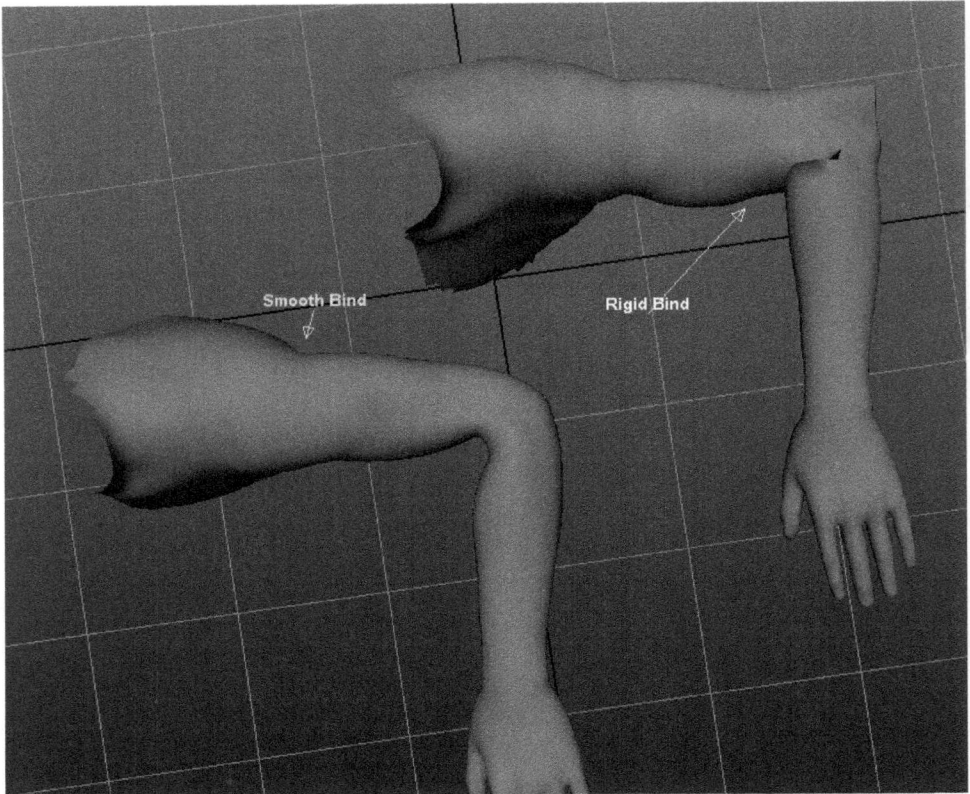

Figure 164. Rigid versus smooth bind.

As before, each vertex is compared to each controlling joint in the default position and the distance is stored in the default bind pose dataset. This time when the joints move, the controlling joints motions are averaged together, or "smoothed", resulting in a weighted average position of each vertex.

One can easily see how this solution per vertex can become increasingly more complex as the amount of influencing joints increases. It is for this reason that it is heartily recommended that you try to keep your influences to as few as possible. A general rule is to start with 3 influences and add more only if required. Doing so not only increases the speed of which your deformations will perform, but also reduces the complication and challenge of trying to control the deformations. This will allow you to simply work faster.

There are other differences of course, for instance flexors are a rigid binding term and are required to be created in different methods for smooth binding. However, the other major difference that one should be aware of is how the relationships between the joints control over the vertices is managed. This brings us to our next topic, painting weights.

Painting Weights: The Tool Explained

Earlier, we discussed weight lists and weight maps when we entered our description of the cluster. In a cluster, each point has a value associated with it which is termed the "weight" since it is a value that must range from zero to one and can be considered a percentage of influence or weight. When we discuss painting weights, we must first talk about the differences of weights in a cluster and weights in a skin cluster. In a smooth skin cluster, you can have multiple influences. This means that for each vertex, there is a full value of 100% or 1.0 that can be distributed amongst the total number of influences for that vertex. This is different from the cluster, where there is only one "influence", and a vertex has simply one weight associated with it. In a skin cluster, each vertex can have several weights that all combine together for the overall weighting of that vertex.

When working with weights, it is important to remember that the sum of the weights will always add to 100% or 1.0 if normalized. This means that whenever a portion of the weight is removed from one influence, Maya will automatically distribute that portion that was removed to other influences in order to maintain the total as a constant 100% or 1.0. Knowing this piece of information is absolutely crucial for you to be able to work with weights in a predictable and successful manner. Normalization is highly recommended. This means that the float number will always total 1.0. It is possible to tell Maya that you would like to have the weights not normalized, but rather totaling to any number you like such as 5.0. In that example, a weight of 100% would equal 5.0. While this is possible, it is also confusing for many people. It is for this reason, it is highly recommended to keep things simple and normalize your weights so they always totally up to 1.0. A number in the 0 to 1 range is far easier to quickly understand the exact percentage it equates to. Either way normalized or not, remember that Maya will always maintain the total as a constant 100%. This is what makes using thing "smooth" function of the paint tool a blessing in cluster weight painting but a problem in smooth weight painting. But we are getting ahead of ourselves. Let us start by talking about the tool.

When we refer to painting weights, we are talking about the "paint weights tool" which can be found as:

Skin -> Edit Smooth Skin -> Paint Skin Weights Tool []

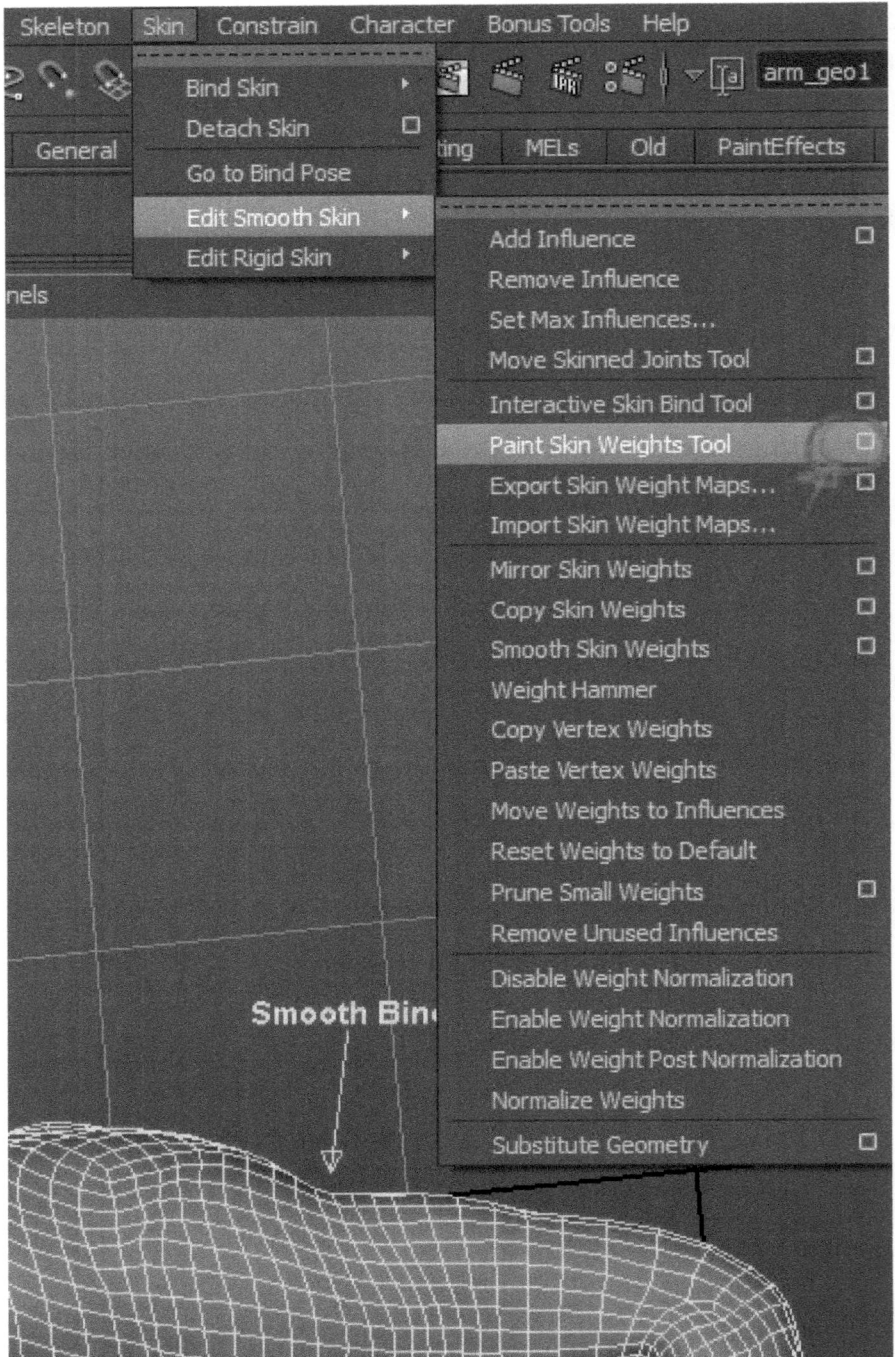

Figure 165. Smooth tool.

weights tool, you will almost always want to use the options provided in the menu, so it is important to choose the [] option box.

Selecting your object and then running the paint skin weights tool command will result in your skinned object turning a black and white colour. In this case, Maya is showing you

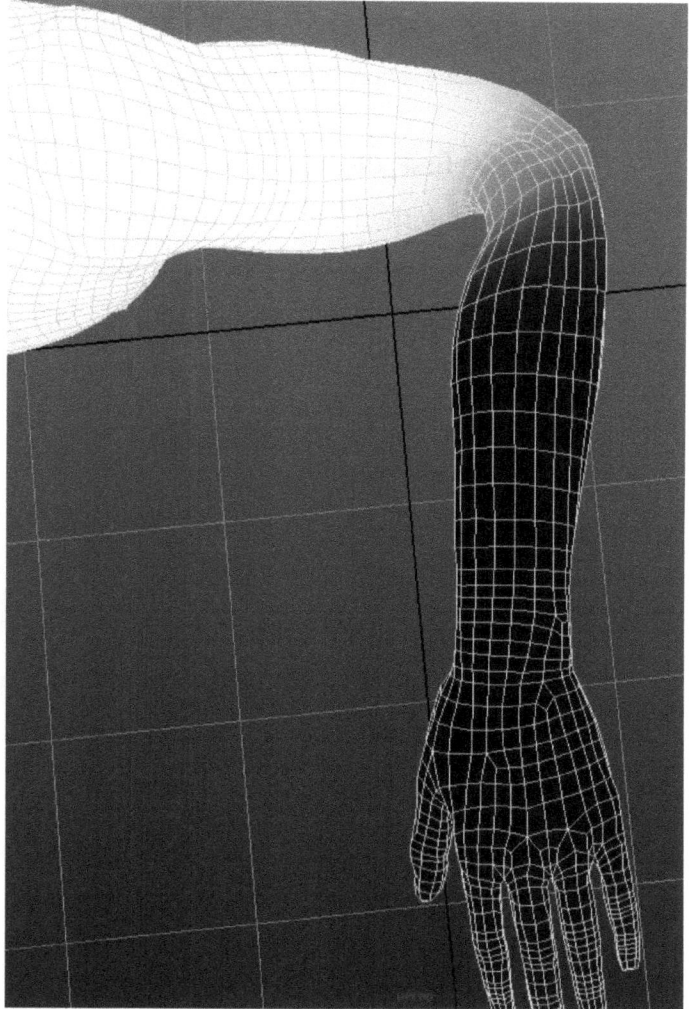

Figure 166. Painting weights.

the results of the skinning by reflecting the weight information as a grayscale image where a weight of zero is black and a weight of one is pure white. Any percentage in between will result in the corresponding percentage of grey.

Let us first discuss how each of the settings of the tool function, and then we will discuss overall methodologies that work the best when painting weights. The first section of the option box deals with how your brush is shaped and sized.

Figure 167. Brush size.

While you can dial in these numbers to affect your brush, the easiest way to do so is to use the pre-assigned hotkey. This key by default is "b" and extremely useful to remember. You can remember this by saying to yourself "b for brush" 3 times daily (maybe while brushing your teeth!) Holding down the b key and dragging with your left mouse button will change the cursor to two horizontal arrows which will then allow you to easily drag the brush to the size that you would like to use. B for brush. If the icon doesn't change when you hold b, you may have to select something to make the viewport active.

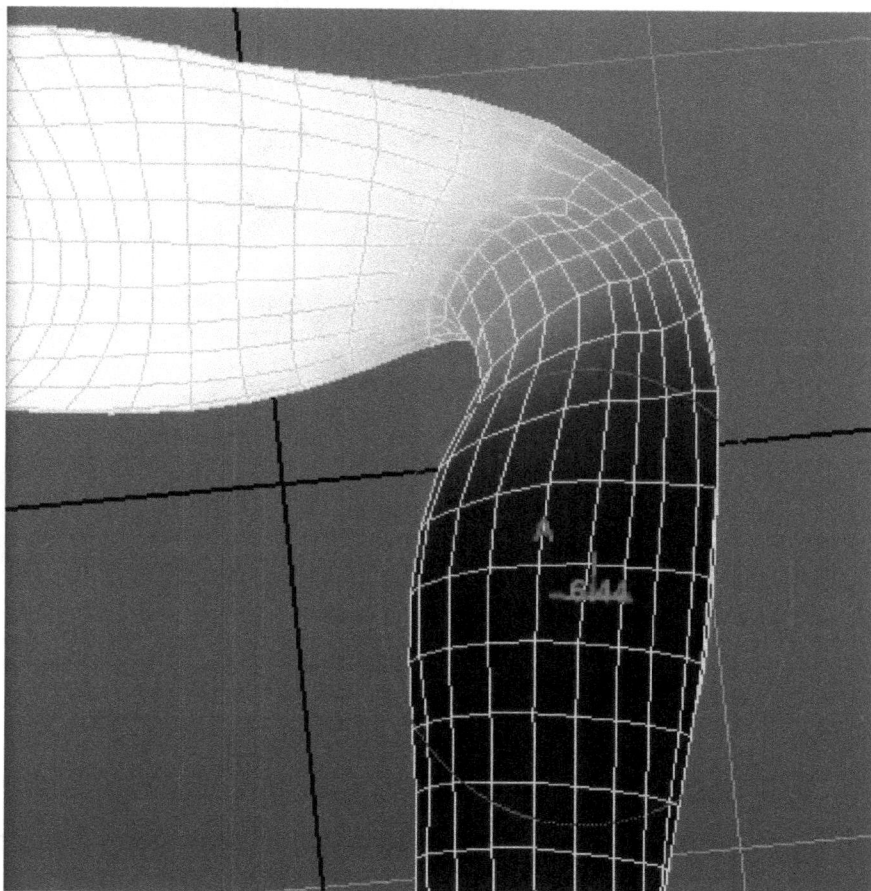

Figure 168. Bigger brush.

The next portion of the tool lists the various joints that are affecting the vertices.

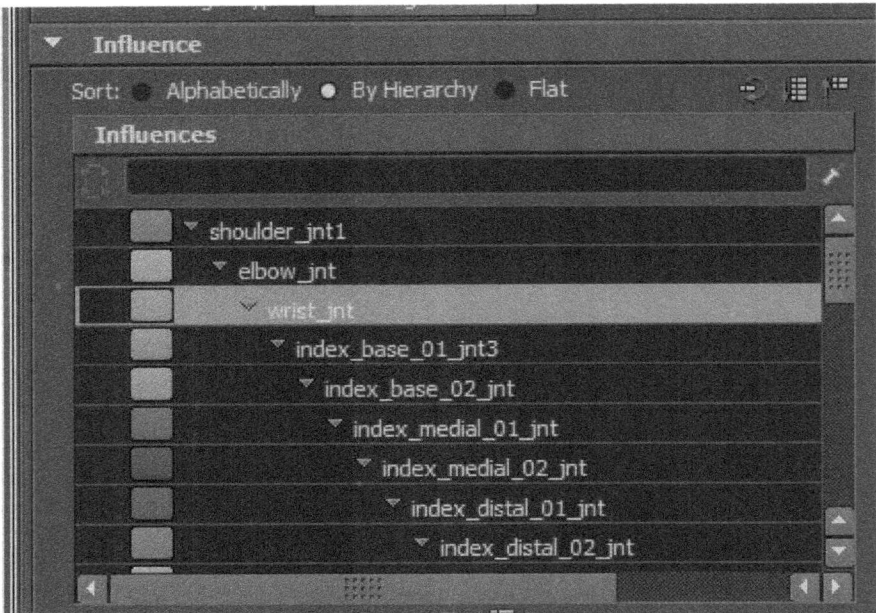

Figure 169. Joints listed in the paint weights tool.

By selecting an item in this list, you are then working on how that item affects the vertices in your model. These items almost always are joints, but other objects like influence objects can appear here. You will see the radio box choices of sorting this list by either alphabetical or hierarchical which will of course sort your list as you choose. At this point, you will find that having named your joints properly will prove to make your life a lot easier. Rather than searching through for "joint27", you can easily look for and find "lf_elbow" much more readily. If you have not named your joints yet, take a few minutes and make sure your scene is clean and named properly.

The next section of the option box for the paint weights tool refers to the actual operations that you will be performing with the tool.

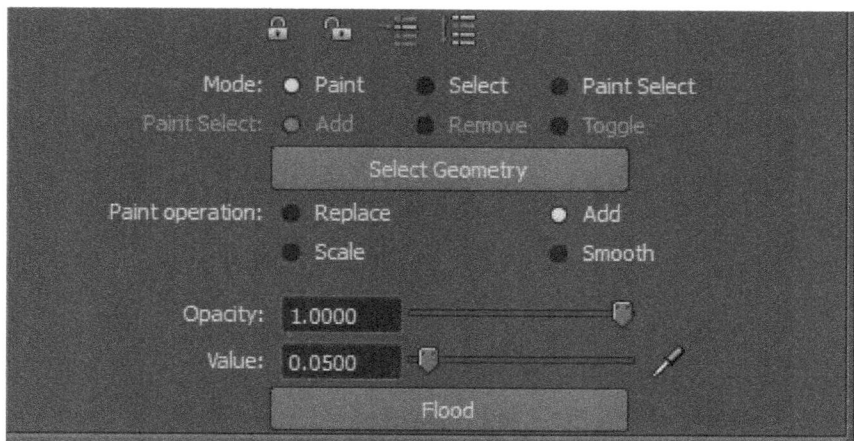

Figure 170. Paint weights tool options.

The mode choices are paint, select, or paint select. This allows you to quickly move from painting weights to selecting vertices by either dragging a marquee box or by painting on the vertices to select them. It is often extremely critical to influence only specific vertices, so by making these options easily available it speeds up your rigging workflow. Many senior rigging technical directors will have all of these mapped to hotkeys to flip back and forth from selecting vertices to painting weights even more quickly.

There are four paint operations: replace, add, scale and smooth.

The replace function will take the value that you have chosen and automatically replaces the current value with the chosen value for whatever vertices you paint on. This can be quite handy to quickly zero out areas or to lock them to a range that you are looking for quickly.

The add function will take the value that you have chosen and add it to the current value. While you hold down your left mouse button during painting, it will only add it once.

Repeatedly clicking with the button will allow you to repeatedly add. Thus, if you have chosen a value of 0.1, and if the current value on a particular vertex is 0.3, by painting it you will change the value to 0.4. Once you have let go of the left mouse button and clicked down again, you will then bring the value to

0.5, then 0.6, and so on. The add function is another function that is used often during painting weights.

The scale function can be a bit strange for many people. This function will multiply the value you have chosen with the current value and assign the result. The best way of thinking about this process is as a reduction of a percentage. In other words, if you chose a value of 0.8, you will effectively be reducing any current value by 20%. Unlike the add function, this is always a percentage, so the results will get progressively less and less. For example, if the current value is white, all the way to 1, and you chose a scale value of 0.8, by scaling your vertex, the result will be 0.8 then 0.64, 0.512, 0.410, and so on. You are effectively taking away 20% of what is already there, and so this portion of reduction gets smaller and smaller as the current value gets smaller. In other words, 20% of 0.1 is only 0.02, but 20% of 1 is 0.2. But if you scaled 0.1 by a value of 0.8, you will actually result in a value of 0.08 (0.1 – 0.02 = 0.08).

As you can see, even the explanation of the scale function can be confusing, and so making use of this and keeping complicated numbers in your head all while painting can be quite a challenge. It is for this reason that many people choose to avoid using the scale function all together. While it can be useful to take gradual pieces away from areas using the scale function, adding or replacing can serve the same purpose but with much more precision. For example, if you are trying to reduce an area, simply replacing that area to the lowest influence you want, and adding in tiny amounts to "soften" the effect will allow you to know precisely what the weight is at any spot. This will become clearer during the tutorials and with practice.

The final function in this section is "smooth". While our friend Mr. Smooth can be useful in some scenarios, it typically is a function that you will want to avoid using. That is because of how Maya handles the assignments of weights. The smooth function works by averaging out the influence in the local area, effectively removing any spikes in values. In other words, if your vertex that you're working on is at 0.6 in value, and the others around it are at 0.4, by using smooth the value will decrease to 0.5 and then 0.45, and so on, to make it more like its' neighbours.

This at face value seems like a great tool to have and quite useful, but we must remember the caveat. As explained above, all of your vertices must have a total weight of 1. That means, as we smooth our value downwards, the remainder of the weight that we have taken away has to go somewhere. In our example, we have smoothed from 0.6 to 0.45. This means that there is 15% or 0.15 of the weight that Maya will automatically reassign for us and this automatic reassignment can be quite a dangerous thing.

This is because Maya will try to guess where the weights should go, and is often wrong. It is a tricky thing to know for the program after all to know where you actually WANT the weight. That means all the time you have spent painting and adding in weights can be automatically overwritten in order to "help" you smooth out the areas when using smooth. This will also become clearer in our tutorials and with practice, but suffice it to say that once you're using smooth, you are less in control and are relying on the computer to make critical decisions for you and while this can work sometimes, it is often wrong. It is for that reason that most seasoned veterans in painting weights avoid using the smooth function. In fact, typically it is wisest to avoid any function that removes weight (like scale or smooth) and to instead rely on ADDING weight by yourself. This can take a little longer, but often the results are far better.

The remainder of the option box typically can be left at the defaults. The documentation explains it quite clearly, but suffice it to say that you will likely only use the value box to change it. You will want to keep your weights between 0 and 1, so setting the maximum and minimum to this, as well as clamping them at 0 and 1 is strongly encouraged which is why of course they are the default settings. Going beyond this range is called having weights that are not "normalized", which is a fancy mathematical way of saying that your weights are not between 0 and 1. Having non-normalized weights will result within Maya essentially normalizing them behind the scenes and running an extra step of calculations for you. Avoiding extra math will speed up how you work in your scenes, so let us leave them normalized and between 0 and 1. The easiest way to do this is to keep the normalize weights option set to "interactive" and hit yes if Maya asks whether you want to do this now.

Figure 171. Selecting normalize raises a prompt window.

The gradient section allows you to choose either the default black and white greyscale, or to pick a colour ramp.

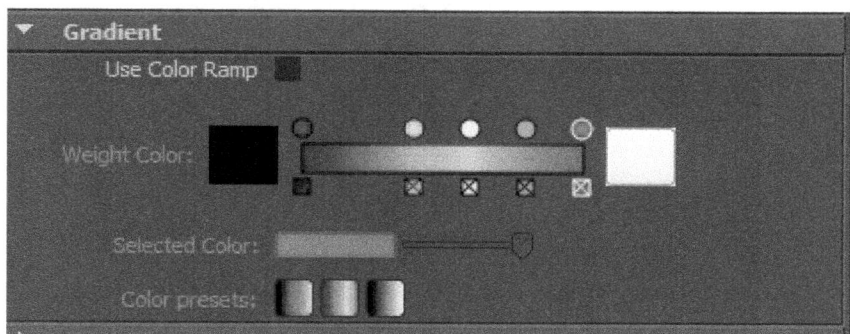

Figure 172. Gradient section.

This colour ramp option can easily show small differences that are harder to spot with low levels of grey. Some find it confusing, so experiment with turning it on and off as you progress and find the mode that you are able to work the quickest in. We will continue to explain everything in the default greyscale mode so as to not further confuse the subject.

There is only one last thing to know until we move on to putting this section in to practice. That is the "hold weights" button. In later versions of Maya, this is shown as either a locked lock icon or an unlocked lock icon.

Figure 173. Locked/unlocked icon.

By pressing these buttons for any selected joint, you will notice a little lock (hold in older versions of Maya) appears behind the name of the joint in the menu.

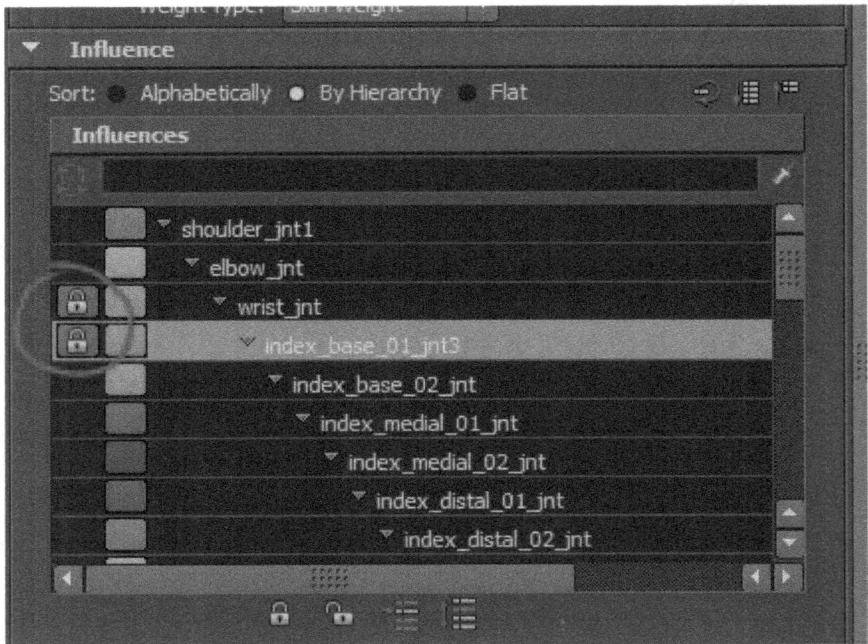

Figure 174. Locked joints in the tool window.

This means that whatever weights have been assigned to that joint when this button has been hit will be the weights that stay with that joint despite using any other tools. Some people refer to this as locking weights because the value is locked in and will not change. This is a good way of controlling how Maya (or even yourself!) continues to assign weights to the vertices. Essentially, any joint that has the "hold" flag showing has been locked out of having any changes affect it. Later on, you will also see how this is useful when adding in new joints to the skin. By adding in new joints as "hold" to 0, the new joints will not change any of the weighting you have already done until you toggle the hold off and start working on the new joint.

Painting Weights: Tips and Tricks

Now that we have outlined how the tool works, let us finally begin talking about what the best ways to paint weights are. But before we can get in to that, we should review how weights are assigned by Maya.

Once you have bound your geometry, every vertex in that geometry, whether it is made with NURBS or polygons, will have weights assigned to it. Each vertex will have 100% weight assigned to it, likely across multiple influences. Each of these influences will be a number between 0 and 1, reflecting that percentage. For instance if your elbow is effecting the vertex in question by 80%, the weight will be 0.8. The remainder 0.2 will likely be applied to the next closest joint(s), perhaps the shoulder and wrist. We have touched on this concept before, but it is an important one to remember. All vertices will have a total weight of 1. This means, if you take away weight from one influence, Maya will automatically add it to another to ensure the total stays at 1.

Knowing this concept is the key to being able to manage painting weights with ease. If you rely on this knowledge, you can see how adding weights is far better than taking weights away. Using Add or Replace will leave you in control, but using

Smooth or Remove will take weights away and thus rely on Maya's automatic help. While this help can be right in some cases, it can also be wrong in many cases. Rather than take the risk, it makes sense to just avoid it.

One of the best ways to work is to flood sections of your model to one for one joint. This will essentially make your model look like it has been rigid bound. From there, you can then slowly add weights back in for the other joints and thus have explicit control over just how the deformation and blending between joints works. In the following tutorial about weighting the fingers of a hand, you can see just how well this process works.

Tutorial: Painting Weights Using Flood and Add on Fingers

1. Create a hand skeleton and model using the tutorial outlined earlier in the book.
2. If you watch your own hands, you see that our fingers

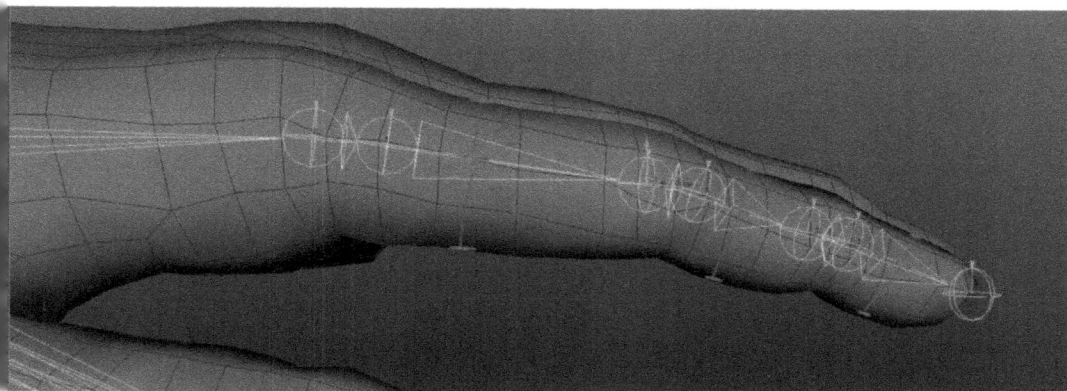

Figure 175. One third from the top.

tend to be rigid on the top and squishy on the bottom. Position the joints so that they are about two-thirds of the way up from the bottom as outlined in the image.

3. This will allow for the squishy deformations to happen on the inside of the fingers and will help you get better deformations right out of the gate.

4. Once you have your skeleton in place, frozen your transformations and your LRA's all in the correct spot, the next step is to bind the skeleton:

   a. Select the joints for your hand.

   b. Hold shift and select your model.

   c. **Skin -> Bind Skin -> Smooth Bind []**

      i. Bind to: Selected joints

      ii. Bind Method: Closest in Hierarchy

      iii. Skinning Method: Classic Linear

      iv. Normalize Weights: Interactive

      v. Max influences = 3

      vi. Drop off Rate = 4

5. Bend the fingers by rotating the joints to try out your default bind. Make sure to set them back to 0 once you are done.

6. Go to frame 1, and set a key for all your joints at the default pose.

   a. Select the joints

   b. s (key selected)

7. Go to frame 30 and rotate the fingers in to a fist.

8. Set a key for your joints at frame 30 in the fist pose.

9. Go to frame 60 and hyperextend your fingers. Make sure to push the pose a little further than the animation ever will. This will ensure that your deformations will always look great.

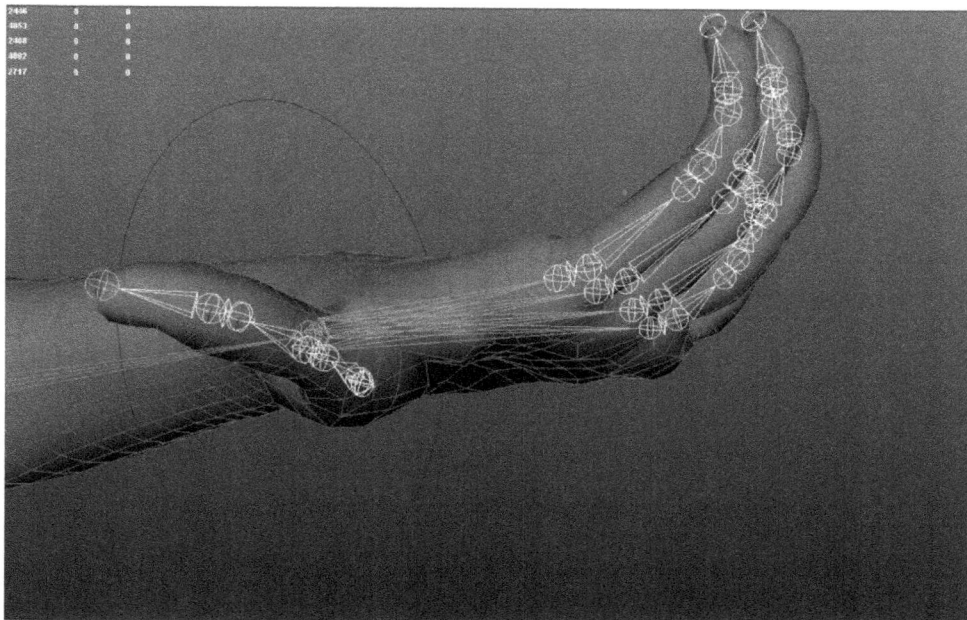

Figure 176. Hyperextend the joints.

10. Set a key for your joints at frame 60 in the hyper extended pose.

11. Now you are able to drag the time slider to change the positions back and forth between the default pose, a fist, and hyperextension. So people prefer to have this

in a better order, with hyperextension at frame 0, default at frame 30, and fist at frame 60. Either method is fine, so long as you can eventually get back easily to the default pose.

12. You will notice that your fingers will bend like sausages or tubes, and not very much like fingers. The next step is to paint the weights to get results that are far more realistic.

13. Select the mesh, and open the paint weights window:

    a. **Skin -> Edit Smooth Skin -> Paint Skin Weights Tool []**

14. Let us get the basic bind working well first. Set your options to:

    a. Replace

    b. Opacity = 1

    c. Value = 1

15. Select the vertices at the tip of your index finger. This is a great time to make use of the lasso tool.

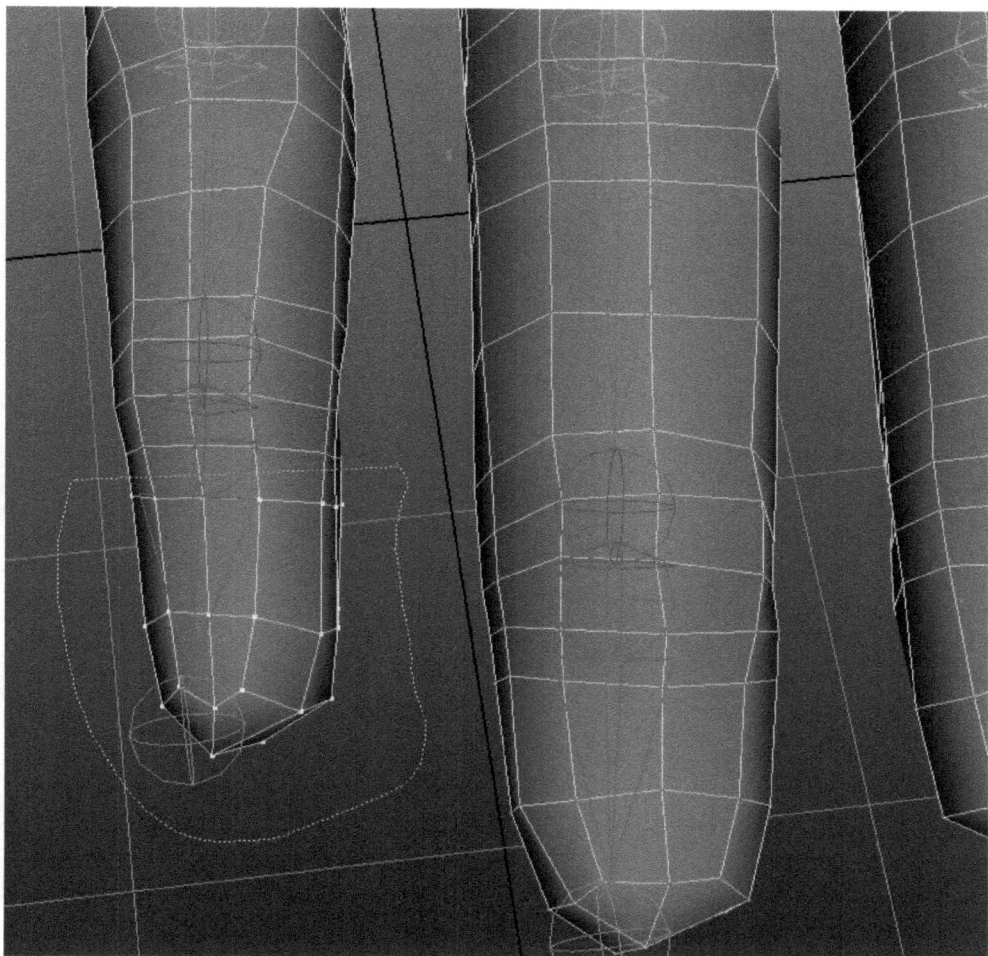

Figure 177. Using the lasso tool.

16. Select the proper joint in the list of the Paint Smooth Skin Options. In our example file it is the joint "index_tip_jnt".

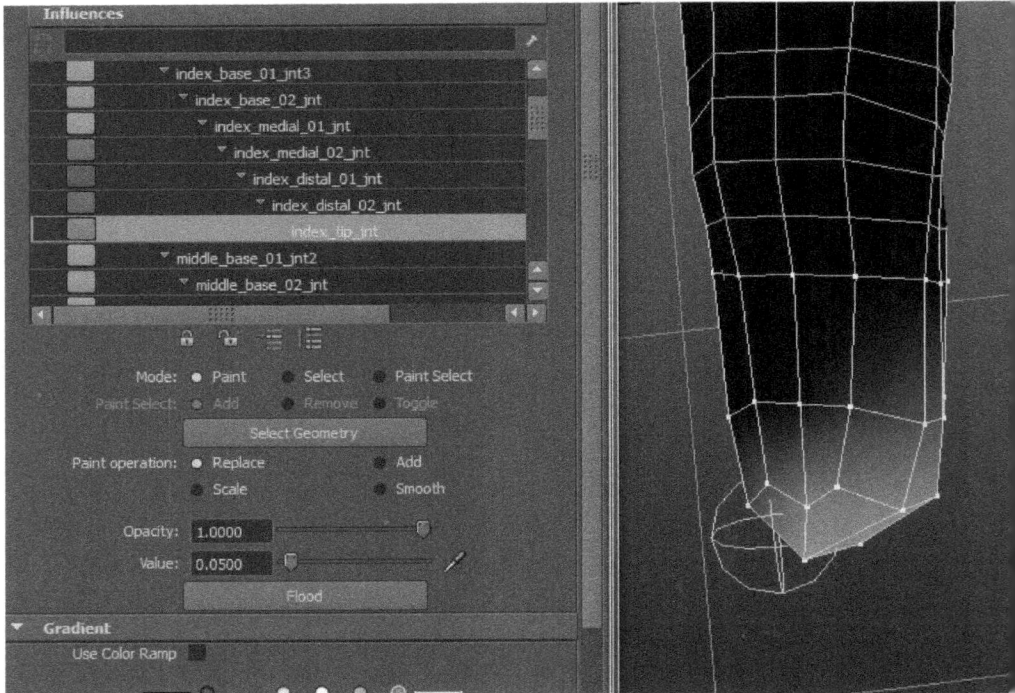

Figure 178. Selecting the joint in the tool.

17. Click the flood button in the tool.

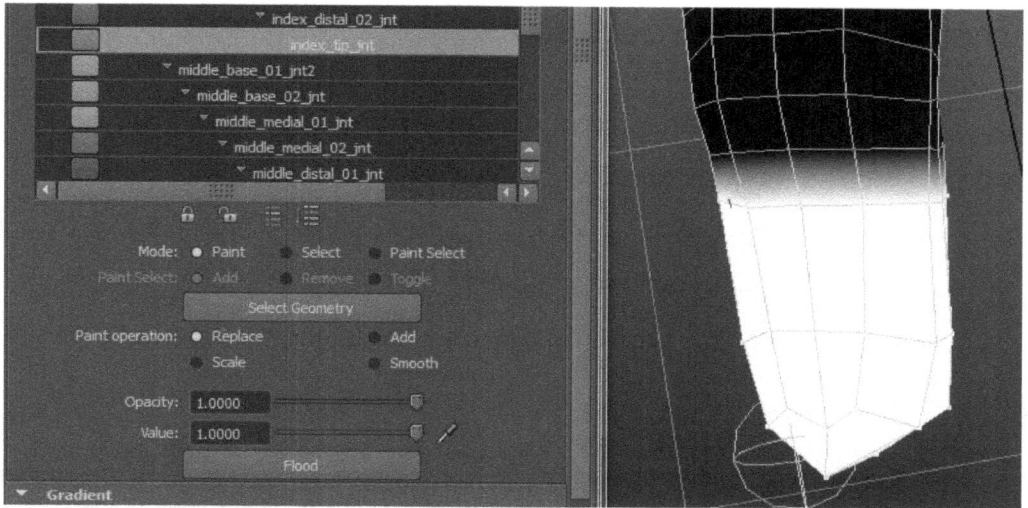

Figure 180. Flooding the tip.

18. Select the next section of vertices in your finger with the lasso and repeat the process for the next joint

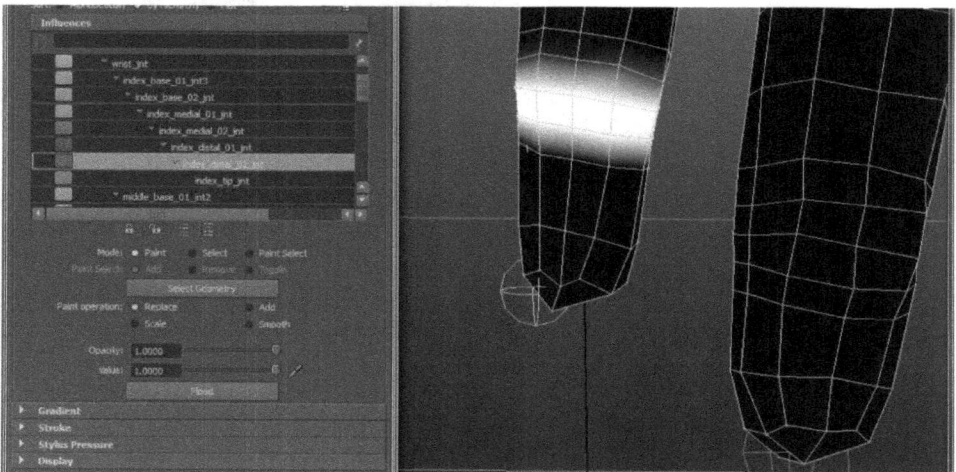

Figure 179. Next ring of vertices.

19. After doing all of this for all of your fingers, you will have a decently deforming model that will already look more realistic. Ensure this is the case by scrubbing your animation time slider to see the hand in action

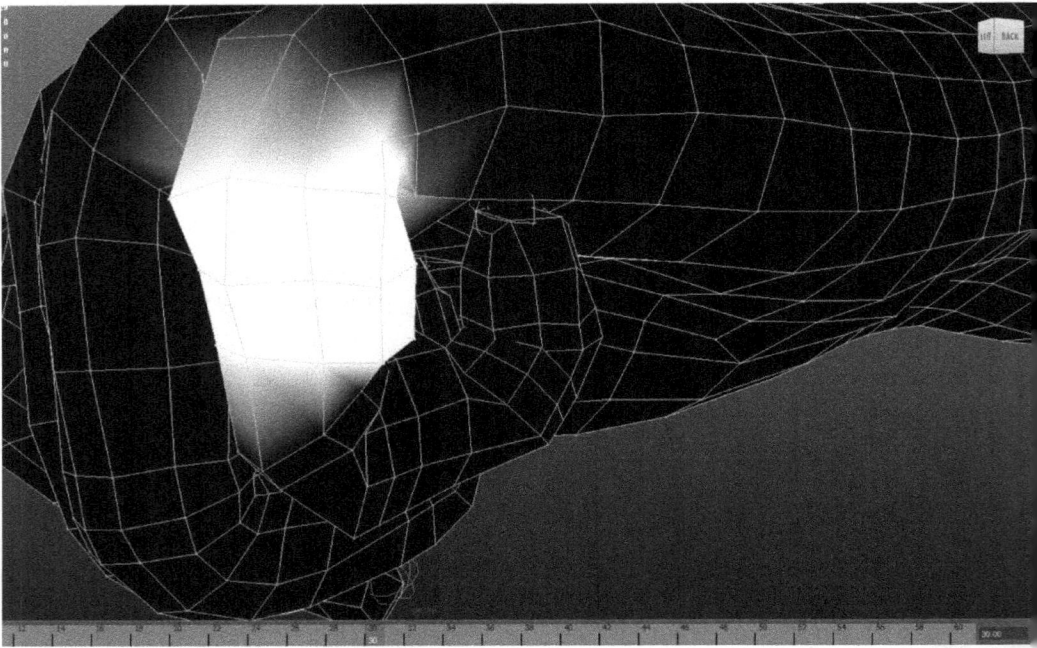

Figure 181. Pinky weights shown.

20. You'll notice that even with very harsh weighting like

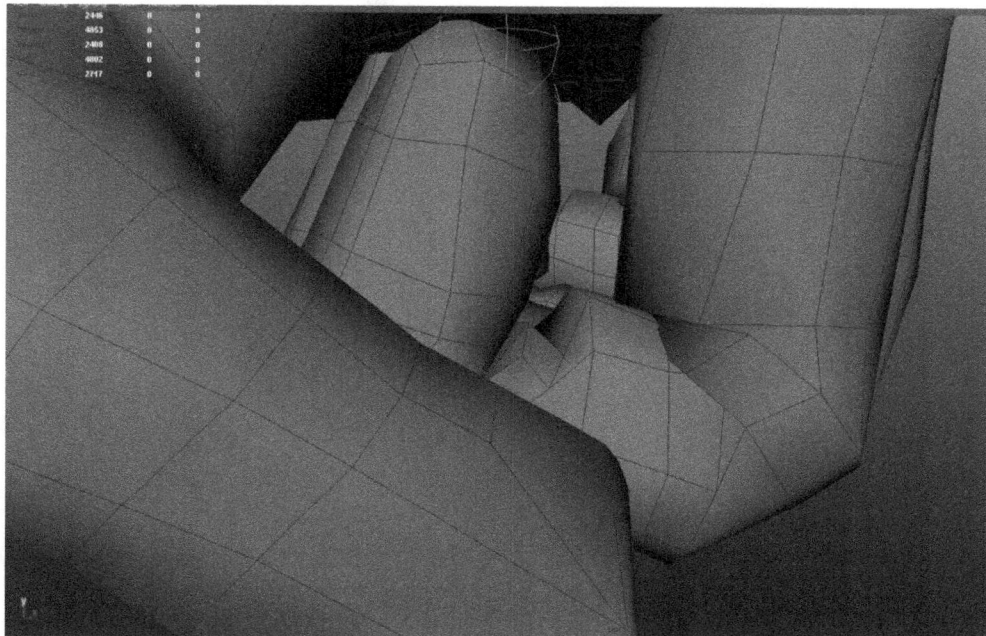

Figure 182. Harsh weights.

this, you can get some very nice wrinkles appearing if the mesh is smoothed a couple of divisions. Try adding a smooth node and checking out your results.

    a. Select your mesh

    b. Mesh -> Smooth

    c. Try changing the divisions attribute in the channel box to 2.

Figure 183. When smoothed, the harsh weights work well for wrinkles.

21. Undo or delete your smooth node.

22. Next, select your model in the object (green) mode and open the paint weights tool again.

23. Select a small value this time, like 0.05.

24. Select the distal joint of your pinky finger

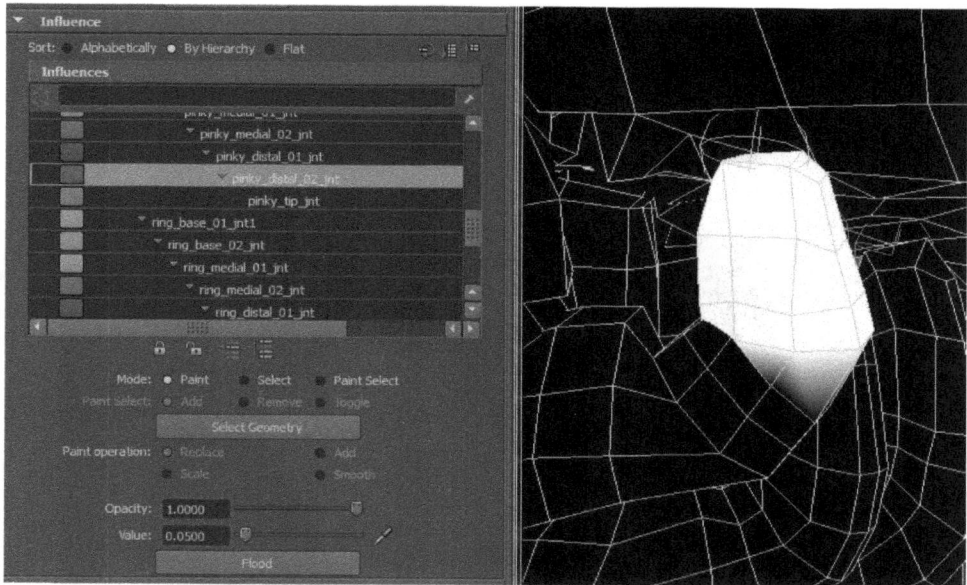

Figure 184. Distal pinky joint selected.

25. Find a bent position of your finger as it nears the fist position that still allows you access to all angles.

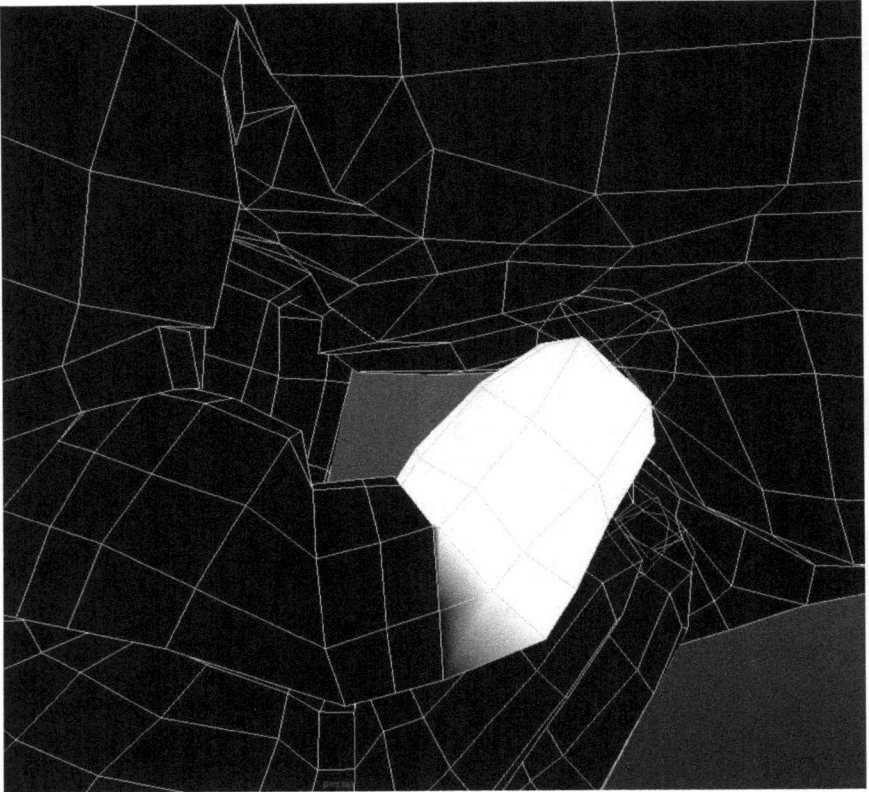

Figure 185. Scrubbing the animation to find a better frame for painting.

26. Slowly work out the hard bend by adding some weight to the joint by using the add function to slowly add 0.05 weight at a time.

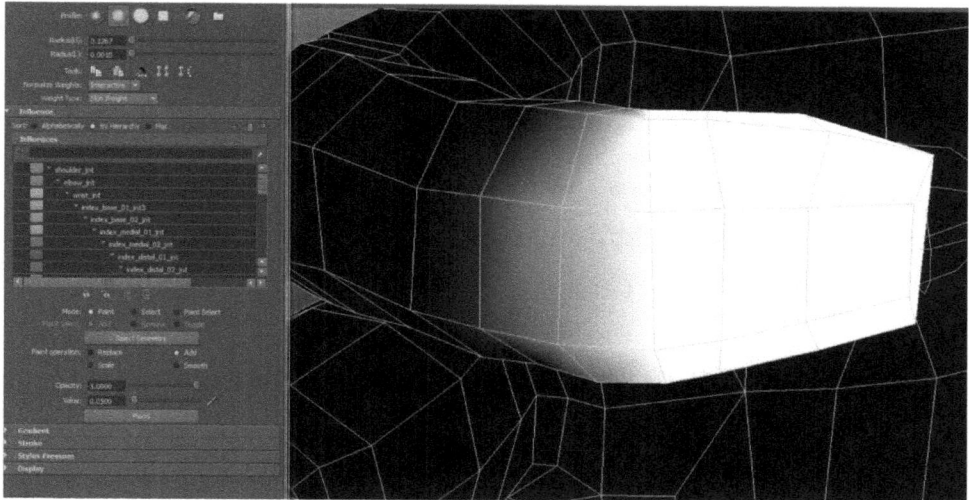

Figure 186. Fixing the weights slowly.

27. As you paint, scrub the time slider from time to time to ensure your fingers look good in all poses. This is the main reason we took the time to add this animation. Note that you can scrub the time slider and see the results without having to leave the paint weights tool. This will help make the whole process that much easier

and is far faster than exiting the tool and rotating the joints each time.

28. Continue to work up the fingers, slowly adding weight until you achieve the results you are after. This will be time consuming, but patience is the key to good weight painting. You can go up to 0.1 if you want, but eventually you will want to be painting the nuances at a 0.05 or even smaller level. All the major deformations and wrinkles can easily be achieved by a good weight painter, so take your time and the results will shine. Go slow to go fast.

Example File: 20_smooth_bind_01_initial_bind.ma

Example File: 21_smooth_bind_02_animating_bind.ma

Example File: 22_smooth_bind_03_replacing_weights.ma

As you can see in the tutorial, by working in this method, you have quite a bit of control of how the weights are being distributed. By doing so, you control just what weight gets assigned to what joint, and you are not relying on Maya to do so. But what if you want to have even MORE control? This brings us to the next section, the Component Editor and Pruning Weights.

Component Editor and Pruning Weights

The component editor is an editor within Maya that allows you to see and edit all sorts of numerical data. In our context of painting weights, the component editor will allow you to manually enter and edit the weights for any given vertex. You can bring up the editor by using:

Window -> General Editors -> Component Editor

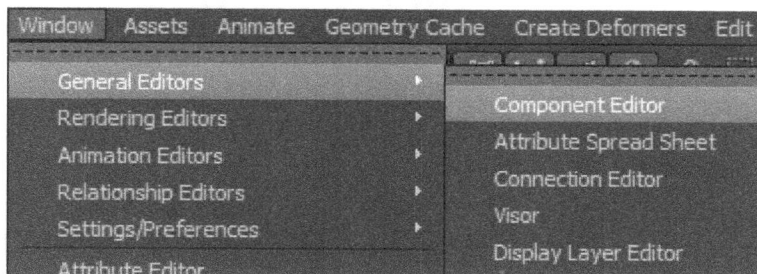

Figure 187. Component editor.

This will open the editor. If you select your model and then choose the "smooth skin" column, you would assume that you would see all the weights in a numerical display. Often viewing all of the weights is both slow and overwhelming, so by default Maya requires you to select the vertices you want to display from your model in order to narrow down just how many things you will get displayed. In order to do so, first select the vertices you want to display on your model, and then hit the "load components" button in the component editor. For this reason, it is important to keep the "Auto Update" not checked on.

Another good tip for using the component editor has to do

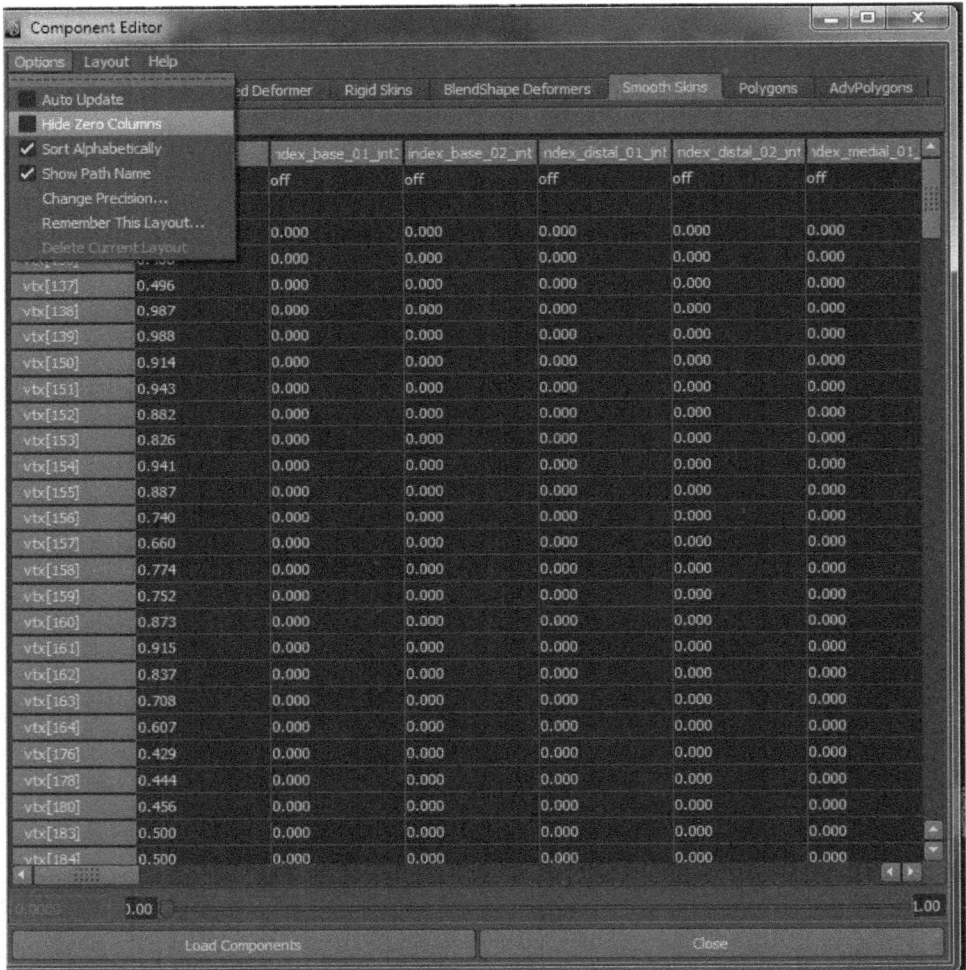

Figure 188. Turning off "auto update".

with reducing even more of what is displayed. When the columns along the top display all the bones in your bind, it can take quite a while to find the right column. To reduce this, you can turn off the columns that have no influence, or hide the "zero columns". By using the option menu at the top (hit the combination of "shift + m" if the menu is not being displayed), you can toggle on or off "hide zero columns". By having these columns hidden, the editor becomes even faster to use. It should be noted that the performance of this editor has vastly improved over the years and a few versions ago, toggling this option was an important step, but one you carefully thought about doing because it could take quite a while to calculate. So depending on the version of Maya you are using, this may have more impact for you.

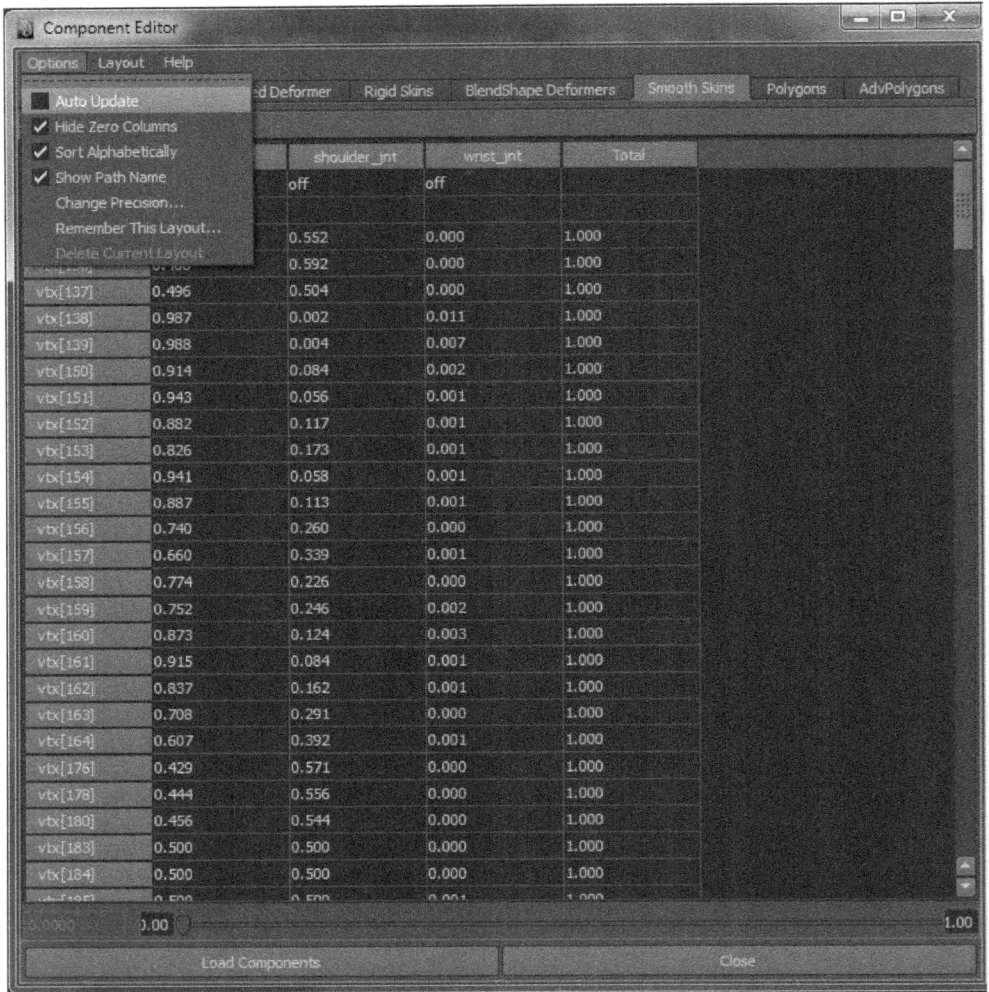

Figure 189. Hide zero columns.

The last concept we will cover with numerical weights is that of "small weights". When opening your component editor, you may have noticed some weights that were really tiny values of less than 0.01. These weights can actually cause problems when your models move very large distances. This is due to the fact that the calculations are being forced to extremely large numbers by that large distance, and will magnify these numbers that would otherwise be so small as to not be noticed. The results can be "spikes" of geometry showing up, or even jiggling in "random" fashions. Of course, neither of which are desirable.

In order to get around these problems, a common step is to "prune small weights" or remove these tiny values. You can do so by using the tool within Maya:

Skin -> Edit Smooth Skin -> Prune Small Weights []

Opening this editor, you will be able to enter in a small value. Any weights below this specified value will be removed when the tool is run. Because it outright deletes these small weights and moves them onto other joints, one should be careful just how big a number is used when pruning.

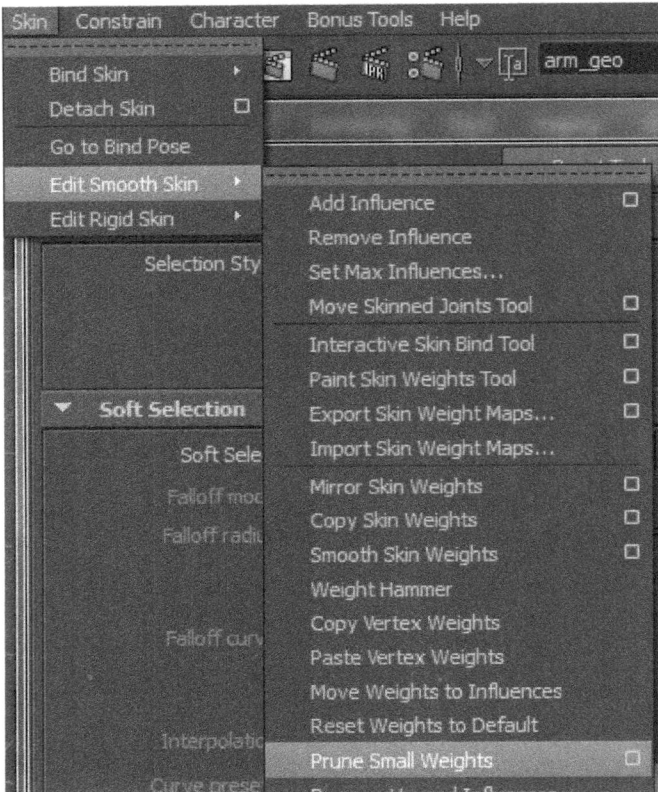

Figure 190. Prune small weights.

Let us examine the last few concepts in a practical manner, and use them in the following tutorial.

Tutorial: Component Editor and Pruning Small Weights

1. Continue on from the weight tutorial explained previously. When you get to a point where you need to fine tune some of your weights, it can become easier

to use the component editor. Select the vertices you want to edit (and not all of them!) then use the command:

    a. Window -> General Editors -> Component Editor

2. Select the Smooth Skins tab.

3. Choose "hide zero columns" in the Options.

4. The result is a spreadsheet of your selected vertices and the weights that they have. You can enter in new weights by hand and have the ultimate control that is far more precise than painting.

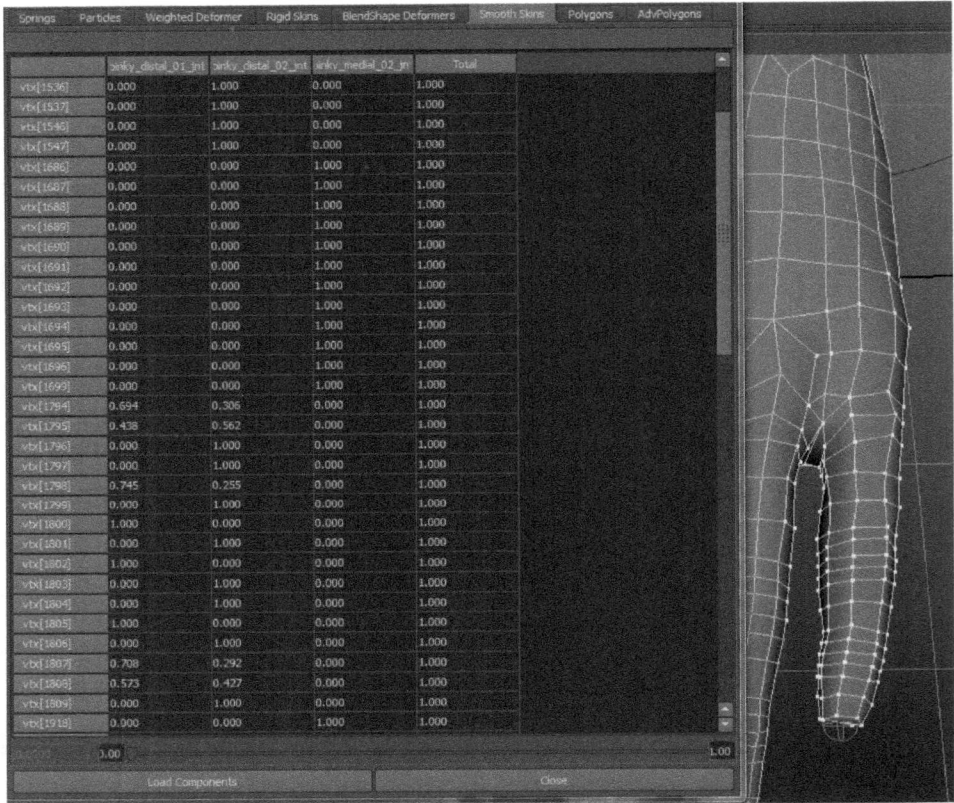

Springs	Particles	Weighted Deformer	Rigid Skins	BlendShape Deformers	Smooth Skins	Polygons	AdvPolygons

	anky_distal_01_jnt	anky_distal_02_jnt	anky_medial_02_jnt	Total
vtx[1536]	0.000	1.000	0.000	1.000
vtx[1537]	0.000	1.000	0.000	1.000
vtx[1546]	0.000	1.000	0.000	1.000
vtx[1547]	0.000	1.000	0.000	1.000
vtx[1686]	0.000	0.000	1.000	1.000
vtx[1687]	0.000	0.000	1.000	1.000
vtx[1688]	0.000	0.000	1.000	1.000
vtx[1689]	0.000	0.000	1.000	1.000
vtx[1690]	0.000	0.000	1.000	1.000
vtx[1691]	0.000	0.000	1.000	1.000
vtx[1692]	0.000	0.000	1.000	1.000
vtx[1693]	0.000	0.000	1.000	1.000
vtx[1694]	0.000	0.000	1.000	1.000
vtx[1695]	0.000	0.000	1.000	1.000
vtx[1696]	0.000	0.000	1.000	1.000
vtx[1693]	0.000	0.000	1.000	1.000
vtx[1794]	0.694	0.306	0.000	1.000
vtx[1795]	0.438	0.562	0.000	1.000
vtx[1796]	0.000	1.000	0.000	1.000
vtx[1797]	0.000	1.000	0.000	1.000
vtx[1798]	0.745	0.255	0.000	1.000
vtx[1799]	0.000	1.000	0.000	1.000
vtx[1800]	1.000	0.000	0.000	1.000
vtx[1801]	0.000	1.000	0.000	1.000
vtx[1802]	1.000	0.000	0.000	1.000
vtx[1803]	0.000	1.000	0.000	1.000
vtx[1804]	0.000	1.000	0.000	1.000
vtx[1805]	1.000	0.000	0.000	1.000
vtx[1806]	0.000	1.000	0.000	1.000
vtx[1807]	0.708	0.292	0.000	1.000
vtx[1808]	0.573	0.427	0.000	1.000
vtx[1809]	0.000	1.000	0.000	1.000
vtx[1918]	0.000	0.000	1.000	1.000

| 1.00 | | | | 1.00 |

Load Components	Close

Figure 191. Component editor provides ultimate control.

Note that while the component editor gives you extreme control, it can also be quite slow to use. It is definitely required at times, but by adding weights carefully while painting, you will reduce the amount of time you need to spend in the component editor.

There are also times when small values have appeared on vertices that throw off your precise deformations. These can easily be removed using the prune weights as explained above.

1. Continuing on from your weight tutorial, save your file.

2. Now let us play with the smooth option in the paint weights. Pick on various joints and paint "smoothness" on the deformations.

3. Scrub your animation in the time slider. Quite quickly, you will start seeing errors showing up and your precision going way. Oh, the joys of the using the smooth option. Remove some of these errors by:

    a. **Skin -> Edit Smooth Skin -> Prune Small Weights []**

    b. Pick a value slightly larger than 0.01. Try 0.1 this time.

4. Scrub your animation and see how pruning off some of the small weights has cleaned up some of the errors.

As you can see, both of these tools are handy to know how to use. An alternative to pruning the small weights would be to edit the vertices' weight values in the component editor by typing zero in the columns of the joints that you do not want to have control over your vertices.

Bind Pose

Now that we have covered binding your model and editing the weights for that bind, we should cover the concept of a bind pose. With the later versions of Maya, this bind pose has become a much less restrictive concept, but it is still important to understand how a bind pose works. When you bind your model, the pose that it is originally in when you run the skinning tool becomes what is known as your "bind pose". The bind pose tells Maya where all the vertices and everything related to the skin's envelope was at the start of the process. By knowing this, Maya can calculate how to move the items around.

A good way to visualize this is to picture a steal beam welded in and running from each vertex to the joint that influences it. If it is a rigid bind, this one to one relationship is accurate. This means if the joint moves, it moves the vertex in exactly the same way.

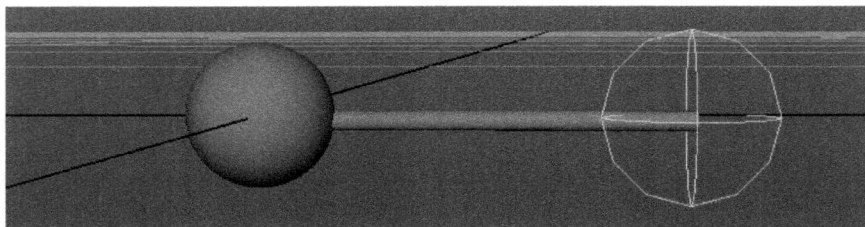

Figure 192. Welded together.

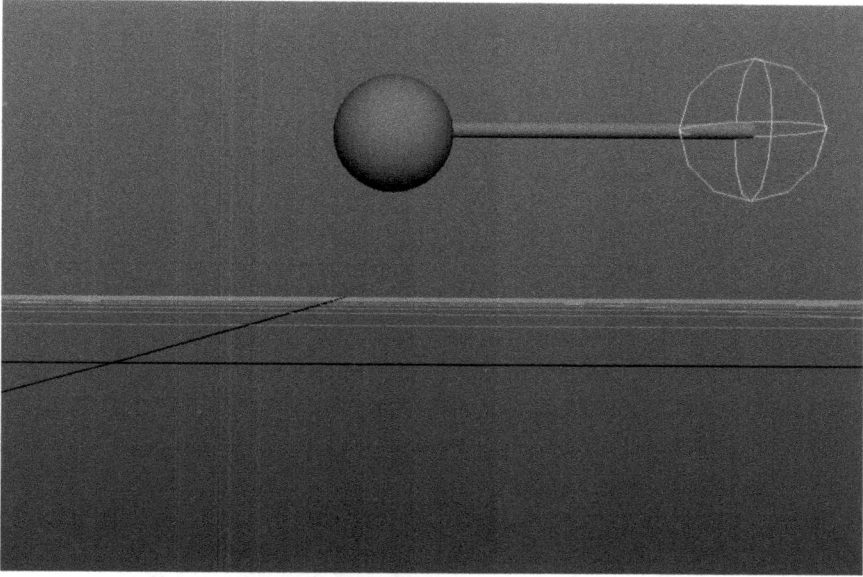

Figure 194. Vertex moves 1:1 with joint.

Now, picture that beam as a spring. This is how a smooth bind works. If the springs are the equal strength and your vertex has a second spring welded to a second joint, it is essentially the same as having two joints with a 0.5 weight on both. When one moves, the springs stretch and ultimately settle on the vertex being halfway in between.

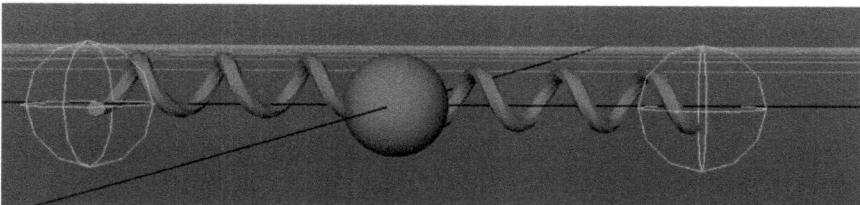

Figure 193. Vertex held by springs.

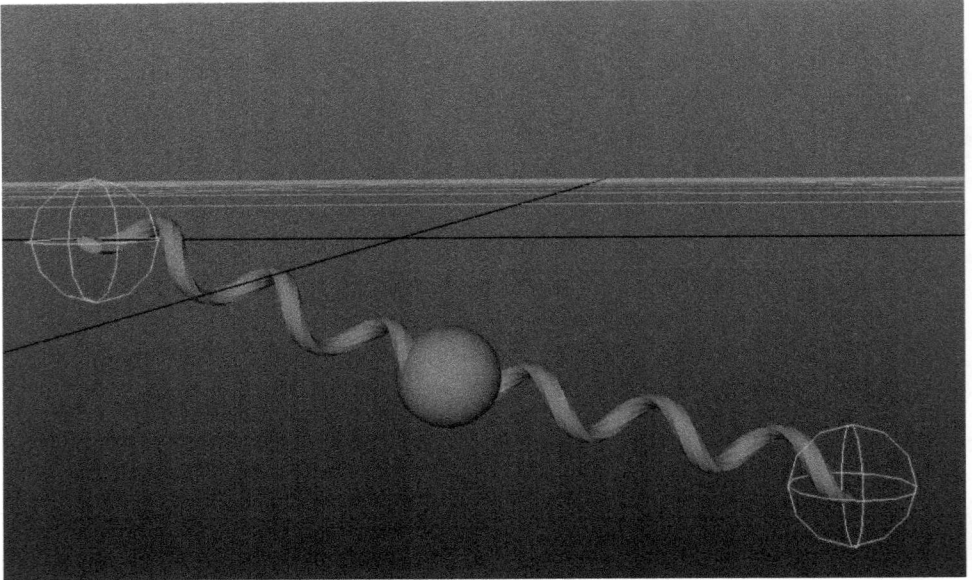

Figure 195. Springs stretch, the vertex stays in the middle between the two joints.

Of course, these examples are quite simple, but you can see that as each joint moves, it is important for the computer to be able to figure out exactly how it moved and tie that movement back to each vertex. In order to do so, the bind pose has to be established.

This bind pose is so important, that there is even a tool to help you get back to the bind pose.

Skin -> Go To Bind Pose

This tool will work most of the time, but if you have added in more advanced controls like Inverse Kinematics, it may not work. This is because there is a conflict that happens between the tool saying "please go back to the original pose" and the other tools saying "please calculate the joint angles based on the position of this IK handle".

If you cannot get back to your bind pose, you can use some MEL to override the pose and set a new one. The following tutorial will show you how. The important part is to try to get as close to the bind pose as possible prior to using this trick because you will literally override where the vertices will think their own particular origin is.

Tutorial: How to Reset the Bind Pose

1. Create a simple skeleton of an arm, with a shoulder, elbow, and wrist.
2. Bind a simple model to your skeleton for a simple arm.
3. Bend your elbow by rotating the elbow joint.
4. Select the mesh and use the command:
   a. **Skin -> Edit Smooth Skin -> Go to Bind Pose**
5. Your skeleton will snap back to the pose you created your bind in.
6. If you are not able to go back to your bind pose, you can chose to reset the pose and force the pose you are

currently in to become the new bind pose. Select all the bones in the skeleton that need to be reset and then use the MEL command for doing so is:

```
dagPose -reset -name "bindPose1";
```

Note: this MEL command requires entering the name of the bind pose that you want to reset. Typically, you will be working with one bind pose and "bindPose1" will be correct, but it is important to know that the proper name should be substituted into the command above.

In later versions of Maya (2008 and on), you are able to add joints and move joints around even if you are not in the bind pose. It is always best however to try to get back to the bind pose if possible.

This brings us to our next section, just how do you add influences or new joints to the already established skin and bind pose?

Adding Influences

Adding influences has gotten far simpler with later versions of Maya. In recent developments, Maya no longer requires you to get exactly back to the bind pose. However, it is a good idea to get back to your bind pose or as closely as possible prior to adding in any new joints or influences. Once you are there, it is also a good idea to reset your pose. While this is not a requirement, there are few downsides of doing so. How to do so is outlined in the tutorial found in the Bind Pose section found above.

Now that you are in your (new) bind pose, let us add in some new joints. The first step is to create some new joints and parent them in properly. Then you can select your model and then your new joint, and run the tool:

Skin -> Edit Smooth Skin -> Add Influence []

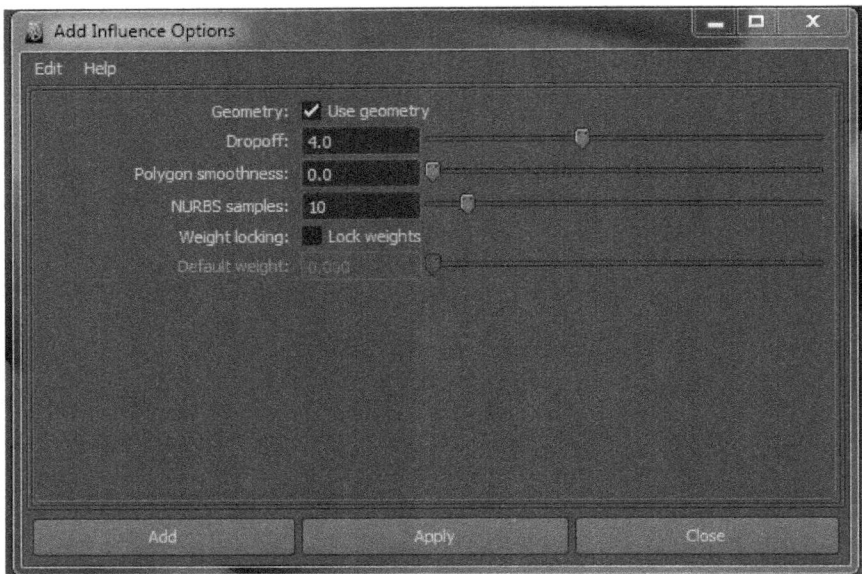

Figure 197. Add influence options.

When you open up your option box, you will notice the first entry is "Use Geometry". If you turn this to off, you are telling Maya you would like to add in a new joint to the skin.

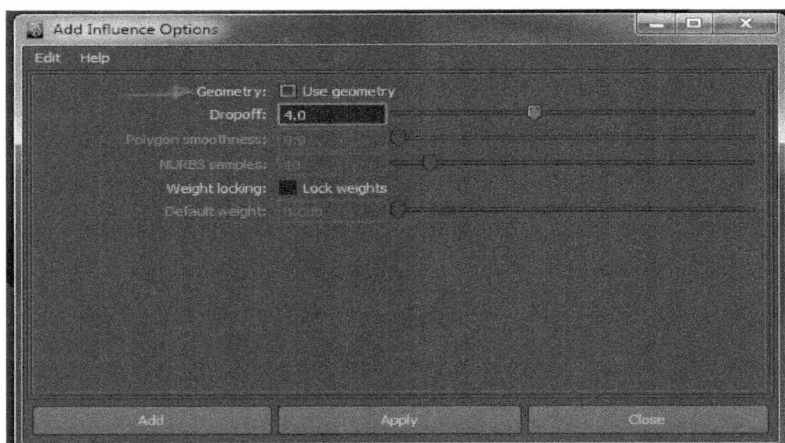

Figure 196. Turn use geometry off.

The first thing to check after that prior to running the tool is to ensure that you toggle on "Weight Locking" and ensuring your weights are locked to 0.0.

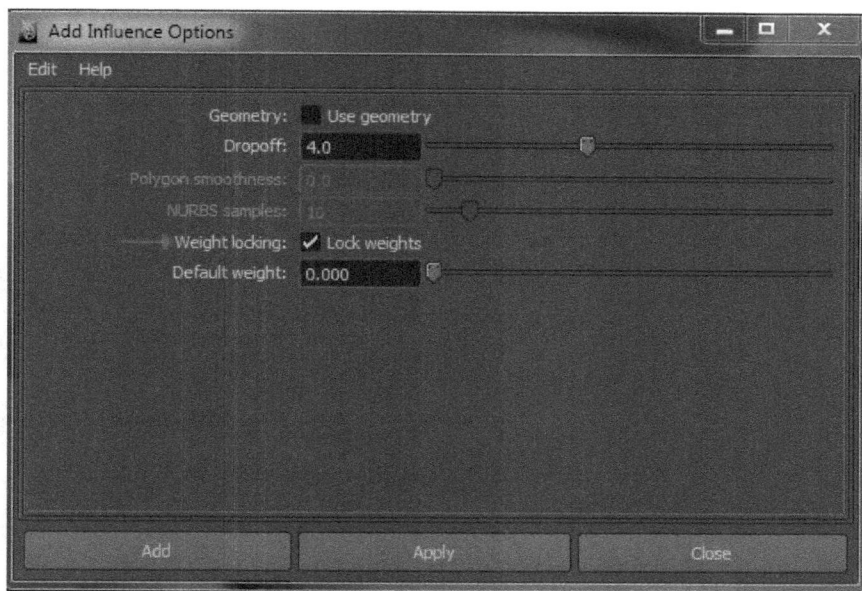

Figure 198. Lock weights turned on and set to 0.

Toggling this on with a default weight of 0.000 will essentially add in your new joint with zero weights and thus preserve the weighting you have done already. You can then go in to the painting weights tool and toggle the hold off and add weights as you choose. Doing so will of course ensure you do not lose any of the work you have already done. Remember from before that you toggle this off by clicking on the padlock icon in the painting weights tool. Select the joint in the painting weights menu that is locked (held) and click the unlock icon to toggle the hold off.

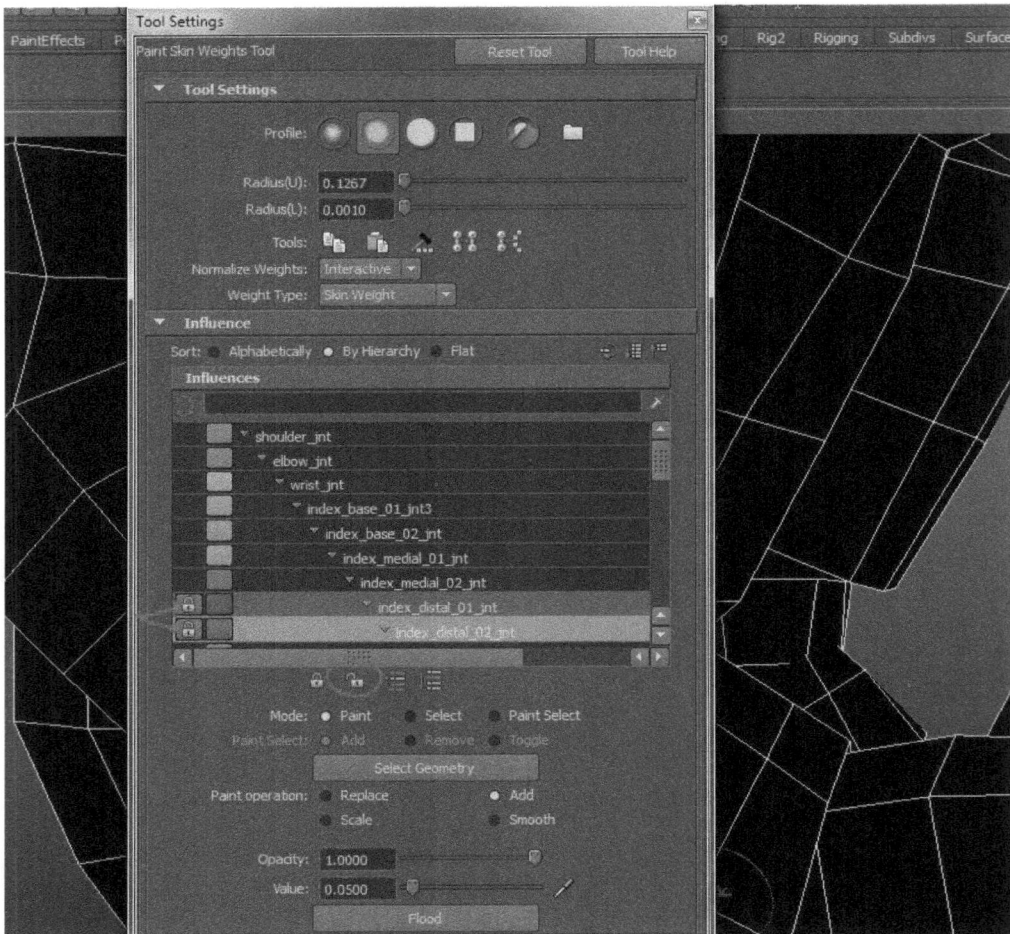

Figure 199. Click to unlock the locked status.

Tutorial: How to Add a Joint to a Skinned Model

1. Open a skinned scene, or create a simple model and add some joints. In our case, I will use one of the scenes with a hand from before.

2. Let us add a joint into the metacarpal area of the palm. Start by going to the bind pose:

   a. **Skin -> Go To Bind Pose**

3. Draw a joint and hit enter.

4. Move the joint in to position where you would like it in the palm and parent it into the hierarchy as appropriate.

5. Select your joint then, holding shift select the skin.

6. **Skin -> Edit Smooth Skin -> Add Influence []**

   a. Turn off "use geometry"

   b. Turn on "lock weights"

   c. Set the weight value to 0.

7. This will add your joint into the skin. The next step is to be able to add weight to it. Select the model and open the paint weights tool.

8. Find the joint in the list (it will likely be at the very top) and hit the unlocked padlock button. This will unlock the joint and allow you to add weights just like any other joint to it.

a. Pro tip: the MEL command is "setAttr joint_name.liw 0". You can easily write a script to turn the .liw attribute to zero for selected joints once you become more familiar with using MEL.

Adding a piece of geometry as an influence is also done using this same tool. These are often referred to as "influence objects". Influence objects are a great way to add a level of visualization to just how the skin is being controlled. To add your influence object, first create your geometry. Next, select your skinned geometry and then your new influence geometry and finally run the tool with the option of "use geometry" turned on. Doing so will also open the choices of Polygon smoothness and NURBS samples. The higher these values, the better the results will be but also the slower the results will be. You can play with these numbers to find the optimal choice for your particular scenario, as it never is the same. A good default value to start with is a polygon smoothness of 1.0 if you are using polygons, or a NURBS sample of 16 if you are using NURBS.

When you add in your influence, it often is a good idea to NOT lock your weights, and allowing Maya to calculate the initial assignment for you.

When you get right down to it, adding in an influence object can give practically the same results as a adding in a joint. The main difference is being able to visualize the shape you want to control, and this does allow some users to get the weights painted more quickly. In the following tutorial, you will see how adding in an influence object can help hold the shape of a boot despite how it bends. In this case, we use a ball shape to maintain the ankle volume of our boot.

Tutorial: Fix a Heel of a Boot With an Influence Object

1. Model a boot.
2. Enter the side view and draw a skeleton for the leg and foot.
3. Bind your boot to the skeleton using a smooth bind as we have done in previous tutorials.
4. Rotate your ankle and you will see the boot does not preserve its' volume very well. It would be nice to see a large area of the boot NOT deform.
5. Create a Nurbs sphere and position it in the area where the boot should not deform but rather should preserve its volume (around the ankle area). Model and/or scale the ball to fit properly.
6. Select the ball, then the model and use the command:

   a. **Skin -> Edit Smooth Skin -> Add Influence []**

b. Ensure the "use geometry" is ticked on.

c. Increase the Nurbs sampling to 16

d. Turn off "lock weights" so weights will be added.

7. Parent the ball to the heel so it preserves the positioning and stays in the right spot when the skeleton is moved around.

8. Try bending the ankle again. This time the ball will exert an influence on the boot and help keep the shape solid as the boot deforms more realistically around the ball.

This is a good time to mention the one limiting factor of an influence object. The relationship of the influence object is essentially a one to one type relationship. This means the vertices that are weighted to the object will follow that object, with however much they follow based on the strength of the weights. What this means is you cannot expect your object to slide under the skinned object. In other words, your model will follow the object and not slide over it based on its position. This is an important note since many people look at using the influence object to do just that for things such as muscles. While you will get a quick rudimentary example of a muscle, you will not get a perfect result as the objects are "sticky" and do not slide underneath.

To learn a good way of just how to make a muscle system, see one of the other books in this series, Advanced Character Rigging: Creating Advanced Tendon and Muscle Systems.

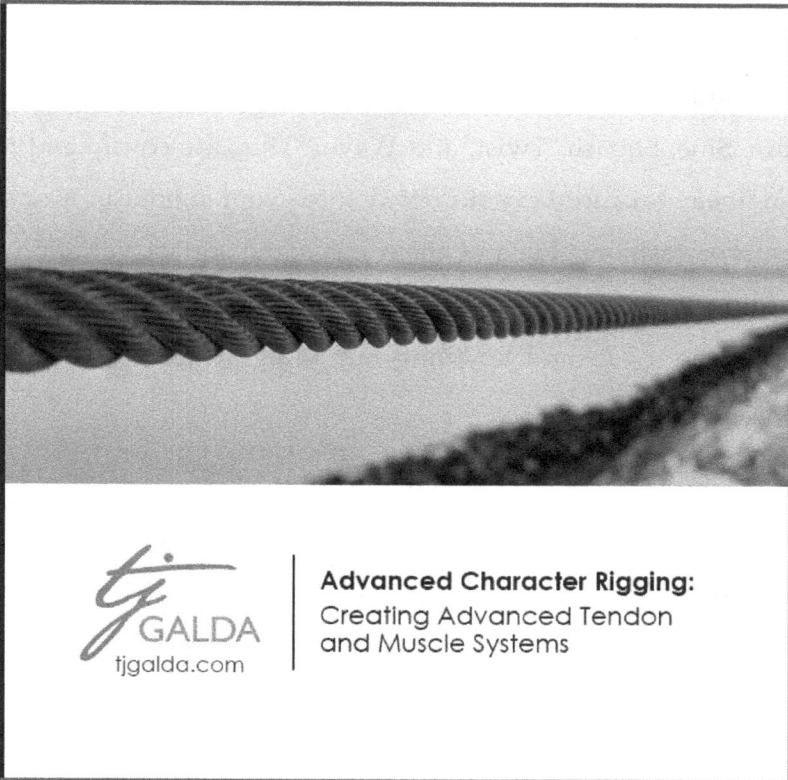

tj
GALDA
tjgalda.com

Advanced Character Rigging:
Creating Advanced Tendon
and Muscle Systems

Non-linear Deformers: Overview

This is a good time to progress beyond using just the typical clusters, lattices and joints/skinning to using even more deformers. Maya has another section of fun deformers called "Non-linear Deformers" and currently ships with 6 of these: Bend, Flare, Sine, Squash, Twist, and Wave. They are considered to be non-linear because they do not deform your model in a straight line type fashion. Each of them has some sort of variation of a twisting, squishing, or rotational force that results in your vertices moving in a fun and anything but straight line. You can find these under the menu:

Create Deformers -> Non-Linear -> (one of six types)

Before we get in to the specifics of each type, let us cover the characteristics they share. Each deformer has an envelope, and non-linear deformers are no exception. The concept of an envelope was covered earlier under our Weights and Envelopes section. By making use of this envelope, you can control the overall influence of the non-linear deformers in your rigs.

When you create your non-linear deformer of choice, you will get a "handle", for example a transform called a "wave1Handle" for a wave deformer. This transform or handle, will allow you to move your deformer and animate the typical transform attributes such as translate, rotate, etcetera.

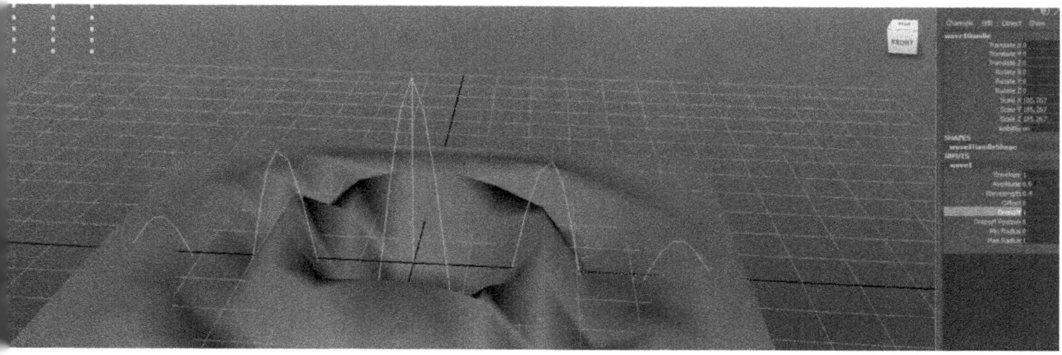

Figure 200. Wave handle.

You will also see that when you select your handle, the deformer type shows up below it in the channel box. Selecting this type will open up the attributes for your deformer which can also be played with and animated.

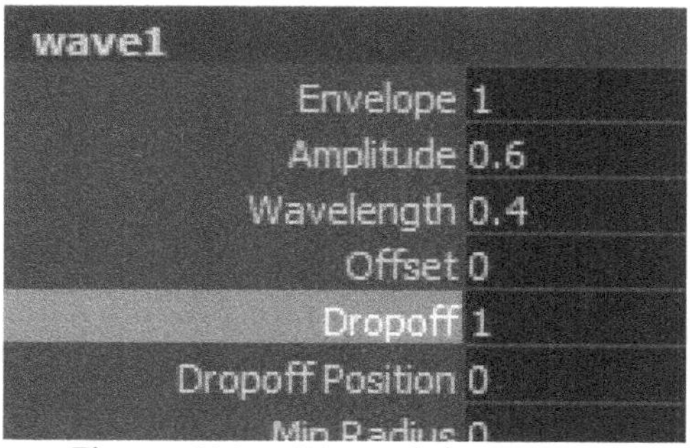

Figure 201.   Wave deformer channel box.

The last thing to keep in mind which is common to all non-linear deformers is just how to control the influence of your non-linear deformers. This is done using the edit membership tool which we discussed earlier in the Rigid Bind and Edit Membership section. By adding or removing vertices to the deformer, you can easily control which ones are affected and which ones are not. This is a quite simple process of first selecting the deformer and then running the tool as discussed above, by running:

Edit Deformers -> Edit Membership Tool

As you can see in the image, the yellow vertices are still being influenced by the deformer while the reddish brown vertices are no longer influenced. The edit membership tool is very simple yet powerful and it is important to remember that it is available for use.

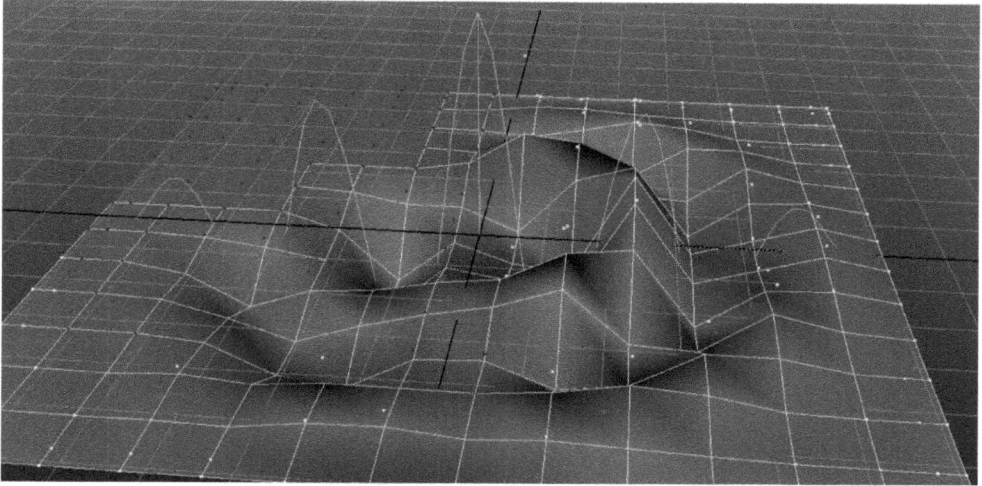

Figure 202. Edit the membership.

Now let us discuss the properties of each non-linear deformer and give some examples of good times to use them.

Non-linear Deformers: Bend

The bend deformer is perhaps the simplest ones to explain. Once added to an object, the bend will, well, bend your object. To create a bend deformer, select your object and then run:

Create Deformers -> Non-Linear -> Bend

Figure 204. Bend options.

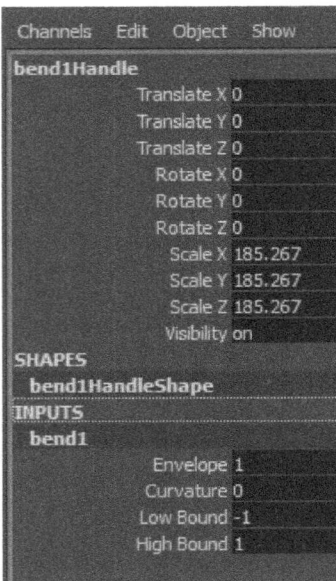

Doing so will create the handle, likely "bend1Handle" as your transform on you object. Selecting the bend handle, you will then be able to select the bend itself in the channel box.

By selecting the bend (likely "bend1"), you will have several options to play with. Try selecting the curvature attribute in the channel box and middle mouse dragging the

Figure 203. Bend channel box.

attribute to make your object bend. This simple bend can be a great thing to use for your simple characters, such as boxes. Take for example a brick. In the tutorial following, you will see just how simple yet effective adding a bend will allow you to animate your brick with some attitude.

The envelope attribute will allow you to dial up and down the overall effect of the bend, while the low and high bound will allow you to choose if you want your bend to be a classic and default C shape, or if you would rather turn a portion of that off. For example, turning the high bound to 0 will result in more of a J shape than a C by essentially removing half of the bend.

Figure 205. High bound attribute of the bend.

The other important thing to remember when using a non-linear deformer is that they affect the model based on their position and proximity. They can even move in and out of an object to cause different effects. Try moving the bend deformer around to see how various positions, scales, and rotations affect how your model deforms. These properties are important to remember when incorporating the deformer into your overall deformation system and hierarchy. In other words, make sure you parent your deformers to the right spot in the hierarchy. Of course, a set driven key on the motion of the deformer can help simplify the deformation for the animators as well. It is often a good idea to connect your various deformers, in this case the bend, to a control object such as the curve around a main joint like the hips.

To make your bend deformer (or any of the non-linear deformers for that matter) even more effective, often creating a lattice first is a good idea. This lattice can then be deformed with the bend, and this will allow you to get a smoother deformation on shapes that are more complex.

Tutorial: Create a Brick that can Bend

1. Create a poly cube and scale it to make it look like a brick.

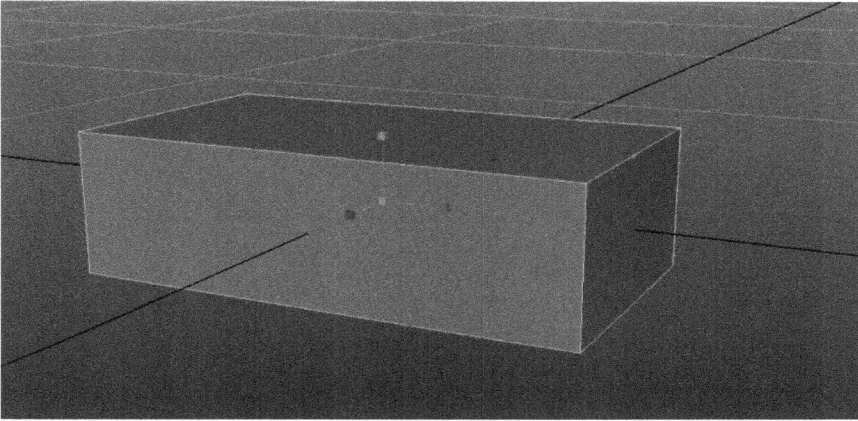

Figure 206. Basic brick.

2. Use the history in the channel box under "polyCube1" to add more subdivisions. We've entered 6 for height, width and depth.

3. Select the brick and use the command:

   a. **Create Deformers -> Non-Linear Deformers -> Bend**

4. Select the bend handle and try using the curvature attribute. Notice how the brick won't bend nicely at first.

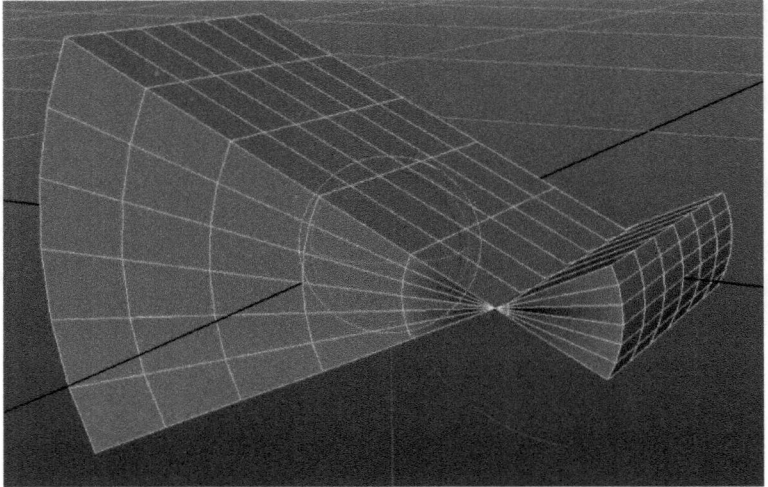

Figure 207. Brick bends poorly.

5. Try moving and rotating the bend handle around and notice how it changes how the object deforms. Notice how the attributes such as low and high bound change where the bend happens as well. Do not forget the overall effect of the envelope. In our example, rotating the bend handle 90 degrees in Z helps the bend out drastically.

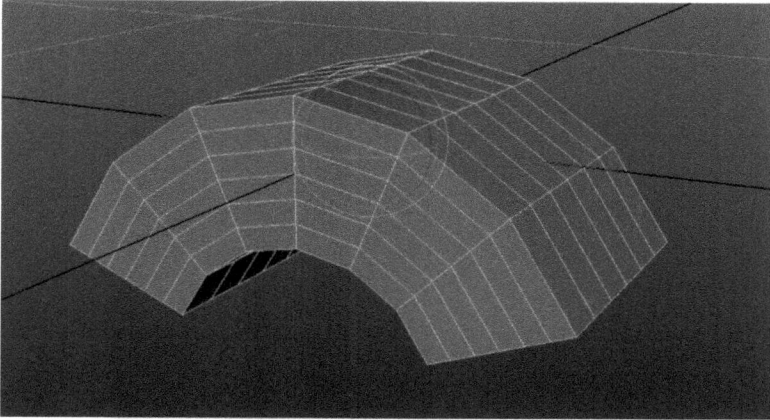

Figure 208. Brick bends nicely.

6. Ensure the bend handle is parented properly, this time to the brick itself. When the brick moves, you want the bend handle to be there. Of course, if the brick is also skinned in a skeleton, then the handle should be parented to the skeleton as well (and not the brick itself).

Example File: 23_bend_deformer_brick.ma

Non-linear Deformers: Flare

The next deformer on the list is the flare deformer.

Create Deformers -> Non-Linear -> Flare

Figure 209. Flare menu.

The flare deformer acts somewhat like a squash but it does not take in to account the volume. In other words, the flare will allow you to stretch or shrink either end of the deformer or both. By using the curve attribute, you will stretch or bulge out the middle. As you play with the attributes, you can quickly make a sphere into a gumdrop shape, or a hot air balloon. In the following tutorial, you will create a chocolate from a sphere by combining what you learned with using the bend deformer and making use of the flare deformer. You will even see how to melt the tip of the chocolate by simply moving the bend deformer.

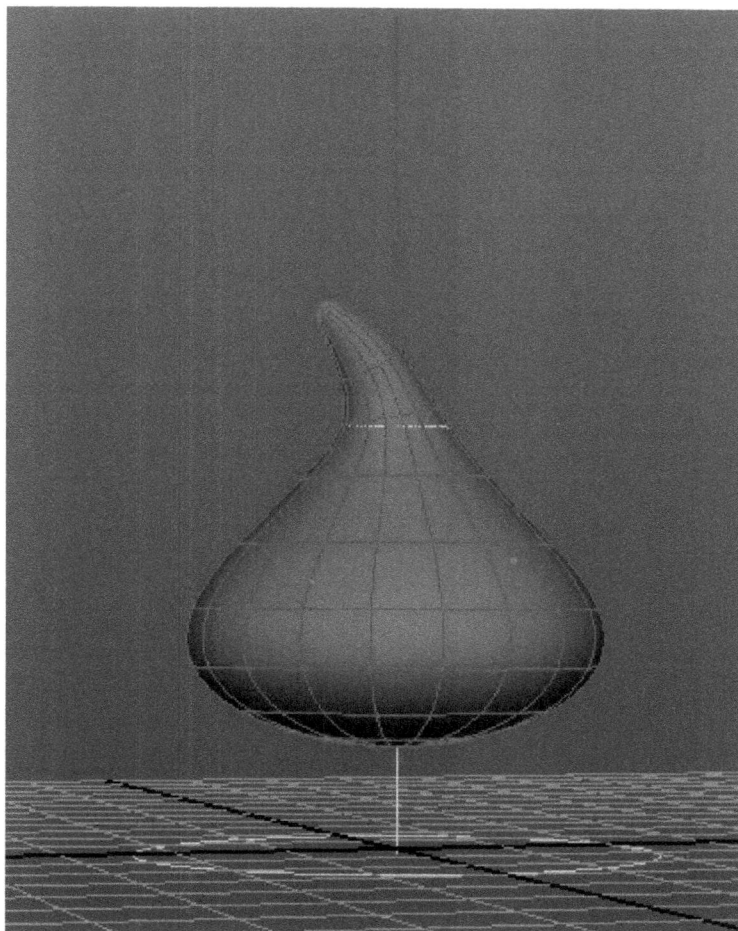

Figure 210. Making a chocolate with a flare and bend.

The flare deformer has a few more attributes than the bend, the start and end flare. These allow even more control on just how the flare is acting on the object beyond the high and low bound.

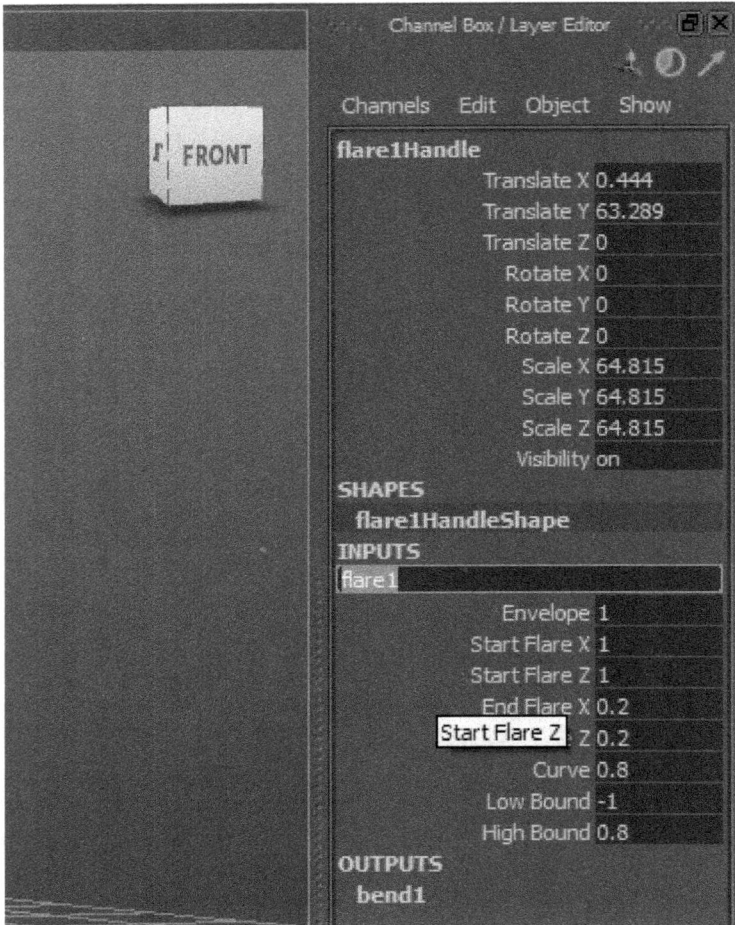

Figure 211. Flare channel box.

The best way to learn how these attributes work is to try different settings for them on your own. You can easily squish one axis down to a flat shape and bulge in the other if you want. This can be a handy thing to remember when you need to subtly tweak a silhouette.

Tutorial: Making a Choclate

1. Create a Nurbs sphere. Ensure that you have enough density in the surface, we used attributes of 19 sections and 11 spans, and did so by altering the settings in the channel box for makeNurbsSphere1.
2. Select the sphere and run the command:
   a. **Create Deformers -> Non-Linear -> Flare**
3. Play with the flare attribute and positioning of the flare handle. This will allow you to create a shape something like what we have in the image. Our settings were end flare x and z as 0.2, curve 0.8, low bound -1 and high bound 0.8.

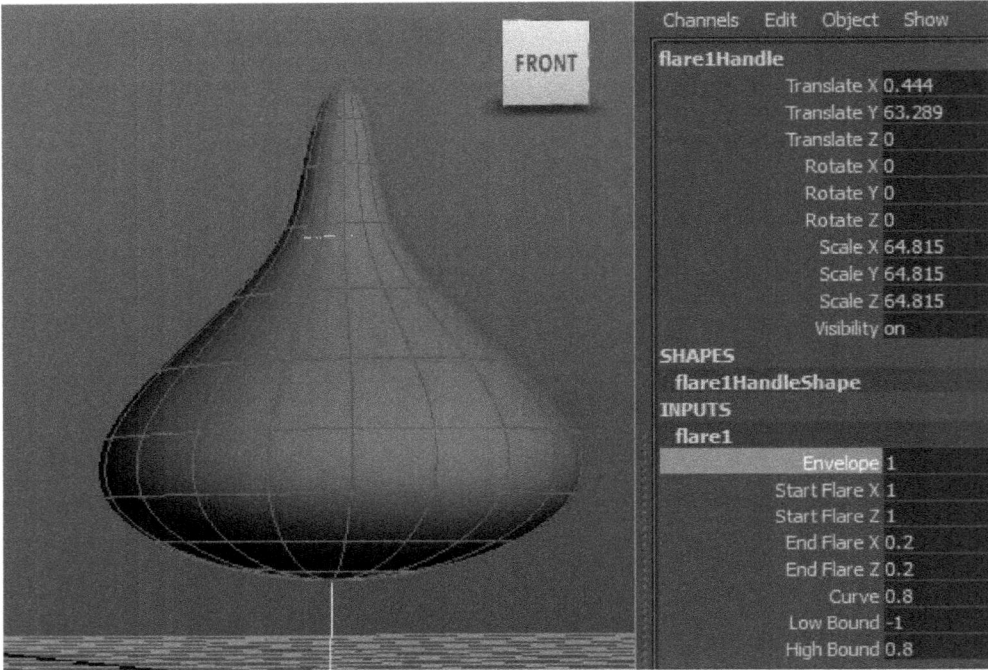

Figure 212. Flare the sphere.

4. Add a bend deformer to melt the top.

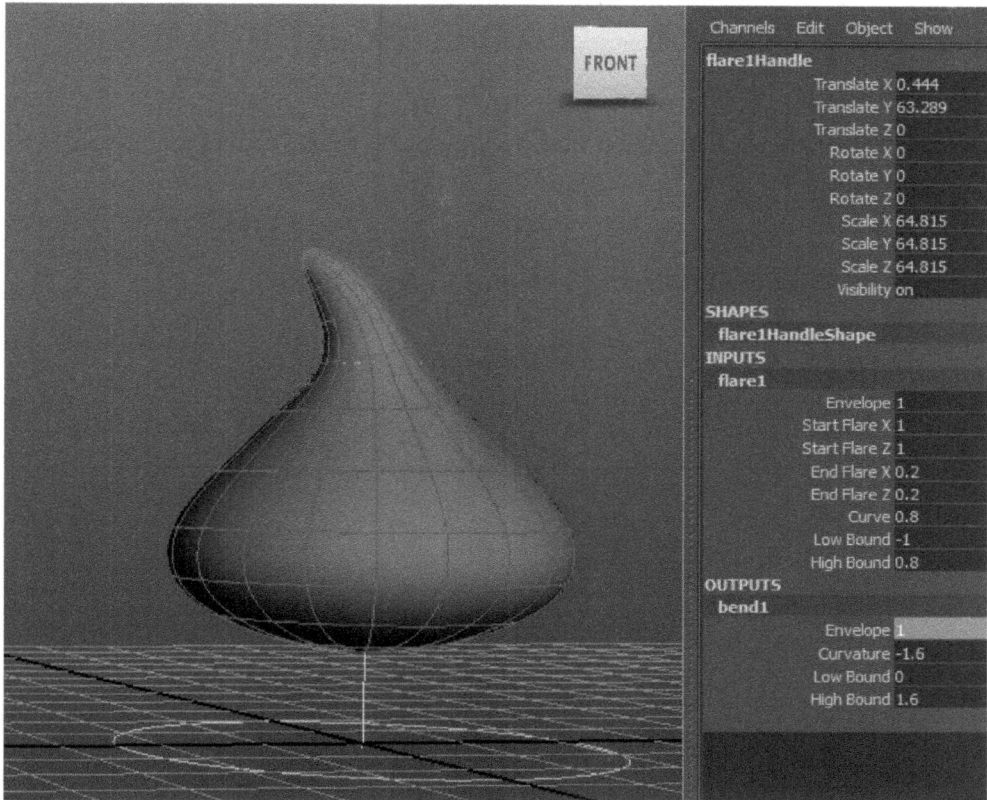

Figure 213. Bend the top.

Example File: 4_bend_deformer_plus_flare_chocolate.ma

Non-linear Deformers: Sine

The sine deformer creates a deformation in your object based on a sine wave.

Create Deformers -> Non-Linear -> Sine

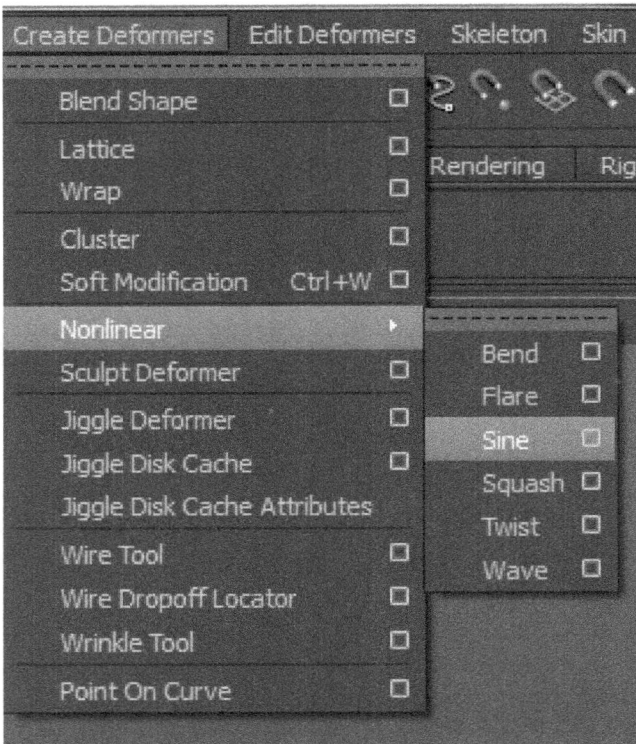

Figure 214. Sine menu.

This deformer is a great way to start creating waves in your surfaces that you can easily and quickly control. It is also a way to quickly create a fake wind. In the following tutorial, you will learn how to easily make a flag flapping in the wind.

Figure 215. Sine to make a flag.

Channels   Edit   Object   Show

sine1Handle

Translate X	-180.768
Translate Y	816.826
Translate Z	-31.855
Rotate X	-55.766
Rotate Y	108.556
Rotate Z	56.784
Scale X	309.87
Scale Y	309.87
Scale Z	309.87
Visibility	on

SHAPES
 sine1HandleShape
INPUTS
 sine1

Envelope	1
Amplitude	0.1
Wavelength	0.6
Offset	-0.6
Dropoff	1
Low Bound	-1.9
High Bound	2.1

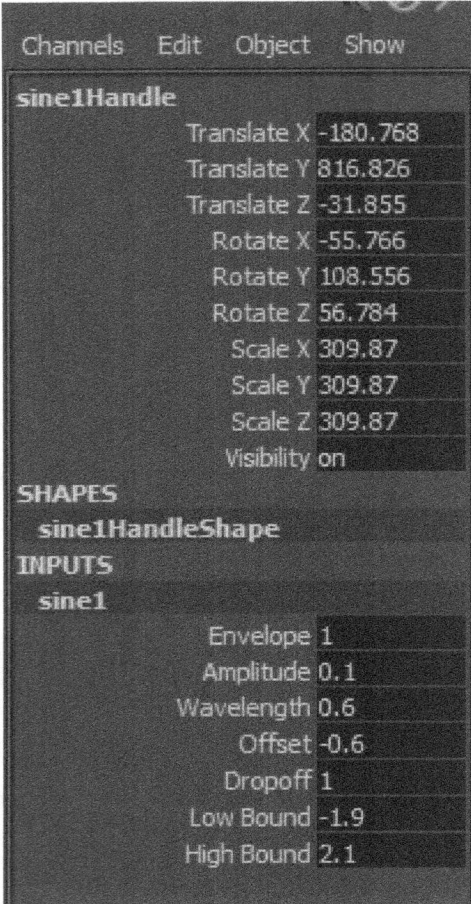

The sine deformer has a variety of attributes that are associated with any wave. The amplitude refers to how high the wave peaks and how low the valleys are. The wavelength refers to the space between each peak and valley. The offset refers to the position of the start of the wave from the deformer.

By increasing the high to above 1 (say 10), or the low bound to well below -1 (say -10), you can easily extend the length of the sine deformer and thus give you ample room to also translate the deformer through the object for even very long animations.

Tutorial: Build and Animate a Flag with a Sine Deformer

1. Create a plane. Scale and model it to be the size and shape of a flat flag. We modeled a simple cylinder for the flag pole and ensured that the flag has a lot of density.

Figure 216. Dense flag.

2. Create a sine deformer on the flag by running the command:

   a. Create Deformers -> Non-Linear -> Sine

3. Select the sine handle and play with the attributes to make a nice wiggly shape such as the image. We used the amplitude of 0.1 and a wavelength of 0.6. The offset is useful for animating the motion and the drop off can control how much the flag will flatten out further from the center of the sine handle. We turned the dropoff all the way to 1. A larger low bound and high bound will extend the effect, so we used -1.9 and 2.1.

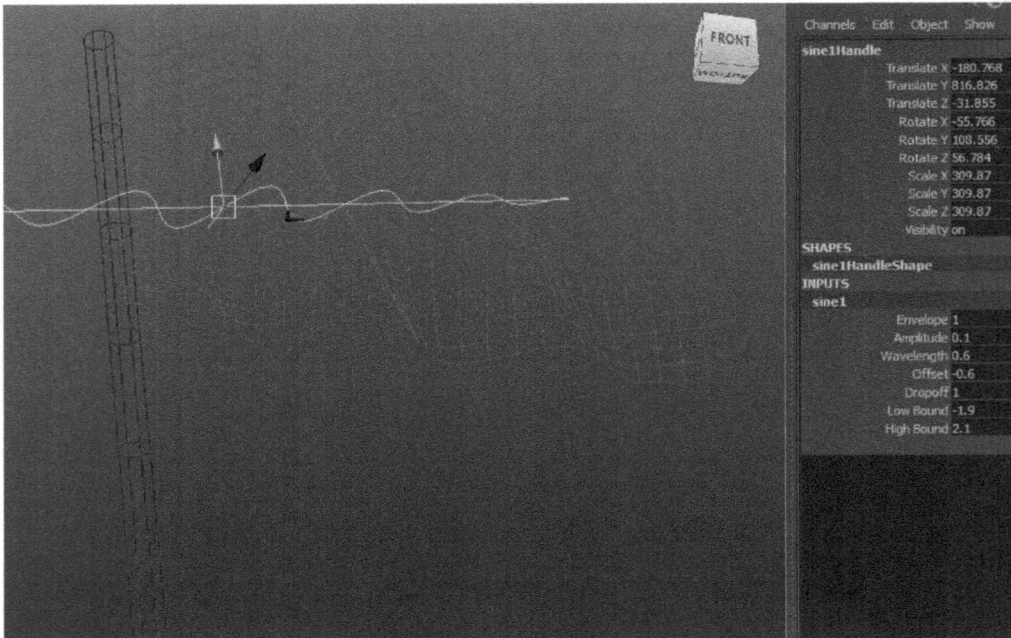

Figure 217. Use the deformer to ripple the flag.

4. Transform and rotate the sine handle towards one end of the flag. Notice how the flag moves but rips away from the flagpole. We can control this end via the edit membership tool.

5. **Edit Deformers -> Edit Membership Tool**
   a. Select the sine deformer with the tool
   b. Control select a few rows of vertices to turn them reddish brown

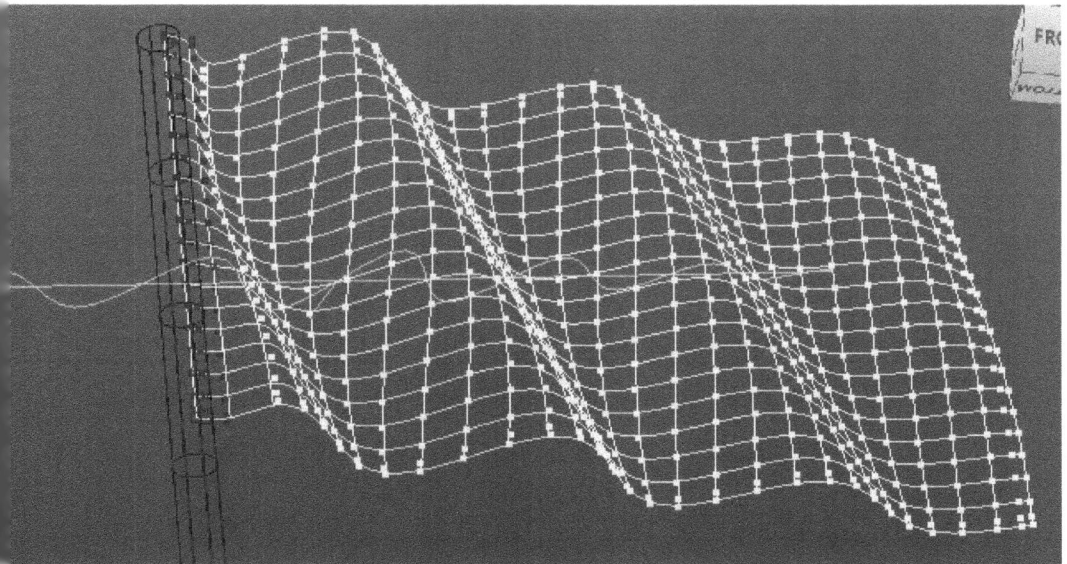

Figure 218. Remove the vertices from the membership.

6. Set a key on the position of the sine handle at frame 1 by:

   a. Go to frame 1

   b. Select the sine handle

   c. s (set keyframe)

7. Go to frame 60 and move the handle to the other end of the flag. Set another key to finish your animation.

   a. Go to frame 60

   b. Select, rotate and move the sine handle

   c. s (set keyframe)

8. Scrubbing the animation slider will show your flag flapping. Modify the animation by adjusting and/or animating the sine handle's attributes or adding additional keys throughout the timeline for rotation. The offset attribute in particular will be useful to control wind speed effects.

9. Play around with adding additional sine deformers to get more noise in the animation and produce a very realistic wind effect with very little memory requirements.

Example File: 25_sine_flag.ma

Non-linear Deformers: Squash

The squash deformer is perhaps the most fun of the non-linear deformers for animators. The tool is found by running:

Create Deformers -> Non-Linear -> Squash

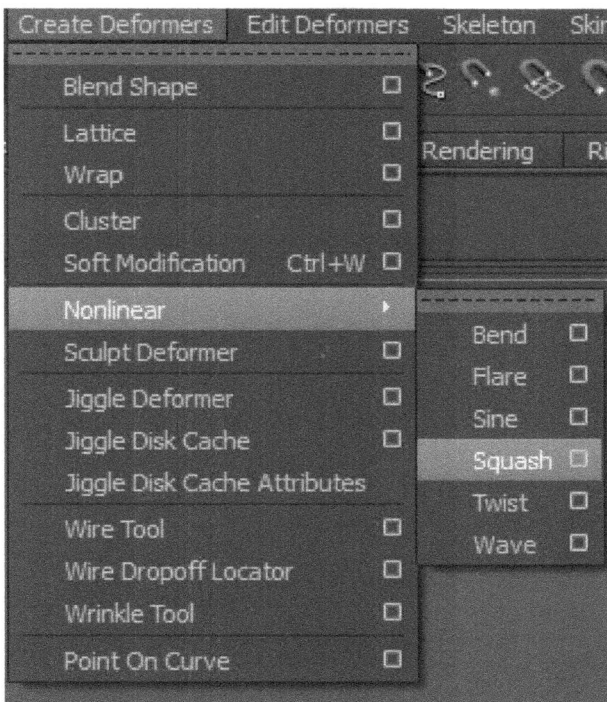

Figure 219. Squash menu.

The squash deformer is similar to the flare deformer, but in with one distinct difference. It attempts to retain the volume of your shape as the squash or stretch acts on the object. That means that by simply dialing in one attribute, the factor, your model will grow and shrink in a pleasing manner. Perhaps the first animation exercise most animators encounter is the bouncing ball. The squash deformer will make this exercise far more fun to animate and easier to allow the ball to act in a squishy manner. This is outlined in the following tutorial. The following image shows how a ball can squash or stretch depending on the squash factor of the deformer.

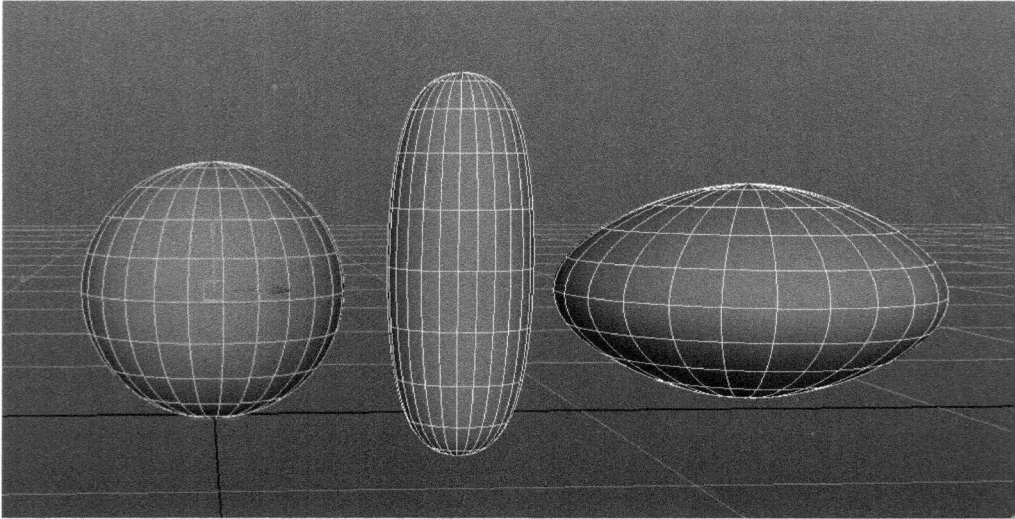

Figure 220. Squash and stretch a ball.

New attributes to take in to account with the squash is the maxExpandPos which stands for maximum expand position. This attribute will control the position from where the maximum expansion will occur. This is different than the factor attribute, which controls the amount of squash or squish. The expand attribute will allow you to control the amount of expansion that occurs with your models. The smoothness attributes allows for control of the smooth versus sharp deformation of your object.

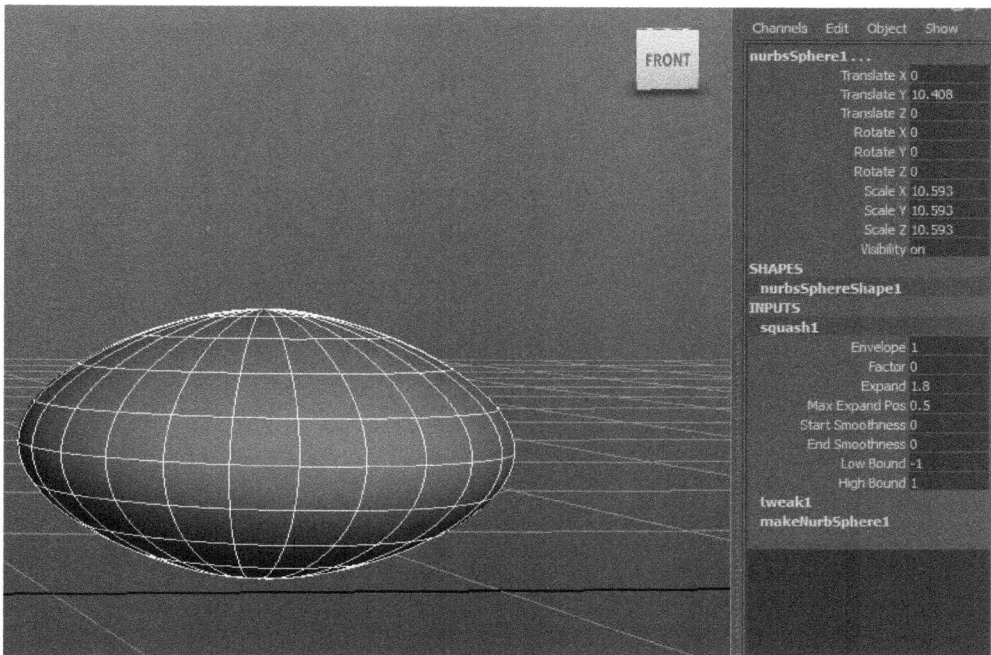

Figure 221. Squash attributes.

Like the other non-linear deformers, it is best to try the various attributes to see exactly what each of them do and how they work together.

Tutorial: Create a Bouncing Ball

1. Create a ball and make sure it is fairly dense with divisions.

2. This time we will make the ball squash without using a fancy expression. Select the ball and run the command:

   a. **Create Deformers -> Non-Linear -> Squash**

3. Familiarize yourself with the squash handle's deformations by playing with the attributes such as factor and expand. Expand will increase how much the ball will exaggerate the preservation of volume.

4. Parent the squash handle to the ball:

   a. Select the handle then holding shift, the ball.

   b. p (parent)

5. Go to frame one and position the ball up in the air slightly.

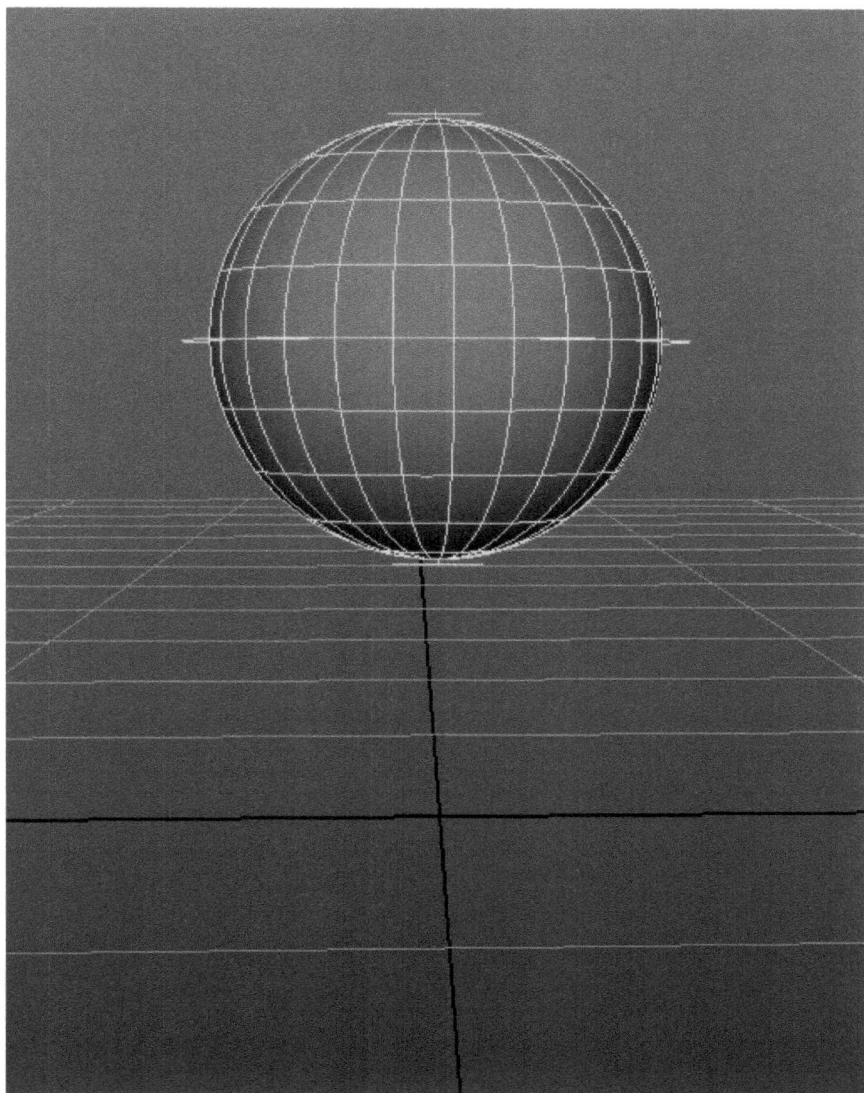

Figure 222. Move the ball into the air.

6. Set a key for the translate attributes of the ball.

    a. Select the attributes in the channel box

    b. Right Click in the Channel Box -> Key Selected

7. Go to frame 30 and move the ball to the bottom of the screen.

8. Key the translate attributes in this position for the ball.

9. Go to frame 45 and move the ball back up into the air. Key this position and scrub the time slider to check your animation.

10.   Now let us add some squash and stretch to the ball. Go back to frame one and use the squash handle to squish the ball a little in anticipation

    a. Factor 0.3

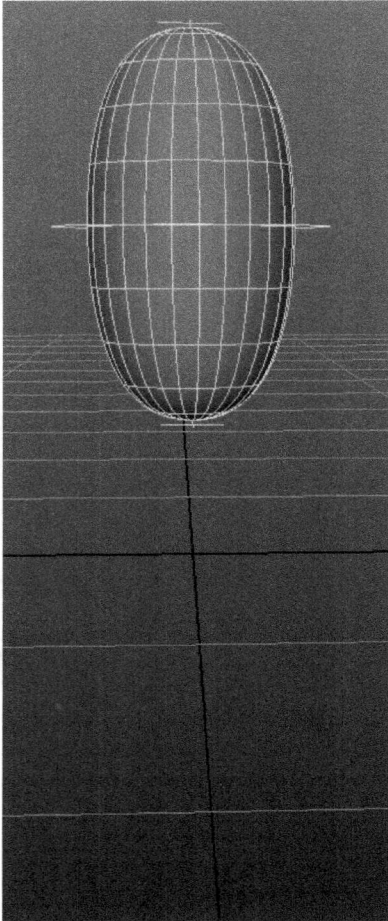

Figure 223.   Ball squishes in anticipation.

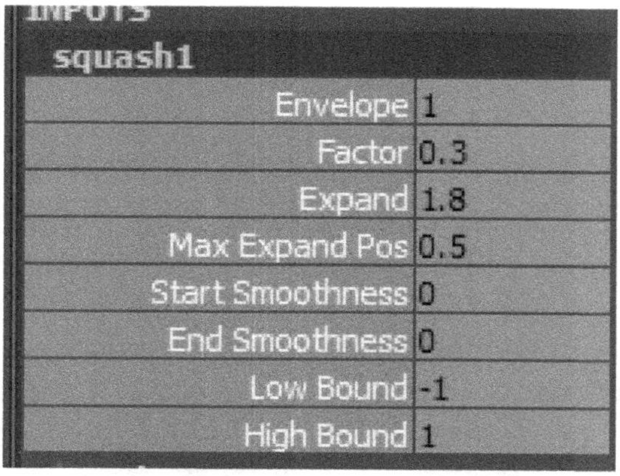

squash1	
Envelope	1
Factor	0.3
Expand	1.8
Max Expand Pos	0.5
Start Smoothness	0
End Smoothness	0
Low Bound	-1
High Bound	1

Figure 224. Squash attributes.

b. Select all the attributes of the squash handle in the channel box

c. Right Click in the Channel Box -> Key Selected

11. Go to frame 29, right before the ball hits the ground. Squish the ball a little more even to increase the anticipation.

    a. Factor 0.657

    b. Select all the attributes of the squash handle in the channel box

    c. Right Click in the Channel Box -> Key Selected

12. Go back to frame 26 and key the factor to the starting level of 0.3 for more cartoony impact.

13. Go to frame 32, giving the ball a few frames to hit the ground. Squash the ball nice and flat and key the attributes using the techniques outlined above and a factor of -0.4.

Figure 225. Ball squashes.

14. Go to frame 37 and squish the ball up to anticipate "jumping" back in the air. Key this in as well. A factor of 0.5 worked well for us.

Figure 226. Ball starts anticipating the jump.

15. Go to frame 43 and return the squash back to 0, to have the ball hit the full round shape by the top of its flight.

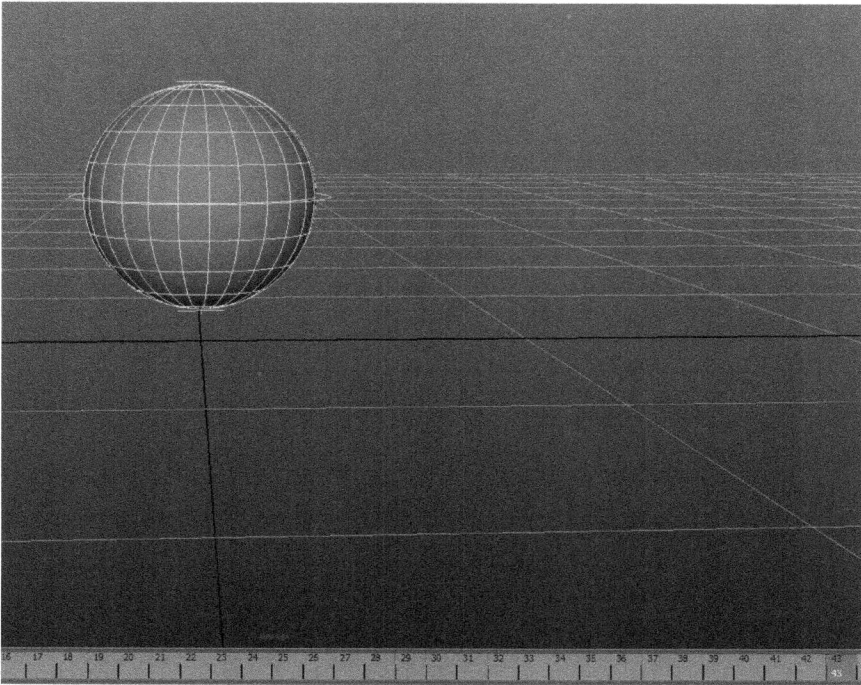

Figure 227. Fully round at the top.

16. Playblast the animation to see your work.

a. **Window -> Playblast []**

b. Adjust the settings to playblast only from frame 1-
    45 using the start/end choice.

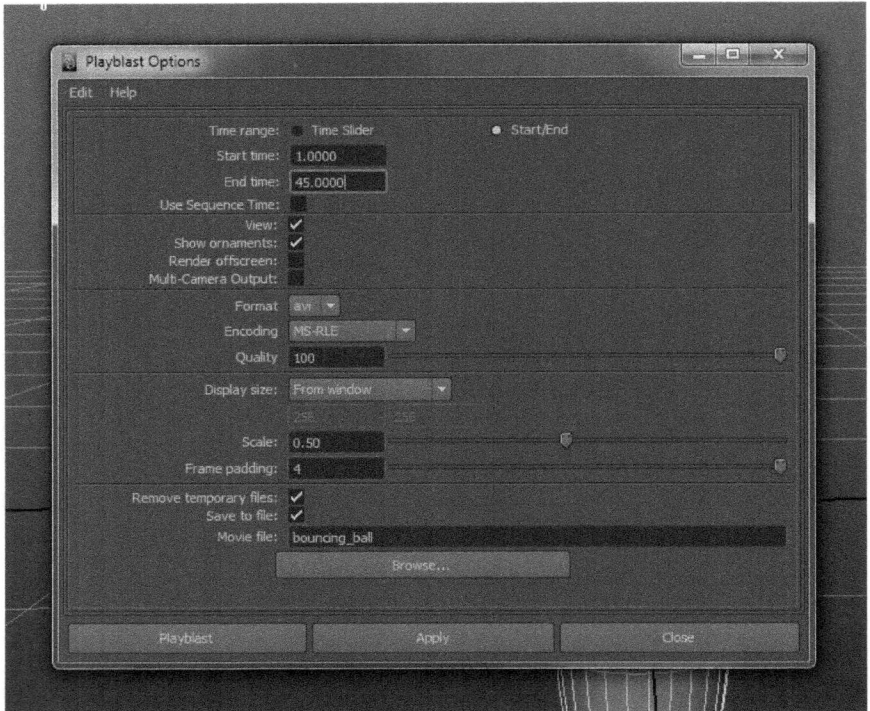

Figure 228. Playblast your animation.

17. Notice that the anticipation happening right on frame 1
    means the animation does not loop well. Adjust your
    animation to be a factor of 0 at frame 1 and fine tune how
    the ball stretches cylindrically before it hits the ground

until you are happy with the motion. For us, that meant keying the factor to 0 at frame 1 and changing our key at frame 29 to be a factor of 0.3.

18. Notice that the squash happens in the middle of the ball and makes the ball not look like it is actually hitting the ground. You can adjust this by either moving the squash handle to the bottom of the ball, or by animating the ball a little lower (known as counter-animating since you have to "over animate" to compensate for something else).

    a. For us this meant moving the handle downwards at frame 15 to give a bulge to the ball at the top.

    b. At frame 28, the handle was centered

    c. At frame 30, the handle moves up to make a bulge at the bottom as the ball hits the ground.

    d. At 31, we centered the handle again.

    e. At 26, we moved the handle up to give the ball a "sticky" feeling to the bottom of the ball. Check our example file to see this in motion as it makes far more sense than a series of images (and saves some paper too!)

19. Playblast your work again and fine tune your squishy ball. You may find that 45 frames is far too slow, so try speeding up your animation 2x. The easiest is to use the playback speed controls in your movie player such as

QuickTime before you do anything in Maya. If you like the results, you can easily squish your keys faster using the dope sheet. For us, changing the animation to take place in 23 frames instead of 45 worked much better.

a. Window -> Animation Editors -> Dope Sheet

b. Select all the animated objects in the scene so they show up in the Dope Sheet

c. Use Alt to zoom the dope sheet out

d. Select all your keys (black bars) so they turn yellow

e. Hit r for scale and a box will appear around your keys

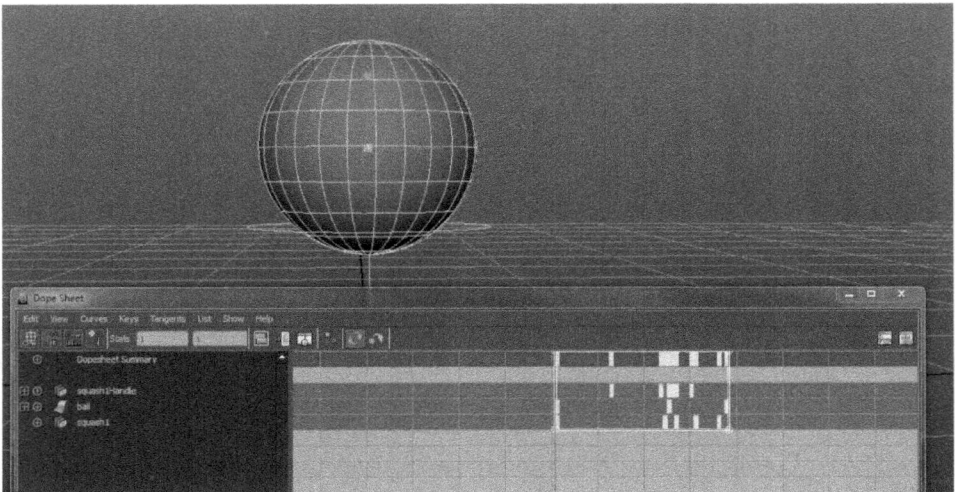

Figure 229. Dope sheet.

f. Use the middle mouse button to squish the box

g. Scrub your animation and view your results.

Example File: 26_bouncy_ball.ma

Example File: 27_bouncy_ball_after_

dopesheet_speed_up.ma

Non-linear Deformers: Twist

The next non-linear deformer is the twist. The twist deformer is created by selecting your object, then running:

Create Deformers -> Non-Linear -> Twist

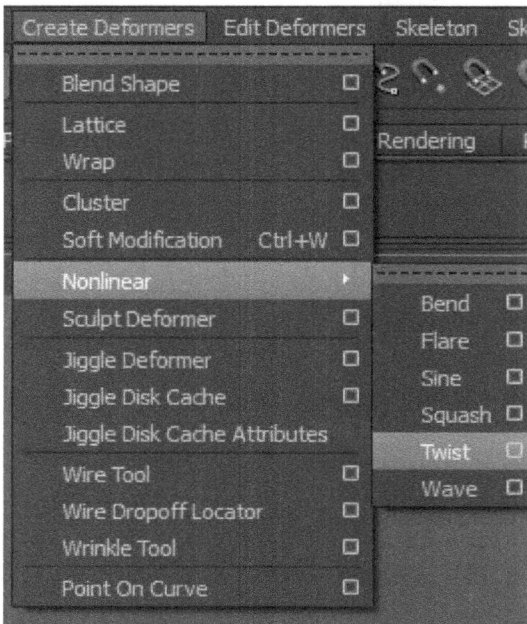

Figure 230. Twist menu.

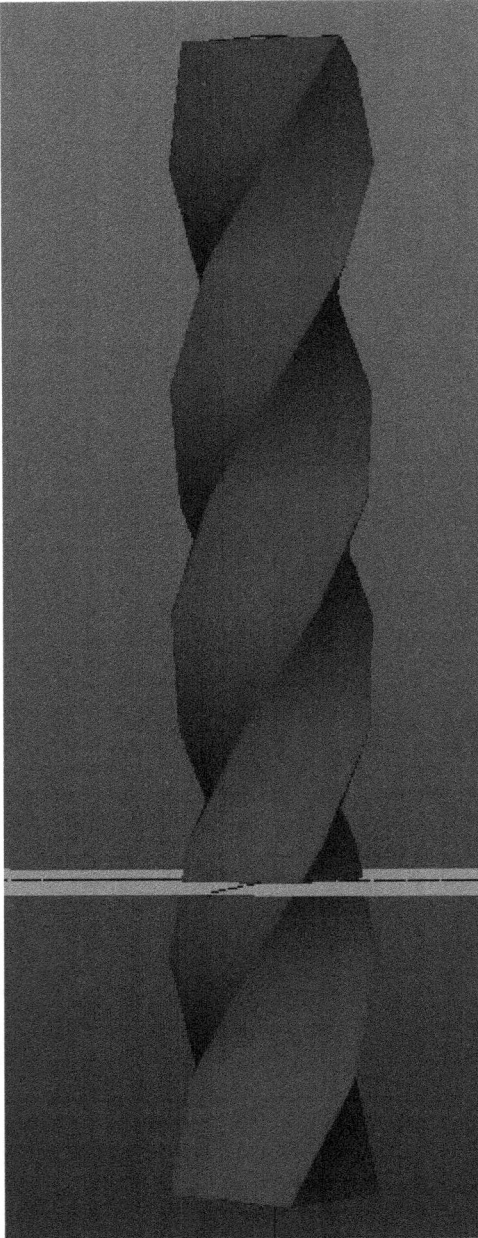

Figure 231. Licorice made the easy way.

This deformer does just like its name suggests, it twists things. This can be great for doing all sorts of things from creating a tornado, wrapping up a dishcloth, or even making a spring. In the following tutorial, you will learn how to create a piece of licorice using the twist deformer.

The new attributes for this deformer are the start and end angles. This allows you to control just how much twist your object will receive at the start or at the end of the deformer. The low and high bounds in this case act like a scale in some senses, extending the length of the deformer and thus the area it affects.

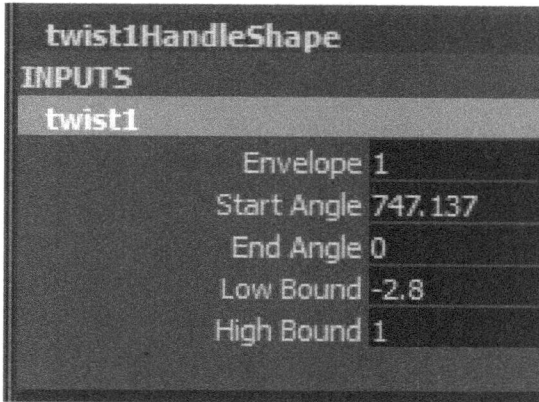

twist1HandleShape
INPUTS
twist1
Envelope 1
Start Angle 747.137
End Angle 0
Low Bound -2.8
High Bound 1

Figure 232. Twist attributes.

Making use of the twist deformer will allow you to get complicated shapes easily. Remember that you can use the deformer to warp your geometry and then go from there to use your geometry as a modeling guide. In other words, you could twist a NURBS cylinder, select an isoparm, duplicate the surface curve, and then delete your deformer and geometry. What you would be left with is a twisted curve that can then be used to make a spring for example. This is a handy way to get a symmetrical twisted object without trying to figure out just how to draw it by hand. Using the deformer is far faster in case such as that, and it works quite well.

Tutorial: Making licorice the easy way

1. Start by creating a polygon primitive of a cube. Scale it long and somewhat flat so that your cube is almost a

cylinder and resembles the image. We changed the default shader to be red as well

Figure 233. Basic cube.

2. Ensure you have at least 10 divisions, since we need a complex deformation. Select your cube shape (polyCube1) and check the attributes in the channel box:

a. Subdivisions Width, Height and Depth= 10

3. Now we can begin making the licorice by twisting the cube. Create a twist deformer on the cube by running the command:

a. **Create Deformers -> Non-Linear -> Twist**

4. Play with the Start Angle, and Low Bound to get a nice twist. We also had to scale the cube afterwards to

fine tune the shape. In our example we found these settings to work the best:

   a. Start Angle = 747.137

   b. End Angle = 0

   c. Low Bound = -2.8

   d. High Bound 1

   e. Cube Scale X = 123.9

   f. Cube Scale Y = 1185

   g. Cube Scale Z = 161

   h. Twist Handle Scale X = 217

   i. Twist Handle Scale Y = 533

   j. Twist Handle Scale Z = 217

5. Try adding a smooth node to the mesh and playing with the attributes to get some very interesting results:

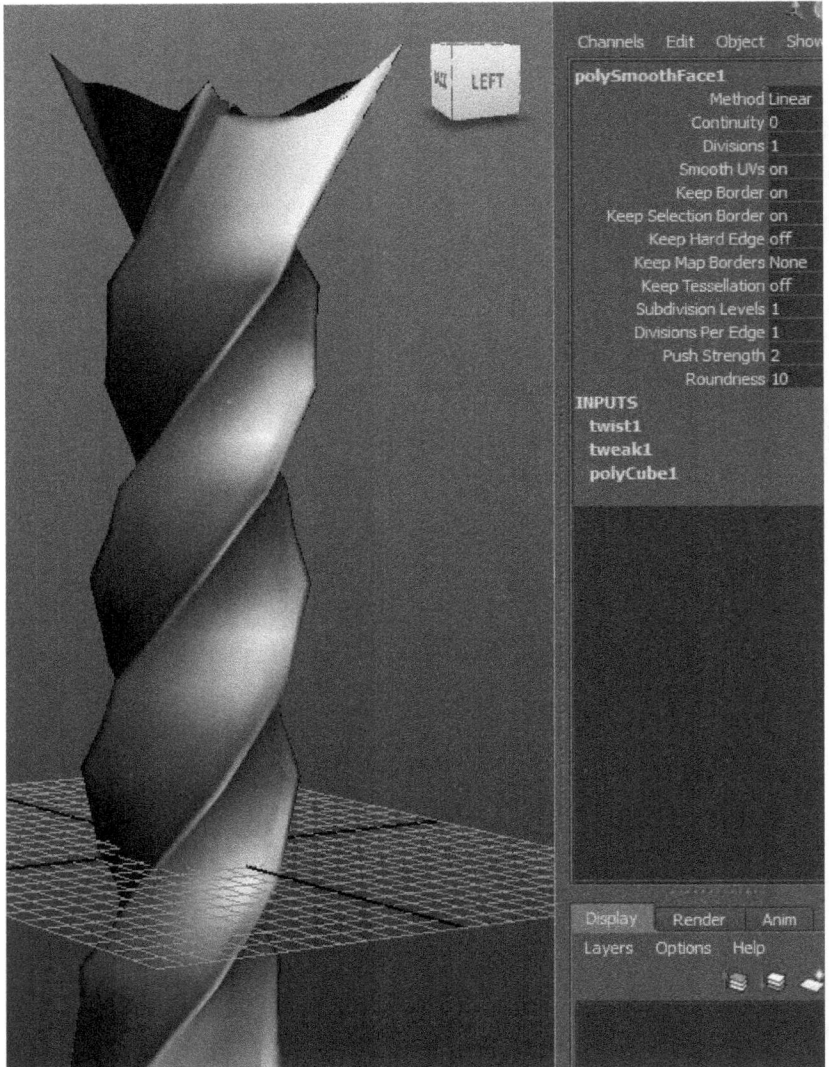

Figure 234. Licorice is formed.

Example File: 28_licorice.ma

Non-linear Deformers: Wave

The last deformer is the wave. You can make a wave by running:

Create Deformers -> Non-Linear -> Wave

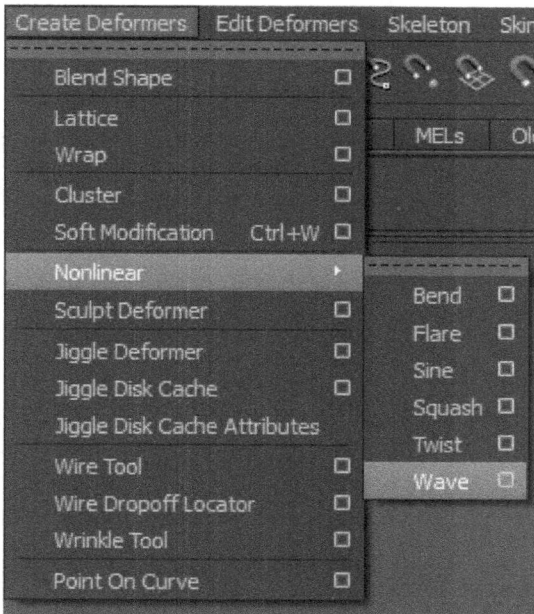

Figure 235. Wave menu.

The wave deformer is much like the sine deformer in that it creates waves. In fact, you could look at this deformer as the exact same, but a cosine wave versus the regular sine. In other words, it has a peak in the middle and on either end versus a zero value or a flat spot in the middle and either end. This can be great for doing all sorts of things that are different than the sine wave such as a drop of water hitting a puddle or a trampoline bouncing, or even a pizza that bends and twists in the air as it is thrown high to make the pizza. In the tutorial that follows, you will learn how to create a speaker for a sound system using the wave.

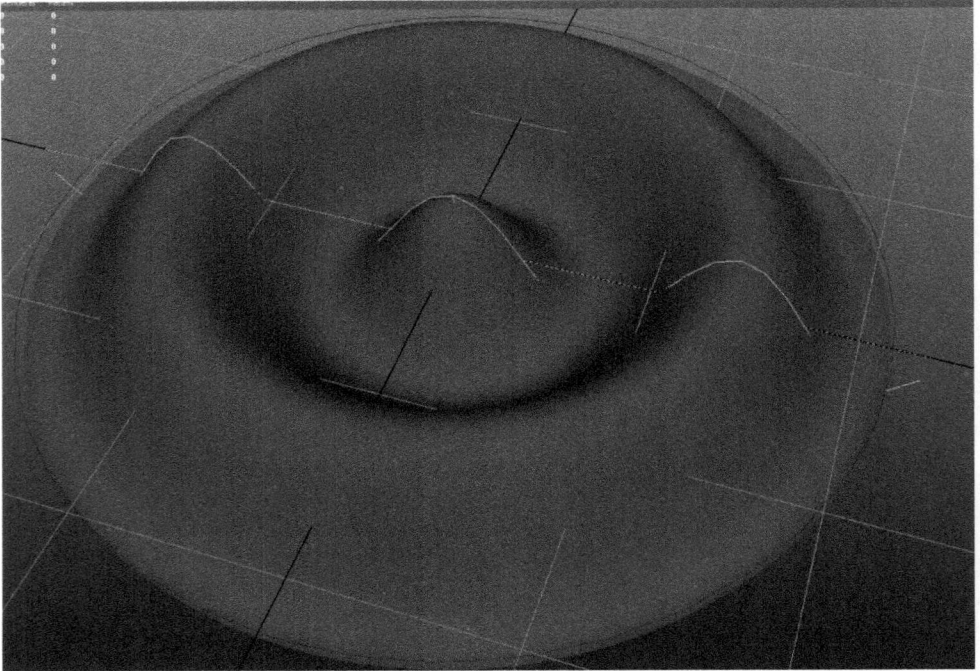

Figure 236. Making a speaker.

The attributes are similar to that of the sine, and correspond to the mathematical properties of a wave: the wavelength and amplitude. To refresh, the amplitude is the size of the wave's peaks and valleys, the bigger the number, the larger these are. The wavelength refers to the amount of peaks and valleys in the wave, the higher the wavelength, the more of these will occur. The new attributes show another difference in the wave versus the sine. The minimum and maximum radius refers to where the wave affects your model, as it acts in a circular manner radiating outwards from the center. In the sine, we saw this in a slightly different manner, with a low and high bound, which allowed the wave to stretch on for a distance away from the deformer. In the case of the radius, we are effecting how the wave leaves the center area.

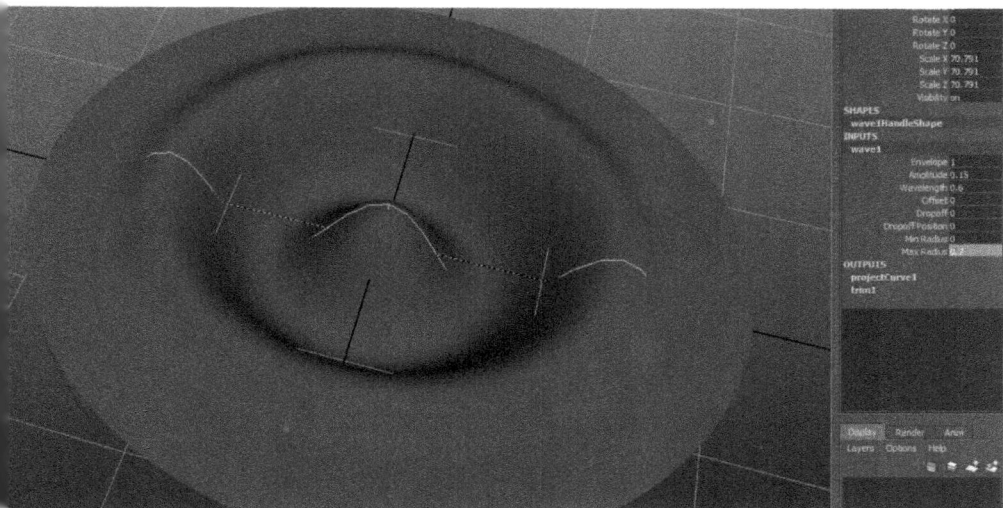

Figure 237. Speaker attributes via the deformer.

Note that your geometry will have to be somewhat dense to show the fidelity of this deformer. If your geometry is not dense enough, the deformer will still affect it, but in a more course manner.

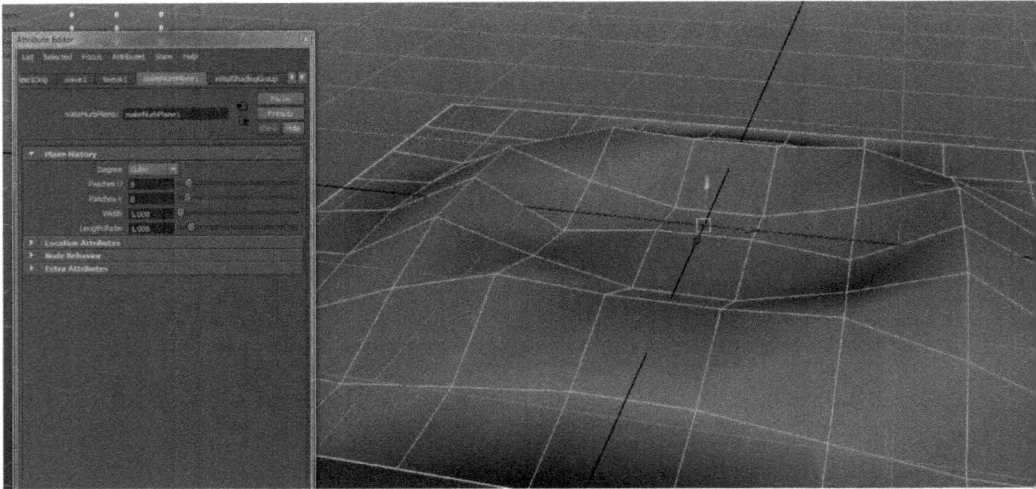

Figure 238. With less density, the shape is obscured.

Let us examine how the wave deformer can be used for modeling interesting shapes such as the speaker in a sound system.

The interesting part is that once you have used this deformer to create the model, you also have your object already rigged. This is because you can easily change the values on the deformer to make your speaker shake, bounce and react as if sound was emanating from it. However, in our example we build on previous knowledge and show this by adding in another deformer, the squash deformer. We will need to control the edges of our speaker force them to stay still and this is achieved by using the edit membership tool which we discussed earlier in the Rigid Bind and Edit Membership section. By editing the membership of the deformer, we show how to control what areas are affected by our deformer.

Tutorial: Create a Speaker

1. Start by creating a Nurbs plane:
   a. **Create -> NURBS Primitive -> Plane**
2. Next, we make the plane a bit larger so it's easier to see:
   a. Channel Box -> Scale X, Y,Z to reasonable size, we used 500
3. To make a complex shape, we will need a fair bit of geometry. Select your new planar surface and change the attributes in the channel box under makeNurbPlane1:
   a. Patches U = 30
   b. Patches V = 30

Figure 239. High density in the square.

4. Ensure to name your new surface. Rename your planar surface to "speaker_nrb".

5. Now we will start deforming the new speaker into its final shape. Begin with a wave deformer by running the command:

   a. **Create Deformers -> Non-Linear -> Wave**

6. Play with the attributes in the wave deformer to make a speaker shape appear in the plane as shown in the image. We used the attribute settings of:

   a. Amplitude = 0.12

   b. Wavelength = 0.55

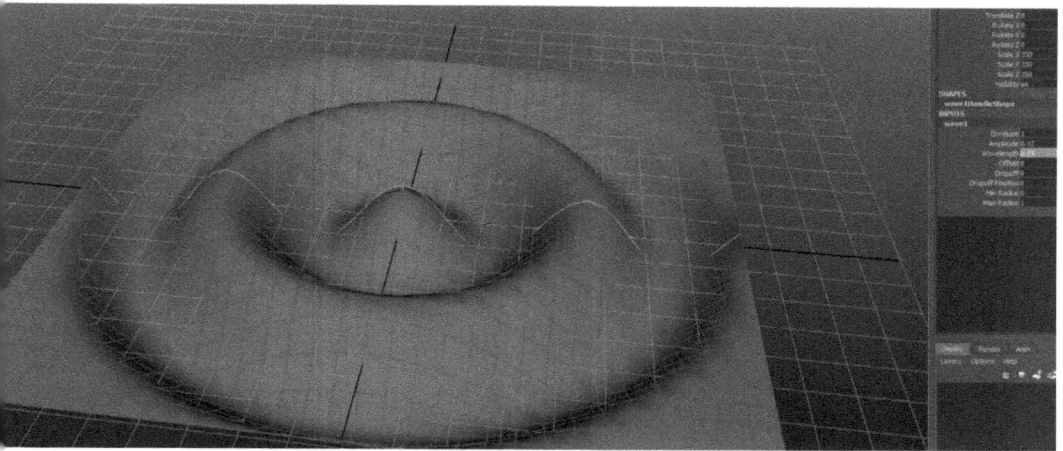

Figure 240. Start of a speaker.

7. You can animate the speaker by playing with the amplitude. In our example file, we animated 5 keys over 7 frames of making the speaker bounce a little more and a little less in amplitude.

    a. Set keys at various frames going from 0.12 to 0.9 or 0.15

    b. Ensure the last and the first key are both 0.12

    c. Animation Editor -> Graph Editor

8. Select the curve

    a. Graph Editor Menu -> View -> View Infinity

    b. Graph Editor Menu -> Curves -> Post Infinity -> Oscillate

9. Press play and view your animation

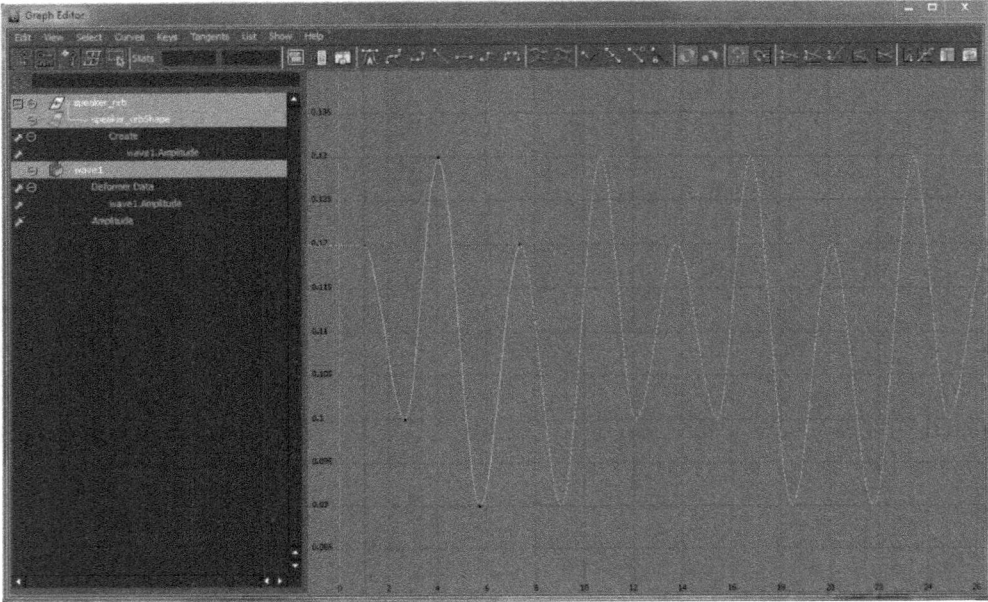

Figure 241. Oscilating the graph.

10. The last thing left is to cut your speaker out of the plane so
that it is round. Start by creating a circle that is the
appropriate size.

   a. **Create -> NURBS Primitive -> Circle**

11. Scale to the size that you would like your speaker

12. Translate the circle slightly above the surface

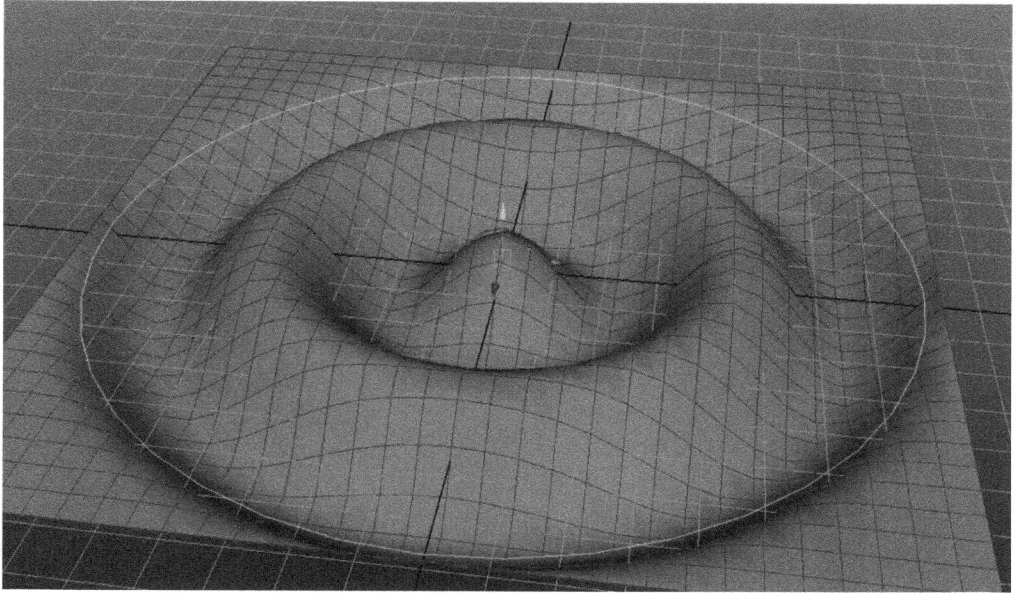

Figure 242. Fitting a circle.

13. Move the camera so that you're looking down on your plane.

14. Select the circle, then shift select your speaker_nrb (the plane you created).

15. The next step is to put the circle directly on the surface so we can use it to cut out the speaker like a cookie cutter.

    a. **Edit NURBS -> Project Curve On Surface**

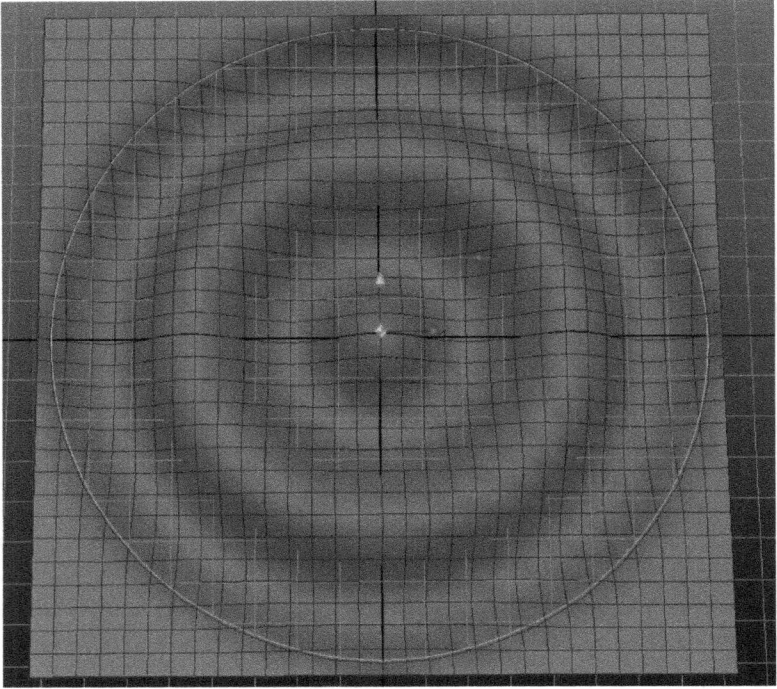

Figure 243. Project top down.

16. Next we will cut out the speaker.

    a. Clear your selection by clicking out in space somewhere.

    b. Edit NURBS -> Trim Tool

    c. Click on the center of your speaker, the surface will change to white with dotted lines and a solid white line where your projected curve was.

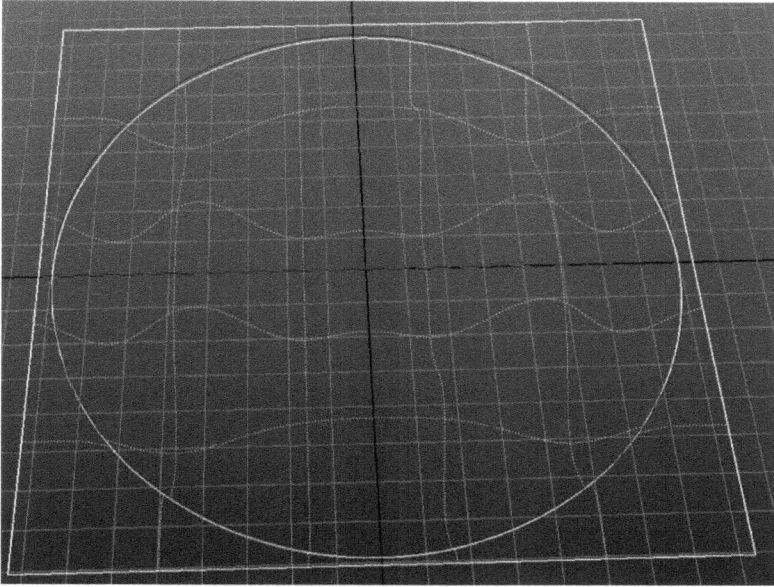

Figure 244. Trim tool started.

    d. Click the center of the speaker and a yellow icon will appear. This signifies that you would like to keep the middle.

    e. Hit Enter to exit the tool and keep only the middle.

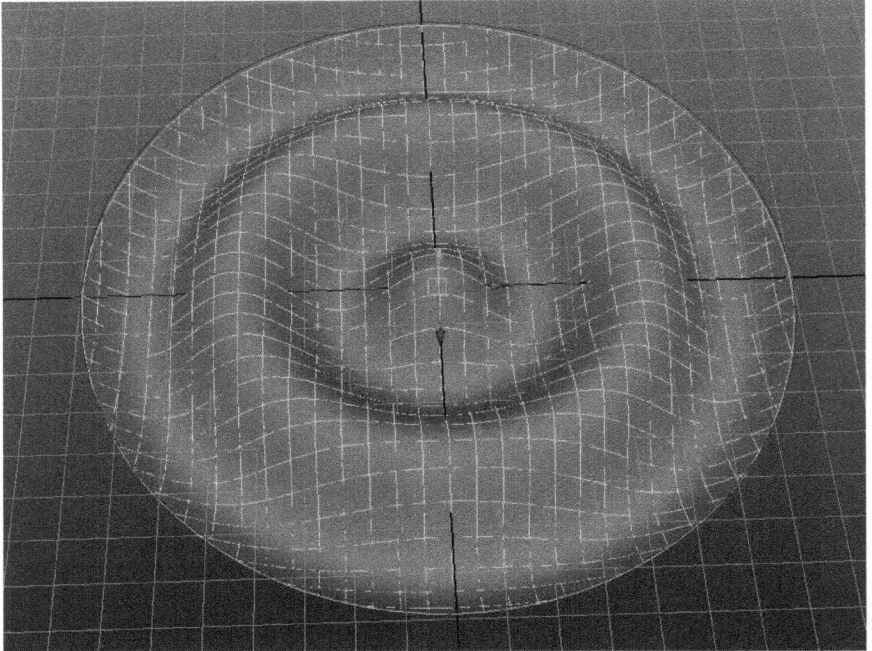

Figure 245. Trim the edges off.

17. You should now have an animated, trimmed out speaker. You can adjust your animations via the history on the wave deformer. You can adjust your speaker size by adjusting the projection curve that you used.

18. If you notice that the speaker animation is too slow, try repeating this tutorial but doing the trim first, deleting history, and THEN applying the wave deformer.

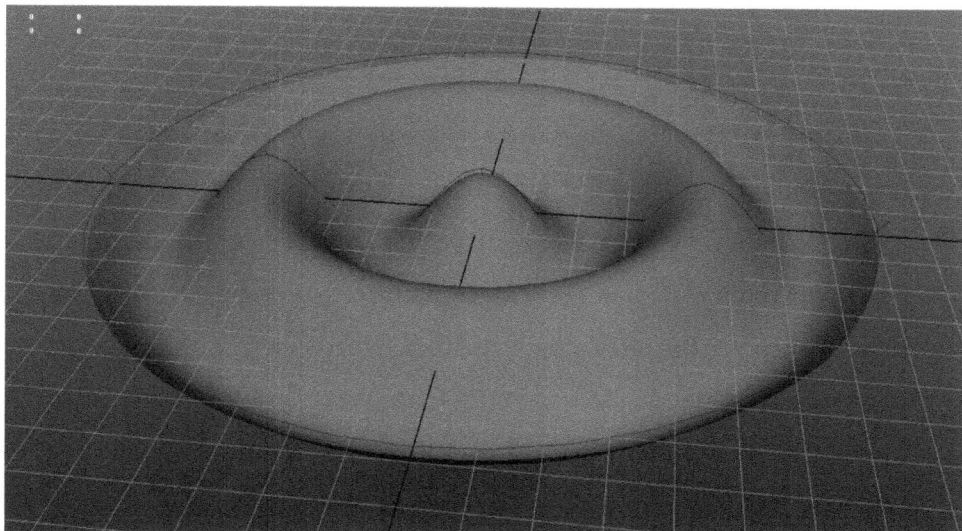

Figure 246. Speaker done.

Example File: 29_wave_deformer_speaker.ma

Wires

Wires are the last deformers we will cover in this book, and thus we can draw on what was discussed up until now to explain them. Wires are essentially a curve that controls a surface much like a lattice or a cluster. A wire is a curve that has a closest point relationship to the surface. In other words, as you move the wire's vertices, the surface vertices that are assigned to it will also move. The assignment has a drop-off rate and is much like how a lattice works in this respect. The benefit of a wire over a lattice is that, since it is a curve, it can have a curvilinear shape. This makes it a lot easier to control shapes that require more detail than a box. A perfect example is your lips. A curve drawn along the profile of the lips can be converted into a wire using the command:

Create Deformers -> Wire Tool

This curve can then be pulled and shaped, and the lips will follow suit. This is ideal since the curve can be drawn with far fewer vertices so that pulling only one point on your curve can pull many on your surface, complete with a nice drop-off.

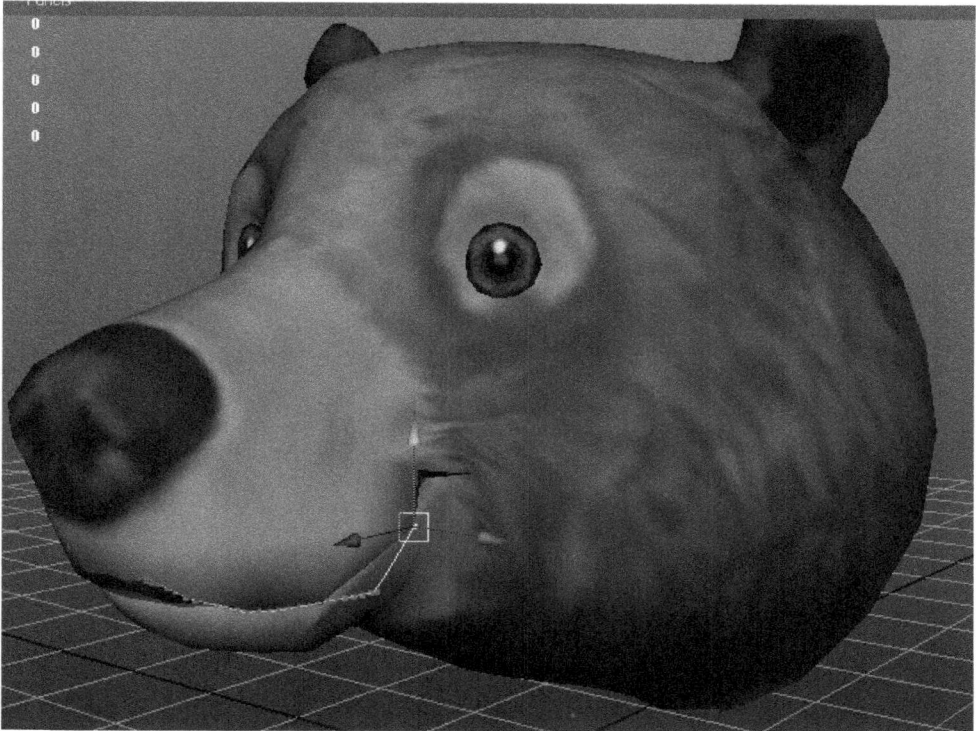

Figure 247. Bear lips controlled by wire.

Of course, you could do the same with a lattice, but in this example, having a curved shape in front is far more intuitive and understandable to the artist than a big box of points that a lattice would have.

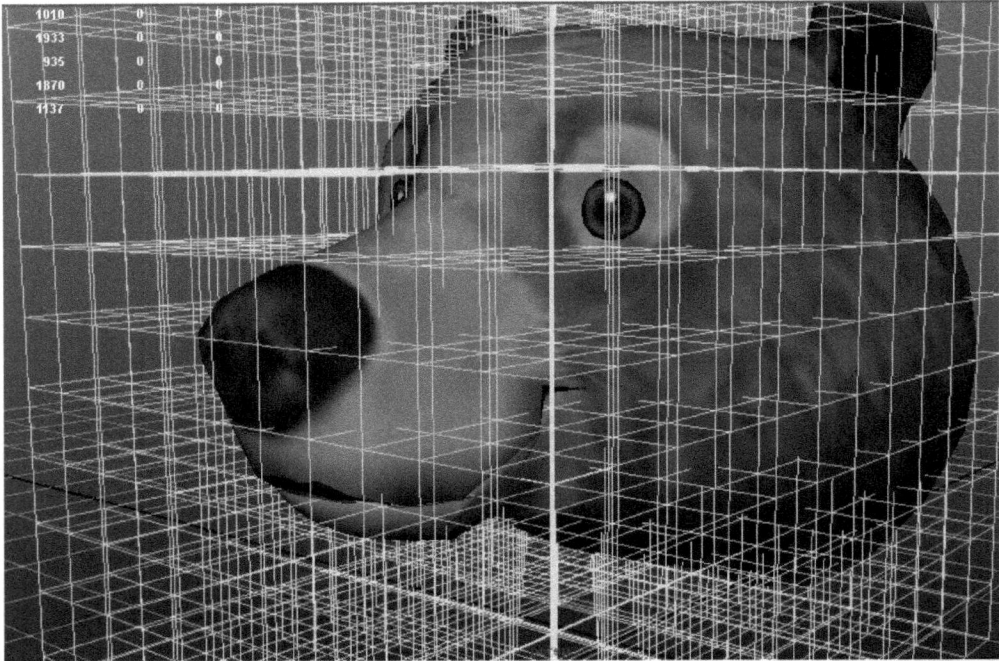

Figure 248. Bear with lattice is far too complex.

You could also make use of our friend the cluster, but in this example, having a curve makes it easier to discern what shape the lips are moving in to and the drop off is more intuitive than a multitude of clusters with overlapping drop-offs.

The irony is of course, that it is often easier to control the vertices on the wire by a cluster. In other words, if you have drawn a wire with 5 vertices, a best practice is to make a cluster for each vertex. This would result in 5 clusters that drive the wire. The wire in turn drives your model.

This may sound like the wire is a middle man that could be cut out of the rigging, but remember that your wire is giving you a great drop-off ability and is far faster than setting up the 10 plus clusters that it would take to drive the exact same scenario. As well, having to animate only a curve reduces the amount of things required for the animator to keep track of when animating and thus speeds up the process even more. Finally, having a curve to look at makes it far easier to visualize what is happening than guessing by imagining a line between 10 points if you were using 10 clusters.

A wire is particularly great for controlling any model that needs to be driven in an "organic" or curvy shape. Another example on your face would be your eyebrows or eyelids. Both work great with wires. In our example below, you will learn how to create a wire to drive your eyebrows.

Tutorial: Create a Wire to Deform Eyebrows

1. Create a face with some eyebrows. For the purposes of this tutorial, it does not have to be a particularly fancy model, but it should have some eyebrow ridges.

Figure 249. Simple eyebrows.

2. Let us create the wire to drive the left eyebrow. Go to the front viewport and draw a simple c.v. (control vertice) curve:

   a. **SpaceBar -> Left click and hold in the center -> Drag to downward select the Front**

   b. **Create -> CV Curve Tool**

3. Draw a simple curve with 5 points to match the shape of your eyebrow, then hit enter.

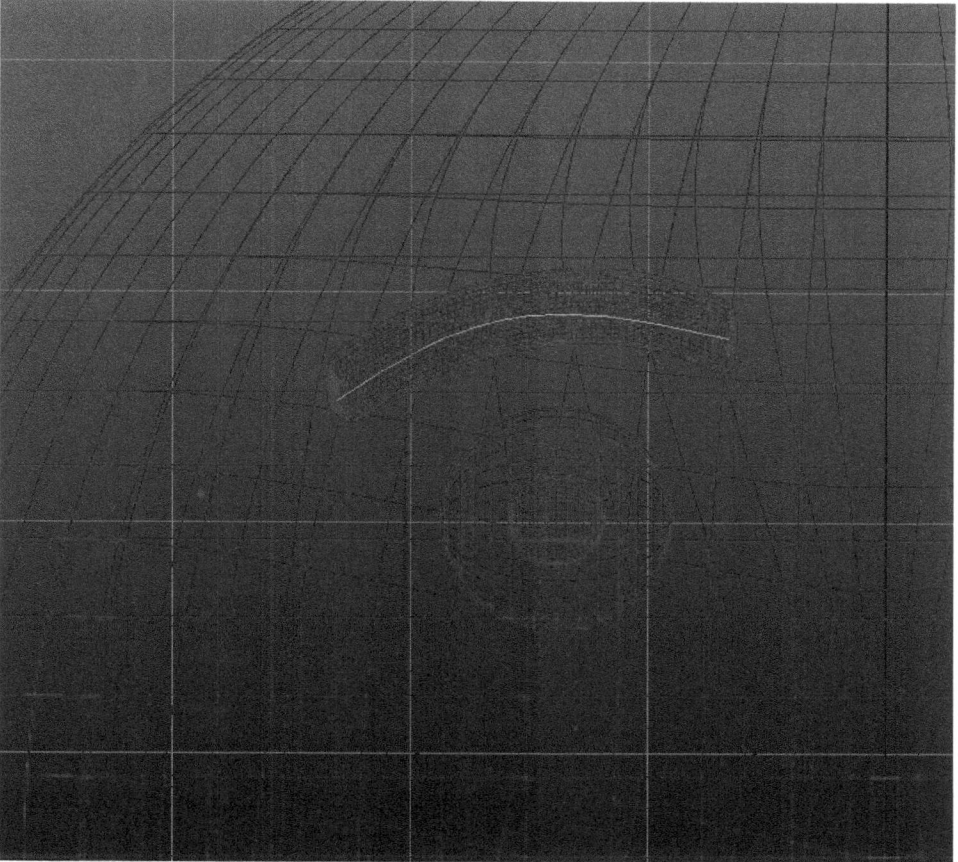

Figure 250. Simple curve for the simple eyebrow.

4. Switch back to your perspective view and zoom around until you can easily select the curve and the mesh.

5. Select your curve and center the pivot:

   a. **Modify -> Center Pivot**

6. Move your curve so that it is just in front of your eyebrow. In our example, we had to slightly rotate the curve as well. Once the curve is in position, remember to freeze the transformations

   a. **Modify -> Freeze Transformations**

Figure 251. Position the curve.

7. Name your new curve "rt_eyebrow_wire_crv".

8. Create the wire by using the command:

   a. **Create Deformer -> Wire Tool**

9. Following the instructions at the bottom of your screen, we select the model and hit enter.

   a. Click on the eyebrow, hit enter

   b. Click on the curve, hit enter

10. Experiment by moving a vertex on your wire (the curve). It should move your eyebrow around nicely. If it doesn't move, this means the drop off distance in your tool was too small. If this is the case, pick a larger dropoff distance in the tool when you first create the wire. In our example, we changed the dropoff distance to 70 after the fact by adjusting the attribute in the channel box.

Figure 252. Wire moves the eyebrow.

11. To make the rig more animator friendly, first we will create some clusters to control the wire. Select the wire and enter the component (blue) mode.

12. Select the first vertex and create a cluster.

   a. **Create Deformer -> Cluster**

13. Select the next vertex and create a second cluster.

   a. **Create Deformer -> Cluster**

14. Repeat this process for the remaining 3 vertices, until you have 5 clusters that can drive each point of the wire individually.

15. Once you have your 5 clusters, you could leave these to be responsible for driving the wire, but we should make this a little nicer for the animators. Let us enter the front view, and draw a nice little icon for the animators for each cluster.

   a. **SpaceBar -> Left click and hold in the center -> Drag downward to select the Front**

   b. **Create -> Pencil Curve Tool**

16. Center the pivot of your icon and position your icon over the first cluster.

   a. **Modify -> Center Pivot**

17. Duplicate the icon and move it over the next cluster. Repeat this process until you have 5 icons, each over their own cluster.

Figure 253. Drawing custom icons.

18. Let us drive the clusters by a direct connect. First, notice that the clusters have a clean transformation matrix right

now, all at 0's (and 1's for scales). Let us do the same for the icons. Select each icon and run the freeze command:

a. **Modify -> Freeze Transformations []**

b. Check to make sure that translate, rotate, and scale are all selected.

19. Once you have frozen your transforms for each icon, we can now connect them up. Remember using the connection editor? Well, let us do so again. Select your first icon, and open the connection editor:

a. **Window -> General Editors -> Connection Editor**

b. Reload the left side with the first icon.

c. Select the first cluster and reload the right side.

d. Connect all of the translates and rotates up from the icon to the cluster.

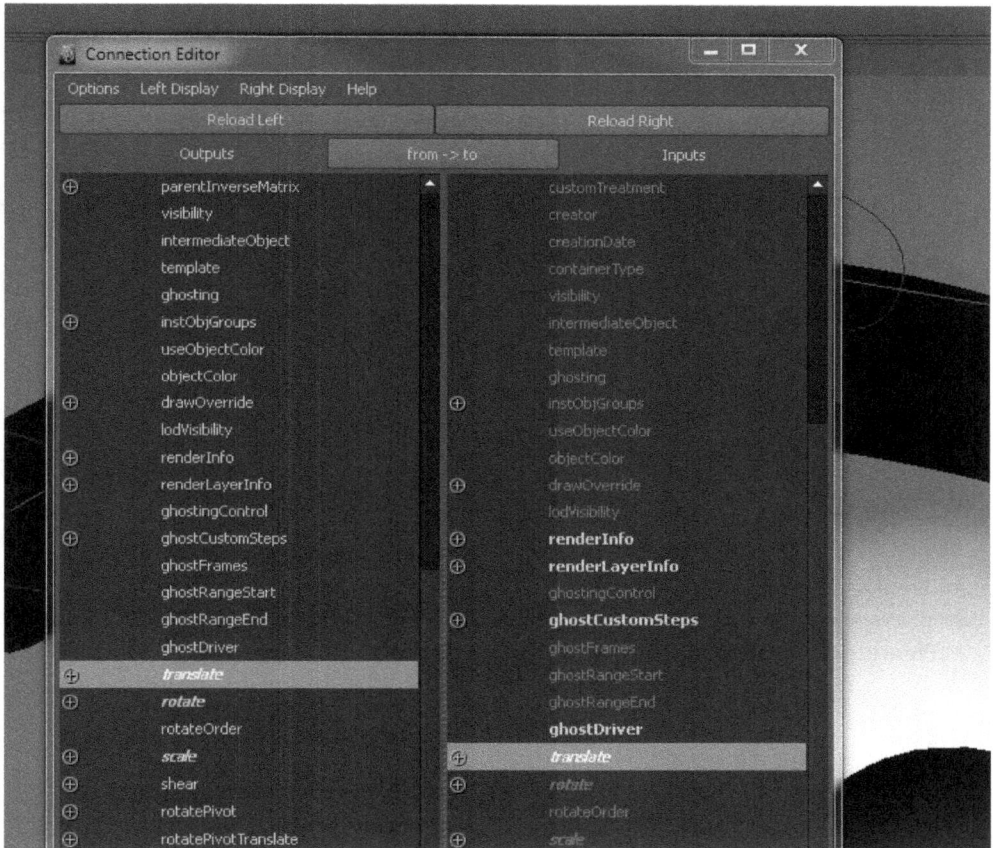

Figure 254. Connection editor to drive the control.

20. Repeat the connection hook-up for each of your remaining four clusters, so that each icon can drive each cluster.

21. Select all the geometry, clusters and wire. Create a layer from selected

   a. **Layers -> Create Layer from Selected**

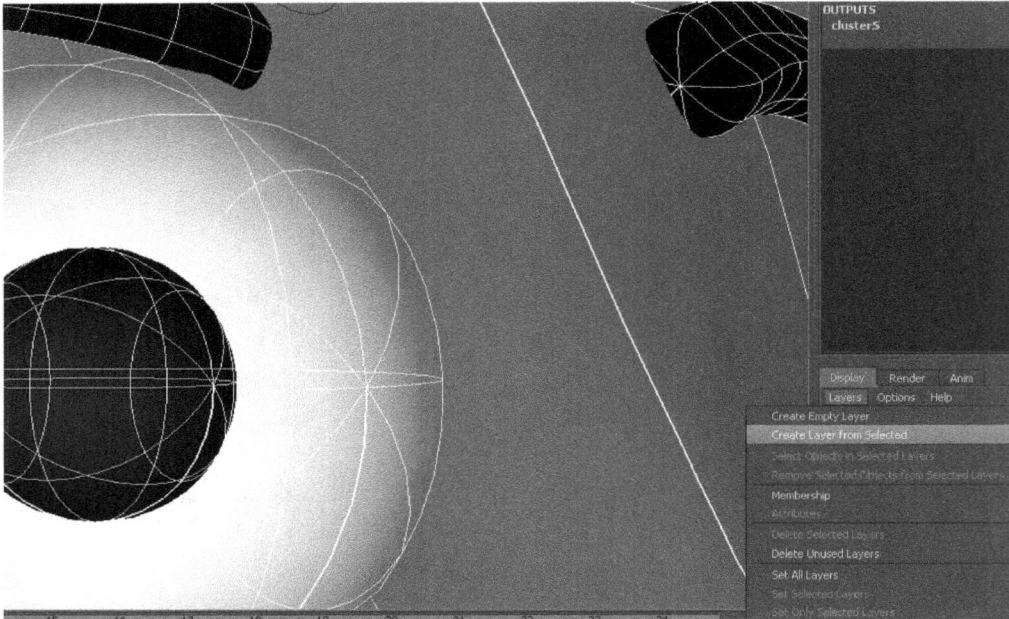

Figure 255. Create a layer.

22. Put the new layer to reference mode so that the only thing that is selectable is your icons.

    a. Click the box on the layer until it shows an R

Figure 256. Turn the "R" on for reference layer.

23. Clean up your scene with renaming your clusters and icons to match your naming conventions.

As you can see, now you have your very own custom icons driving your eyebrow. You can easily hide your clusters and wires, but many people prefer to just hide the cluster. This will leave your icons driving the wire, which in turn drives your model.

Experiment with moving your wire around and then repeat the process for your left eyebrow.

Figure 257. The finished wire.

Example File: 30_eyebrows_wire_01_base_model.ma

Example File: 31_eyebrows_wire_02_curve_positioned.ma

Example File: 32_eyebrows_wire_03_

wire_driven_icons.ma

Deformation Order

After you have moved your eyebrows around, and experimented with moving your face around, you might start noticing that things are not quite working as expected. This brings us to your deformation order. Built in to Maya is a sense of order. There is a mathematical order with rotations called the rotation order, where the rotation of x happens before y and y before z. We took advantage of this earlier with the setup of the local rotation axis in order to reduce the chances of gimbal lock. There are various combinations we have used the order and connections in history for one thing to drive another. And now we will bring this concept to deformations using what is termed the deformation order. This is simply the order in which your deformers happen. In other words, by now you will likely have wires, blendshapes, clusters, non-linear deformers, and even skin clusters all happening to the model. In order for the computer to make heads or tails of what would actually happen to your model when all of these deformers say "Deform!", it must do the math for each one at a time (even if Maya does so very quickly) and solve each deformation in order. This order is merely a list that gets constructed as you make your deformers, much like history. This means that the order in which you have created your deformers will affect the order in which they deform the model.

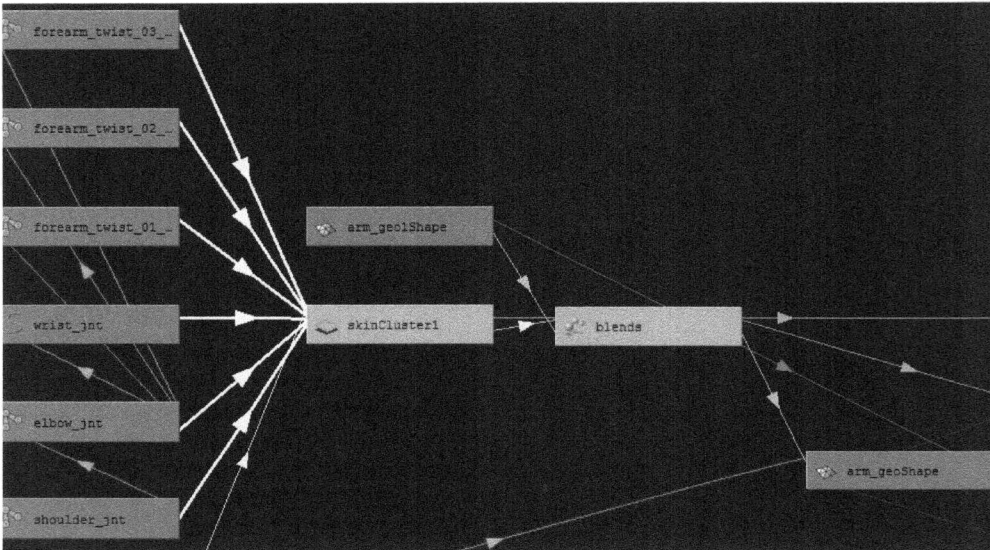

Figure 258. Hypergraph showing the connections.

In many cases, we need to adjust the order to suit our needs since it is far more likely that you will not have created every piece in the exact order that is how you want the model to deform. A perfect example is your blendshapes and your skin clusters. You would like to see something that says "make my character smile, AND THEN turn his head to the left". This means that the blendshape needs to happen BEFORE the skin cluster. In other words, your blendshape says "smile!" and then your bones (via your skin cluster) say "turn to the left".

Being in control of the order makes it possible to mix and match the various combinations you will try as you rig. These deformers all pile into history as "inputs" into the making the model deform, and this brings us to the next section, the input list.

Input List

In order to control the deformation order, we need to control the order of inputs. These are all assembled into the "input list". This list is the deformation order plus all the other inputs that may show up such as "tweak" nodes, etcetera. To see the input list, the easiest way is to:

Right Click on your Model -> Inputs -> All Inputs...

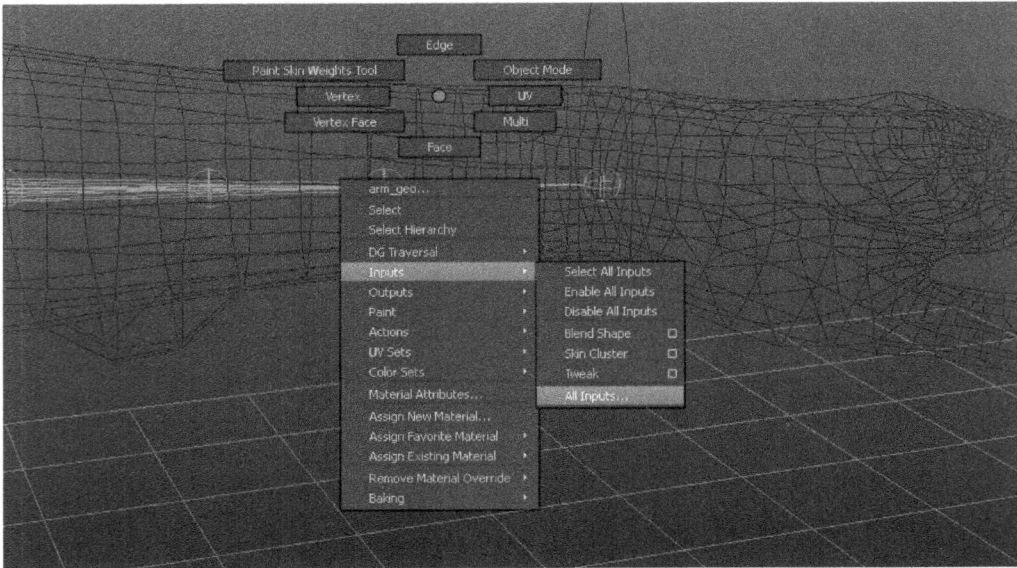

Figure 259. Right click to bring up the menu.

Bringing up the input list will then show you a window that has all of the deformers in it.

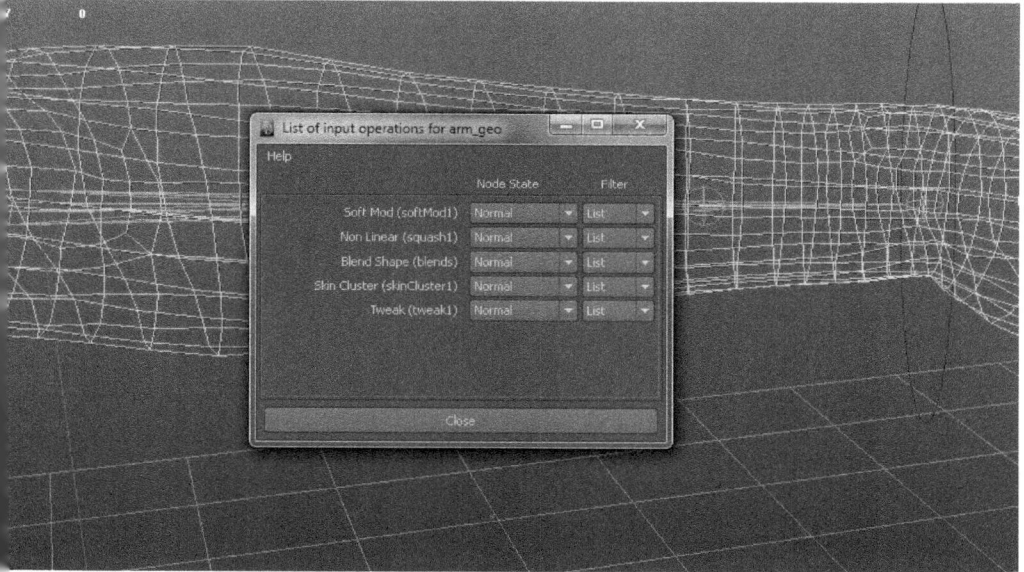

Figure 260. The input list window.

To change the input list, it is as simple as middle mouse dragging the items around until you have them in the order you would like.

Like the example explained above to turn your head and smile, typically you will want your skin cluster to happen at the end. This is because, for most of your deformers, it is easier to set them up at the default position and move them at the default position. This allows for you to ignore what potential angle the head might be in or whether the character has twisted into a strange pose, or even whether the controls of the deformer need to "come along for the ride" or not.

In our other books, where we discuss setting up muscles and more advanced systems, being able to control the deformation order via the input list editor is crucial. This allows you to setup the muscles in the default pose and then not ever have to "worry" about them again. Once they are setup, they are driven automatically by the animation system, and thus can effectively be "forgotten", and allowed to "just work".

The skin in this case essentially bulges into a muscle position and then moves to where the arm says it should be. Of course, all of this happens at each frame almost instantaneously these days, and most people do not even cast a second thought to the fact that things do not actually happen all at once, but in a specific order.

Now that you understand that things happen in an order, and how to adjust that order, you should be able to debug many problems that the beginner rigger will first encounter and you will be well on your way to constructing rigs that "just work".

Other Things to Consider for Deformation

When working with deformations, it is always important to remember your goal. It is easy to spend many, many hours perfecting your deformation and in major studios, this can mean several months' worth of time devoted to each and every character's deformation. The trick to deforming your character in the best way is to first determine just how much time you have to devote to it. If you only have a few days, it is unreasonable to assume you will get full muscle systems up and running AND looking good unless you have a lot of automation tools to assist you. Of course, you can easily put these in, but it takes time to make your deformations look great and many would argue it is well worth taking the time.

The second biggest tip is to make sure you understand what your rig needs to do before you start on your deformations. There is no point wasting time making sure a wrinkle or a fold looks great and works well if the rig will never hit that pose or the camera will never see it. For instance, if you are working on how your ankle moves and bends on a character that is only ever in a close up for a dialogue shot, you are wasting your time. This example is a bit exaggerated of course, and often you may not know all of your rig requirements, but it is ALWAYS a good exercise to find out as much as you can about the movement and demands before you start. Just like a good engineer, a rigger needs to define their requirements carefully before beginning if they want to not waste effort or time.

Third, once you have determined how your rig will move, construct some animation to put your rig through those paces to the extreme. Pose out your extreme positions and keyframe them into an animation that will push your model as far as it needs to go, and then go just a little further. This is often referred to as an exercise test. By watching your deformations go through these various extreme poses, you will get to see just how the model is deforming. A great workflow is to have your rig keyed at frame 0 in the default pose, and then have this exercise test run for several hundred frames after. You can then scrub through the timeline while you paint weights and see how your weights affect each pose. The great thing about working this way is you can move your model into different poses through scrubbing and Maya does not consider this as a selection change. What this means is simply that as you are painting weights, you can move to different poses and the paint weights tool and selection will stay open and at the right spot. This simple little tip can drastically speed up how fast you work. Once you are happy with your weights, you can simply return to the default pose by going to frame zero. Just remember to delete your animation before you save off your final rig!

The fourth tip is to work in layers. Start with your smooth bind and painting your weights to achieve all the major bends, twists, wrinkles, and folds. Your weights should be able to handle the vast majority of your demands. Once you get to a point where you are ready to look at finer details, only then you should consider layering in more deformers such as clusters, wires, blendshapes, non-linear deformers, and the others that we have discussed here. By mixing in the layers after you have spent some quality time with the weights, your rig will start to shine with nuances. Often, you can achieve quite a lot with the initial weight pass and reduce the amount of complexity drastically if the original smooth bind weights are painted well.

The final tip to remember is patience. It takes time to get your rig working well, and you will hit times of frustration. Remember though that the time you put in to making your rig look great will always show up in your animations and make them look that much better.

Rigging Deformation Summary

After reading this section, you should understand all the basics of deformation. You will know how to bind in both smooth and rigid binds, and know which is more appropriate for what work.

You will have worked through all sorts of small tutorials to learn how to use clusters and a variety of non-linear deformers, how to use lattices and even wires.

Conclusion

This book is geared towards you learning not just how to hit a button and which button is where, but the actual WHY to hit the button. By understanding the concepts and theories, you will then know how to not only create your own rigs, but much more importantly, you will know how to figure out WHY something may not be working and HOW TO FIX IT. This is the biggest difference between someone who can successfully navigate the production environment with ease, and someone who may struggle. It is critical to understand not just the hows and where's but also the why's.

By now you will not only just know how to troubleshoot a problem and "save the day", but you can also now move beyond just following a tutorial by rote and creating a system exactly how the steps have been laid out. You should be now ready to start to innovate and invent new systems of your very own! Understanding how and why things work will allow you to come up with new ways to combine things that people may not have thought of before. This is another crucial ability that will separate you from people who have to wait for someone else to show them how to do things.

I hope you are now ready to tackle not just the simple rigs, but move into setting up rigs that can do fancy and wonderful new things, faster and far simpler. You will be able to start setting up systems that will make it easier for the animators to do their jobs, and hopefully that will allow them to work faster. Working faster means that you will be able to help people not just get the job done, but have time to make the project look great! The less time it takes for someone to do their job, the more time they have to make it look better and better, and you can also save your project money as well.

All this from just knowing WHY. I hope this book will make you start asking WHY more and more each day!

Key Terms

Binding:

Binding is the term given to creating a skin cluster in Maya. This results in every point in the cluster (typically the whole mesh) being assigned to be influenced (and thus moved) by one or several joints.

Bind Pose:

The position in which the joint(s) were in at the time the binding command was issued. The skin cluster deformation can then be calculated as the delta between the current position and the bind position.

Blend Shape:

Blend shapes, or morph targets, are a deformation technique that relies on modeling. In this technique, one models the end position of how the model should look. This is most often used for facial rigging, and a series of models or targets, are created to simulate the various poses that a face can get in to.

Bones:

Sometimes referred to as bones, joints in Maya are a component of a skeleton. These are nothing more than a point in space, or a "transform", with a special icon that shows the parent/child relationship by drawing an arrow type triangle towards their child. Joints also have their own unique rotational axis, called a local rotation axis (LRA).

Cluster:

A deformer that defines a group of vertices. This group description is stored in a "weight list".

Deformation Order:

The order of events in which the calculations are made to ultimately produce the final deformed results. Editable by using the "list of all inputs" editor.

Deformation Systems:

The deformation system is used to define all the joints, clusters, and other fundamental pieces that work together to allow the rig to change shape or deform. When splitting a rig into two fundamental areas, deformation systems partner with motion systems to make up a rig. Good deformation systems can be quite complex yet fade in to the background and work automatically for the animator regardless of the range or pose the character is put into.

Dynamic Solutions:

The term given to mathematical solutions that are being constantly evaluated at every frame. This evaluation comes at the cost of having to calculate an answer at every single frame.

Expression:

An expression is simply a mathematical way of controlling attributes in Maya. They can be modified using the expression editor and are always evaluated left side equals right side.

Freeze Transformations:

This is the command used reset all the translation, rotations, and/or scale values as displayed to the user. The current information is then forced down to the internal matrix.

Influence Objects:

Any object used to have weight in a new or existing cluster. Joints are often used as influence objects when they are used in a skin cluster. See the section on how to use geometry as influence objects.

Gimbal Lock:

When the rotation tool (gimbal) "breaks" and has one or more axes converging with the other axes rather than staying at 90 degrees. This is caused by certain combinations of orientations that are difficult or impossible to attain. This will result in your rotation gimbal "breaking" to avoid mathematical errors like dividing by zero.

Joints:

Sometimes referred to as bones, joints in Maya are a component of a skeleton. These are nothing more than a point in space, or a "transform", with a special icon that shows the parent/child relationship by drawing an arrow type triangle towards their child. Joints also have their own unique rotational axis, called a local rotation axis (LRA).

LRA: Local Rotation Axis.

This is the local coordinate system for a joint in Maya, allowing the joint to have a second axis in a global coordinate system.

Lattice:

A lattice is also known as a "free form deformer". This FFD or lattice is a way of creating an object (typically a box) around your model that will then deform your model based upon the closest point associations and how you move the lattice's points.

Motion Systems:

The motion system is used to define all the controls, joints, expressions and other fundamental pieces that work together to allow the rig to move. When splitting a rig into two fundamental areas, motion systems partner with deformation systems to make up a rig. Good motion systems can be quite complex while appearing simple and are easy to use.

Non-Linear Deformers:

A class of deformers that come as default with Maya to allow you to quickly modify your geometry using an envelope. Used as basic building blocks to many rigs, they come with abilities to bend, squash, stretch and do a lot more. See the section in the book that walks through each of these deformers, complete with tutorials and examples.

Set Driven Key:

This is a command in Maya that allows you to create an expression in more friendly way. By making use of animation graph nodes, the user creates a relationship between two items and defines how that relationship can change. Set Driven Keys are often used when creating an expression to define the same behaviour becomes a complex mathematical exercise.

Soft Modification Tool:

A tool in Maya that can be used for many purposes. It is designed to ultimately pull or push areas with a drop off. See the section in our Advanced Character Rigging book for more information and detailed tutorials.

Weight List:

An array (a table of numbers) that describes the vertices in a cluster or envelope and how much control something has on the vertices. Weight lists can be singular in fashion where one item controls a list of vertices (for example, a cluster), or complex where many items control many vertices with varying influence (for example a smooth bound skin cluster).

Weight Painting:

This is the interface in which the user assigns the influence or "weight" by using a brush tool. See the section on Weight Painting for more.

Wires:

A type of deformer that uses a curve to control a surface with a paintable range of influence. Wires behave on a closest point methodology, where the vertices are assigned to the controlling point on the wire based on proximity. See the section describing wires that comes with examples and tutorials.

Wrinkles:

Everyone has them and so should any realistic rig.

About the Author

TJ Galda, MBA

TJ Galda has distinguished himself in the field of film, animation, and video games since the '90's. Mr. Galda has been teaching computer graphics for well over a decade. He has worked on character rigging teams for numerous feature films including several that were nominated for Academy Awards®. He was responsible for leading the rigging team who put Mr. Fantastic on screen in the first Fantastic Four feature film and understands how to make rigs that are photorealistic enough to fool the audience as a digital double.

Most notably, TJ was recognized as one of the 2006 Autodesk Maya Master Award recipients, as well as having earned a Lifetime Achievement award from the Ontario Government by the age of 29. In his role as Development Director (promoted from Senior Computer Graphics Supervisor) at Electronic Arts Canada, TJ is in charge of all art and rendering production for several AAA games.

An expert in his field, Mr. Galda is often asked to speak internationally, and has received several notable accolades. His work includes helping with the creation of DreamWorks' newest animated logo, and working on award-winning feature films and television shows such as: Shark Tale, Over the Hedge, Kung Fu Panda, Fantastic Four, Rolie Polie Olie, and Rescue Heroes. His projects have accumulated a total of five Emmy® Awards and two Academy Award® nominations, as well as countless Annies, VGAs (including 3 Game of the Years) and other awards.

TJ is also an active volunteer in the community and has been on the Board of Advisors for Zerofootprint, a not-for-profit environmental agency as well as an Ambassador for the David Suzuki Foundation. TJ currently is an instructor at the Vancouver Film School, and has taught at several other institutions, including Centennial College and Electronic Arts University.

Mr. Galda resides in Port Moody, British Columbia, Canada, with his wife and child, and Beau, their assistance dog that they are helping to train for Pacific Assistance Dogs.

For more information, visit www.tjgalda.com.

Index

A

adding influences......................... 295

attributes 140, 145

B

bend deformer...................... 307, 310

bind pose........................ 231, 290, 293

binding....................................... 61, 231

blend shapes................. 222, 226, 227

bone 60, 94

boolean 141

buttons... 126

C

cloth 173

cluster 195

complex chains............................... 64

component editor.......................... 281

connection editor 150, 155

constraint 36, 58

control curves 127

controls... 120

custom attributes.......................... 140

D

deformation 185, 231, 379

deformation order............... 192, 373

direct connection.................. 150, 174

double transformations............... 191

drawing joints 62

dynamics 173

E

edit membership tool .. 232, 306, 349

enum 143

envelope 202

expression 157, 159, 172, 219

expression editor 158, 165, 219

F

FFD 205

fist 180

FK 80, 90

flare deformer 313

flexor 246

float 140

flow path 214

forward kinematics 80

free form deformer 205

freeze transformations 31

G

gimbal lock 30, 75, 373

graphical user interfaces 120

groups 28

GUI 120

H

hand 65, 81

hierarchies 24

I

icon 131, 371

IK 92

IK handle............................ 92, 94, 96

IK RP Handle................................. 98

IK system 92, 96

influence object............. 256, 300, 302

influences 249, 300

input list 376

integer.. 141

inverse kinematics 92

J

joint chains 62

joint orientation................................ 78

joints 60, 231

L

lattice 205, 207

local rotation axis............ 60, 61, 74, 76

lock and hide selected 183

locked down 182

LRA 61, 76

M

motion path 211

multiple joints................................. 69

muscles 217, 378

N

non-linear deformer............. 234, 304

normalizing.................. 200, 251, 261

O

orient constraint 58

P

paint cluster weights 197, 203

paint skin weights tool 251

painting weights 196, 249, 266

parent constraint 58

parenting 24, 36

pencil tool 137

point constraint 36, 38

pole vector 99, 103, 114, 118

preferred angle 94

primary axis of rotation 75

prune small weights 285

R

relationship editor 231

rigid bind 231, 240, 290

rotation plane 96

rotational plane (RP) solver 94, 95

S

scale constraint 58

selection handle 133, 135, 139

set driven key 174, 175, 177

shelf button 121

shoulder 93

sine deformer 320

single chain (SC) solver 94

skin 378

small weights 284

smooth 260

smooth bind 247, 291

squash deformer 327

sticky 103, 302

string 143

T

templating...................................... 134

tweak 376

twist deformer............................... 339

twist value....................................... 99

two joint chains 64

V

vector 140

W

wave deformer 345

weight...................................... 40, 250

weight list............................. 201, 250

weight map........................... 201, 250

weights 200, 261, 281

wire.............................. 357, 361, 372